Formative Assessment and Feedback in Post-Digital Learning Environments

This fundamental text provides cutting-edge theory and practical insights into how formative assessment and feedback can be used to enhance student learning development through exploring an exciting range of case studies from experts in the field.

Underpinned by relevant theory and real-world advice spanning the global higher education sector, this book examines the importance of technology and digital education in shaping the use of assessment and feedback in higher education. Presented through international perspectives in assessment research and practice across a broad array of subject disciplines, the book focuses on the inclusion of empirical evidence, as well as the contemporary issues and challenges currently facing formative assessment. The case studies bring to life strategies and approaches that utilise a combination of digital and material tools to promote a range of innovative formative assessment practices, including facilitating dialogic formative assessment and supporting peer review and co-production of feedback artefacts. Each case study is divided into the context behind it, the strategy, practice, impact, and key learning outcomes, presenting a series of opportunities for practitioners to consider and embed in their practice.

Aimed at experienced and early career practitioners in higher education, as well as third space practitioners such as learning and educational developers and designers, this text is ideal reading for educators who wish to see evolution in higher education, using the lessons learned from utilising educational technology to focus on student learning in increasingly digital environments.

Sam Elkington is Professor of Learning and Teaching at Teesside University, UK, and is a PFHEA and National Teaching Fellow (NTF).

Alastair Irons is Deputy Principal and Deputy Vice Chancellor and Professor of Computer Science at Abertay University, UK. He previously served as Academic Director for Digital Education and Dean of the Faculty of Technology at the University of Sunderland, UK.

Formative Assessment and Feedback in Post-Digital Learning Environments

Disciplinary Case Studies in Higher Education

Edited by
Sam Elkington and Alastair Irons

Designed cover image: Getty Images

First published 2025
by Routledge
4 Park Square, Milton Park, Abingdon, Oxon OX14 4RN

and by Routledge
605 Third Avenue, New York, NY 10158

Routledge is an imprint of the Taylor & Francis Group, an informa business

© 2025 selection and editorial matter, Sam Elkington and Alastair Irons; individual chapters, the contributors

The right of Sam Elkington and Alastair Irons to be identified as the authors of the editorial material, and of the authors for their individual chapters, has been asserted in accordance with sections 77 and 78 of the Copyright, Designs and Patents Act 1988.

All rights reserved. No part of this book may be reprinted or reproduced or utilised in any form or by any electronic, mechanical, or other means, now known or hereafter invented, including photocopying and recording, or in any information storage or retrieval system, without permission in writing from the publishers.

Trademark notice: Product or corporate names may be trademarks or registered trademarks, and are used only for identification and explanation without intent to infringe.

British Library Cataloguing-in-Publication Data
A catalogue record for this book is available from the British Library

ISBN: 978-1-032-41893-3 (hbk)
ISBN: 978-1-032-41894-0 (pbk)
ISBN: 978-1-003-36025-4 (ebk)

DOI: 10.4324/9781003360254

Typeset in Times New Roman
by Apex CoVantage, LLC

Contents

	Acknowledgements	ix
	About the editors	x
	Meet the case study contributors	xii
1	**Introduction** *Sam Elkington and Alastair Irons*	1
2	**Formative assessment and feedback in post-digital higher education** *Sam Elkington and Alastair Irons*	9
3	**Creating a formative-feedback trialogue by embedding an e-learning theory package into undergraduate music education** *Paul Fleet*	29
4	**Reflective writing online as a powerful formative assessment tool in teacher leadership development** *Phil Quirke and Nadya Moosa*	35
5	**Developing student employability through formative assessment and virtual project learning in the social science curriculum** *Joy Perkins and Stuart Durkin*	42

6	Using formative feedback to scaffold and manage student wellbeing in an accelerated online research course *Natasha van Antwerpen, Deanne Green, John Baranoff, Sara El-Kaissi, and Anastasia Ejova*	50
7	Promoting situated change towards sustainability and climate action through post-digital online distance learning pedagogy *Annabel de Frece and Ros Taplin*	59
8	Conversations in context: reframing assessment for international trainee teachers *Alison McMaster*	69
9	Formative and summative assessment rubrics for a UK postgraduate taught education studies module *Andrew Holmes and Paul Hopkins*	77
10	Implementing ipsative feedback through interconnected tasks and comparison processes in a direct-entry program *Bianka Malecka*	84
11	An online peer assessment tool for embedding authentic feedback literacy in students studying creative subjects *David Anthony Parkinson and Michael Edward Parker*	91
12	Integrating scaffolding instructional strategy through digital tools for improving academic performance among undergraduate finance students *Sandar Win, Eliana Lauretta, Tasneem Joosub, and Jayne Revill*	99
13	Developing an experiential formative assessment activity with the GIST framework *Yusuf Oc*	107
14	Formative feedback for international supply chain post-graduate students combining digital and face-to-face formats to enhance engagement and criticality *Rebecca Page-Tickell and Richard Addo-Tenkorang*	114
15	Meet Zara: An AI-generated teaching assistant for enhancing formative assessment and self-regulated learning *Bronwyn Eager*	120

16	Creating an academic safety net for newly inducted undergraduate medical students using formative assessments and feedback Syeda Sadia Fatima, Romana Idress, Satwat Hashmi, Saniya Sabzwari, Sadaf Khan, Kauser Jabeen, and Kulsoom Ghias	127
17	Using e-portfolios and video reflections to support postgraduate students' personal and professional development Charlotte Chandler	135
18	Using digital multisource feedback to provide medical students with formative feedback on their workplace behaviour and professional progress Sarah Allsop, Joanna Howarth, and Jane Williams	142
19	Formatively assessing competency in practical skills in the biological sciences through direct observations and oral feedback Anna Nousek-McGregor, Laura McCaughey, and Lesley Hamilton	149
20	Embedding formative assessment in the flipped statistics classroom Yeh-Ching Low	158
21	Embedding formative feedback through differentiated instruction using Microsoft OneNote class notebooks Samantha Gooneratne	164
22	Scaling up and automating formative assessment in computer science Neil Gordon	172
23	A data-driven approach to student support using formative feedback and targeted interventions Simon Coupland, Conor Fahy, Graeme Stuart, and Zoë Allman	179
24	Beyond the unit: A course-wide, iterative formative assessment and feedback framework for enhancing learning and employability skills in computer science education Ioannis Benardis, Alan Hayes, and James H. Davenport	186
25	Formative diagnostics for student transitions and success through personalised guidance Jack Hogan and Luke Millard	195

26 **Using an ongoing formative feedback approach to support early career academics make progress towards their end point assessment** 202
Bianca Fox and Adam Tate

27 **Reimagining formative assessment and feedback: propositions for practice** 211
Sam Elkington and Alastair Irons

References 227
Index 249

Acknowledgements

For Noah and Charlie – my own constant source of learning, every day.
Sam

For my wife Marie, for all her love, support, and encouragement.
Alastair

About the editors

Sam Elkington
Sam is Professor of Learning and Teaching at Teesside University, where he leads on the university's learning and teaching enhancement portfolio. Sam is a PFHEA and UK National Teaching Fellow (NTF, 2021). He has worked in higher education for over 15 years and has extensive experience working across teaching, research, and academic leadership and policy domains. Sam has previously worked for Advance HE (formerly the Higher Education Academy), where he was National Lead for Assessment and Feedback and Flexible Learning in Higher Education. He holds the dual role of executive committee member and pedagogic research lead for the Association of National Teaching Fellows and is a visiting professor at Leeds Becket University in England and Abertay University in Scotland.

Sam has published widely on different aspects of higher education assessment. His most recent book (with Professor Alastair Irons) explores contemporary themes in formative assessment and feedback in higher education: Irons and Elkington (2021). *Enhancing Learning Through Formative Assessment and Feedback*. London: Routledge.

Alastair Irons
Professor Alastair Irons is Professor of Computer Science, Deputy Principal, and Deputy Vice Chancellor at Abertay University in Scotland. Before coming to Abertay in July 2022, he was Academic Director for Digital Education at the University of Sunderland, having previously been the Dean for the Faculty of Technology. Prior to joining the University of Sunderland in 2008 he worked at ONE North East, Northumbria University, and ICI.

Alastair became a National Teaching Fellow in 2010. Alastair was a visiting scholar at the University of Cape Town in South Africa from 2013–2017 and is currently a visiting professor at the University of Johannesburg and at the British University in Egypt.

His research interests focus on digital education and digital pedagogies but also on digital forensics and cybersecurity. His current research includes digital skills frameworks for students and academics, digital skills for all, and digital poverty, as well as cybersecurity in the classroom and learning safely in the classroom of the future. Alastair has over 20 refereed journal publications and has over 40 conference papers in the last 5 years. His recent book publications include a text (with Professor Sam Elkington) that explores contemporary themes in formative assessment and feedback in higher education (Irons & Elkington, 2021). He has also published (with Professor Byron Brown) an anthology of issues in higher education in a post-COVID world in 2022, Brown, B., & Irons, A. (2022). *The Emerald Handbook of Higher Education in a Post-Covid World: New Approaches and Technologies for Teaching and Learning*. Emerald Publishing Limited.

Alastair is currently Vice President (academic) of the BCS, the Chartered Institute for IT, and is chair of the BCS Academy board; he also sits on the BCS Council and BCS Trustees, is a member of the BCS Academic Accreditation Committee, and is a founding trustee of the BCS Foundation. Whilst in the northeast he was chair of the Newcastle Branch of the BCS, and since moving to Dundee has been elected chair of the Tayside and Fife Branch of the BCS. He is also currently the UK representative on the International Federation for Information Processing (IFIP) and serves on the IFIP board.

MEET THE CASE STUDY CONTRIBUTORS

Richard Addo-Tenkorang is currently a senior lecturer in engineering design and manufacturing at the University of Hertfordshire. Before that, he was a lecturer and module leader for the MBA Supply-Chain Management pathway at the University of East London. Richard's research area evolves around harnessing the collaborative and competitive advantage of digital manufacturing and enterprise resource planning–digital supply chain management.

Zoë Allman is Associate Dean (Academic) in the Faculty of Computing, Engineering and Media at De Montfort University, UK. Zoë is passionate about ensuring and enhancing educational experiences for students and staff within the university community and as such leads activity in collaboration with academics, professional service colleagues, and students.

Sarah Allsop is a medical academic, with 14 years' teaching and leadership experience in medical and anatomy education and a background as an NHS doctor. She is a specialist in curriculum review leadership, development, and design and lead for the Bristol Medical School Education Research Group (BMERG).

John Baranoff's role as a lecturer at the School of Psychology, the University of Adelaide, involves being an educator and clinician-researcher. John teaches both undergraduate and postgraduate courses on campus as well as online.

Ioannis Benardis is a senior lecturer and Director of Studies at the University of Bath. Beyond learning and teaching, Ioannis is extremely passionate about the student experience, and many of his initiatives under different roles focus on empowering students to co-create their university experience.

Charlotte Chandler is a senior lecturer in sport and exercise psychology and Postgraduate Coordinator for the School of Sport and Exercise Science at the University of Derby, UK. She has expertise in developing and leading postgraduate programmes and modules, and her research focuses on the personal and professional development of practitioners.

Simon Coupland is an associate professor of games, maths and intelligent systems at De Montfort University, UK. Simon's interests are in harnessing, combining, and co-opting existing technologies for use in all aspects of teaching and learning at all levels from the individual classroom to the institution.

James H. Davenport is Hebron and Medlock Professor of Information Technology at the University of Bath, a visiting professor at the University of Coventry, an honorary fellow and former Vice-President of the British Computer Society, and an honorary doctor of science from the University of the West in Timişoara.

Annabel de Frece is Senior Lecturer in Sustainable Development at SOAS, University of London. She holds a PhD in development sociology. Her interests include sustainable development, food systems, intersectionality, and education. Annabel is passionate about transformative learning and its potential for steering us towards a more equitable and sustainable future.

Stuart Durkin is Director of Education based in the School of Social Science at the University of Aberdeen. He teaches politics and international relations and has research interests in student experiences of group work and learning in groups, student perspectives on authentic and alternative assessments, and graduate employability enhancement.

Bronwyn Eager serves as a senior lecturer in Entrepreneurship and Innovation, RMIT University, Australia. She is an internationally recognised multidisciplinary researcher and educator in the areas of applied artificial intelligence (AI), digital skills development, entrepreneurship, and the scholarship of teaching and learning.

Anastasia Ejova is an academic at the University of Adelaide's School of Psychology. Since completing a PhD on gambling decision-making in 2013, Anastasia has worked on experimental, brain imaging-based, and survey-based research projects on gambling and health. Anastasia has designed and taught courses in psychology: health, social, personality, and research methods.

Sara El-Kaissi is a student completing her bachelor's degree in psychology at the University of Adelaide. Sara contributed to the project in the course of a research internship during her second year of study.

Conor Fahy is a senior lecturer in computer games programming at De Montfort University, UK. Conor is interested in innovative, research-based methods which can improve learning outcomes and the overall student experience. He is particularly interested in student-centred, data-focused approaches.

Syeda Sadia Fatima is Associate Professor in the Department of Biological and Biomedical Sciences at the Aga Khan University, Pakistan. She has previously been the Chair of the UGME Year 2 Curriculum Sub-Committee and currently leads the Human Body Systems and Disease course in the Year 1 Foundation module.

Paul Fleet is Professor of Authentic Music Theory at Newcastle University, UK, and is (more importantly) husband to Nathalie and father to Belle and Evan. He is a National Teaching Fellow (2021) and Senior Fellow of the HEA and publishes on music theory, authentic education, embodiment, metatonality, and Ferruccio Busoni.

Bianca Fox is a principal fellow of Advance HE and a senior lecturer in academic practice at Nottingham Trent University. Bianca leads the Academic Professional Apprenticeship (APA)/Postgraduate Certificate of Learning & Teaching in Higher Education (PGCLTHE). Bianca holds a PhD in media and communication studies and has more than 15 years of teaching experience in higher education in the UK and other European countries. Bianca was the academic lead of the ERASMUS+ MeLDE project, contributing to the design of a CPD programme in digital literacy for European educators.

Kulsoom Ghias is Professor and Chair of the Department of Biological and Biomedical Sciences at the Aga Khan University, Pakistan. She led the Year 1 Foundation module and has previously been the Co-Chair of the UGME Curriculum Committee.

Samantha Gooneratne is Principal Lecturer for Staffing and Resources in Engineering at Teesside University, UK. She teaches on their Chemical Engineering courses, focusing on reaction engineering and process simulation. Her pedagogic research interests include authentic assessment of group work, feedback literacy amongst engineers, and the use of EdTech tools.

Neil Gordon is a reader in computer science at the University of Hull, UK. Neil is also a National Teaching Fellow. His research interests include applications of computer science to enable true technology enhanced learning, issues around sustainable development, and the interface of mathematics with computing.

Deanne Green is a lecturer and researcher at the University of Adelaide, lecturing in research methods and perception. Deanne's research focuses on exploring factors contributing to visual perception and memory errors, such as attention, arousal, and emotional valence.

Lesley Hamilton is an eLearning officer at University of Glasgow, delivering instructional design and learning technologies.

Satwat Hashmi is Associate Professor and Vice Chair, Education, in the Department of Biological and Biomedical Sciences at the Aga Khan University, Pakistan. She has previously been the Co-chair of the UGME Year 1 Curriculum Sub-Committee.

Alan Hayes is a professor of computer science education at the University of Bath. He is a National Teaching Fellow and Principal Fellow of the Higher Education Academy. He chaired the National Advisory Group for the review of the QAA Subject Benchmark Statement in Computing (2022).

Jack Hogan is Lecturer in Academic Practice at Abertay University in Scotland. His pedagogic research interests are around the first-year student experience, retention, and employability. His current focus is around personalised learning, diagnostics, and how microcredentials can be used to support student transitions.

Andrew Holmes is a senior lecturer at the University of Hull. His areas of research interest include pedagogy and the scholarship of teaching and learning, particularly assessment theory and practice in higher education.

Paul Hopkins was until recently a lecturer and researcher at the University of Hull. His areas of interest are in pedagogy and practice, science education, and the use of technology to support teaching and learning. He has worked in all sectors of education from primary to HE and nationally and internationally as a consultant, researcher, inspector, and advisor. He is now working again as an independent consultant.

Joanna Howarth is a medical academic with 11 years' teaching and leadership experience in medical and neuroscience education and a background in molecular neuroscience research. She is the current programme co-director for undergraduate medicine at Bristol and has a specialist interest in curriculum innovation and supporting students' professional development.

Romana Idress is Associate Professor in the Department of Pathology and Laboratory Medicine at the Aga Khan University, Pakistan. She has previously been the Chair of the UGME Year 1 Curriculum Sub-Committee and currently leads the Year 1 Foundation module.

Kauser Jabeen is Professor in the Department of Pathology and Laboratory Medicine at the Aga Khan University, Pakistan, and Vice Chair of the UGME Curriculum Committee.

Tasneem Joosub is a senior lecturer at Coventry University. She obtained her chartered accountancy qualification from South Africa and her PhD from the University of the Witwatersrand. Tasneem has made scholarly contributions over the last 15 years and has an interest in auditing, risk management, and pedagogy.

Sadaf Khan is Professor in the Department of Surgery and the Associate Dean of Undergraduate Medical Education at the Aga Khan University, Pakistan.

Eliana Lauretta is an assistant professor in finance at the School of Economics, Finance, and Accounting (EFA) at Coventry University and the EFA Scholarship Development Lead (SDL). She holds a PhD in quantitative methods applied to economic policy and was a post-doc international research fellow at Birmingham Business School, University of Birmingham.

Yeh-Ching Low is an associate professor at Sunway University, Malaysia. Her research interests are in statistical modelling, Monte Carlo methods, statistical methods in data science, and STEM education. She is an active researcher with publications in indexed journals and engagements with the broader scientific community through conference presentations.

Bianka Malecka is a curriculum writer and English language teacher at UNSW College in Sydney, Australia. She holds a PhD in education from CRADLE (Centre for Research in Assessment and Digital Learning), Deakin University. Her research interests include feedback literacy, assessment design, and teacher education.

Laura McCaughey is a lecturer in microbiology at University of Glasgow, investigating employability and work-related learning.

Alison McMaster is a senior lecturer at the University of Sunderland, leading the PGCE iQTS Primary Programme in the International Initial Teacher Training team. Formerly a primary teacher, she champions authentic assessment in teacher education, bridging practice with research for over 500 global students annually in PGCE distance learning programmes.

Luke Millard is Dean of Teaching and Learning at Abertay University in Scotland. He is a professor of student development and Principal Fellow of the UK's Higher Education Academy, which recognised his work on improving the student experience through co-creation work with staff and students.

Nadya Moosa is a lecturer in the Education Faculty at the Higher Colleges of Technology, UAE. She has also held additional roles as System Course Team Leader, Teaching Practicum Coordinator, Acting Program Team Leader, and Quality Assurance Manager in the Faculty of Education over the past 10 years.

Anna Nousek-McGregor is a senior lecturer in ecology at University of Glasgow, exploring fieldwork learning and employability.

Yusuf Oc is an associate professor (senior lecturer) in marketing education at Bayes Business School, City University of London, UK. He is the co-author of the textbook *Consumer Behaviour: Building Marketing Strategy* from McGraw-Hill and serves as the course director of the Marketing Strategy and Innovation MSc program at Bayes.

Rebecca Page-Tickell is a senior lecturer in work-based learning at the University of East London, UK.

Michael Edward Parker is Director of Impact and IP Commercialisation in Research and Innovation Services at Northumbria University, UK.

David Anthony Parkinson is Director of Postgraduate Research for the School of Design and Assistant Professor for Industrial Design Subject Group at Northumbria University, UK.

Joy Perkins is the Educational & Employability Development Adviser based at the University of Aberdeen. She works in partnership with academics to enable cross-fertilisation of employability ideas and practice across the university. Her research interests and recent publications include work-integrated learning and the role of employer engagement in curriculum development.

Phil Quirke is Executive Dean Education at the Higher Colleges of Technology, UAE. He has been in higher education leadership positions for over 20 years and published widely on teacher education, reflective writing, and educational management and leadership.

Jayne Revill is a principal lecturer and teaching and learning portfolio lead in the Department of Finance, Accounting, and Business Systems at Sheffield Business School, Sheffield Hallam University. Her research interests mainly revolve around pedagogic practice in teaching and learning, which includes e-learning, digital skills, and artificial intelligence.

Saniya Sabzwari is Professor in the Department of Family Medicine at the Aga Khan University, Pakistan. She is currently the Chair of the Undergraduate Medical Education Examination and Promotions Committee and has previously been the Co-Chair of the UGME Curriculum Committee.

Graeme Stuart is a senior lecturer in the Faculty of Computing, Engineering and Media at De Montfort University, UK. Graeme leads undergraduate programming and web development modules and has research interests in the influence of data analytics and user-interface design in complex systems.

Ros Taplin is a reader in environmental management in the Centre for Development, Environment and Policy, Department of Development Studies at SOAS, University of London (UK). She is an enthusiastic and committed interdisciplinary educator and researcher and has contributed to the environmental policy, environmental art, and education for sustainability literature.

Adam Tate is a senior lecturer in academic practice. He joined NTU's Academic Practice team in March 2021 and is co-course leader of the Academic Professional Apprenticeship (APA)/Postgraduate Certificate of Learning & Teaching in Higher Education (PGCLTHE). He is passionate about effective education, inclusive practice and policy, and removing barriers to participation.

Natasha van Antwerpen is a lecturer and researcher at the University of Adelaide's School of Psychology. Natasha teaches research methods and global psychology across on-campus, online, and experiential learning experiences. Natasha has also designed interdisciplinary and practice-focused courses, with much of her research focusing on the application of psychology to journalistic reporting.

Jane Williams is a member of the teaching and leadership team for undergraduate medicine at Bristol with 30 years' experience of leading digital education developments supporting health sciences education. Her specialist interests include curriculum development, digital by design, and supporting students' professional development.

Sandar Win is the Head of Division for Economics and Finance at Sheffield Business School, Sheffield Hallam University. She is interested in connecting research and practice. Her primary research interests in pedagogy include integrating and promoting formative feedback and digital technologies in both formative and summative assessments.

1

INTRODUCTION

SAM ELKINGTON AND ALASTAIR IRONS

A great deal has changed in higher education (HE) since our last book on formative assessment and formative feedback in 2021 (Irons & Elkington, 2021). We have emerged from a global pandemic, expectations about modes of delivery in higher education have evolved, and the international geopolitical environment has been transformed, with the demand for different forms of higher education continuing to grow (although the growth might not be as stark in Western Europe). Propelled by this unprecedented sector disruption we have also seen such innovation in digital educational technology that our practice environments are now substantively different compared to where we were even in 2021. The creation of this book has been timed to provide support to practitioners in the increasingly necessary work of (re)considering what meaningful assessment and feedback ought to look like in a changing higher education environment to enhance the student learning experience. More specifically, our aim in developing this book and the collection of case studies it contains is to provide a resource which practitioners can utilise to design and create appropriately future facing assessments at a time when more nuanced, flexible, and responsive assessment approaches are being called for.

ON CHANGING EDUCATIONAL ENVIRONMENTS

It is impossible to ignore the rapid and near-constant innovation in digital technology that has taken place since 2021, with the recent proliferation of generative AI (GenAI) having perhaps the most destabilising impact on the higher education sector. In some higher education institutions, the initial reaction was to ban generative AI and to return to an assessment regime of closed-book, time-constrained examinations. The spirit of this book is one of embracing the use of technology to reframe and restructure how we design and practice the kinds of assessment approaches that encourage students to develop their understanding of using digital technologies (including GenAI applications) for enabling meaningful learning in their disciplines and to develop their creative and critical thinking abilities.

At the time of writing higher education remains in a state of flux. There are many variables to consider, and these variables will differ depending on where in the world higher education provision is taking place. Wherever we are there are pressures on universities such as rising costs (pay rises, inflation, rising utilities, need for digital security) and dealing with government funding policies (in many countries across the world this means real term cuts). We have already mentioned the need to consider alternative modes of study and flexibility in learning pathways. Other equally complex considerations include shifting demographics of students choosing to enter higher education and changing demands for certain subjects. The international student situation continues to fluctuate, and issues such as immigration, availability of post-study work visas, and restrictions on students' ability to bring dependents with them when studying has rendered the student market extremely unpredictable.

As the wider HE environment is changing, so too is the student experience. The choices that students have before them now extend beyond that of selecting the subject they want to study and the location of the university they wish to attend. There are additional decisions students are required to consider, such as the face-to-face nature of their university experience, the on-campus requirements of their studies, the flexibility of delivery patterns, and the range and accessibility of digital resources that are made available to them. Choices in how to access higher education and how to engage with programmes of choice have an impact on the ways universities need to operate and support students. For the purposes of this book, we are most interested in understanding the impact of digital technology on our changing educational environments and how as educators we might approach the concepts of assessment and feedback to effectively and with confidence move university assessment forward in ways that prepare students for a multitude of future possibilities.

A POST-DIGITAL EDUCATION

Education, and by extension how we approach learning, teaching, and assessment, is always affected by the context in which it is enacted (Bearman et al., 2022; Boud et al., 2018). We have now entered an era wherein hybrid education has moved to become almost the de-facto norm for a global higher education sector. The swift proliferation of digital learning technologies accompanying this movement has meant that educators have had to adapt to the demands of changing patterns of work and student learning, with the enactment of academic practice now occurring across a multitude of interconnected, digital, and physical environments (Elkington & Chesterton, 2023; Goodyear, 2020). The 'hybridisation' of higher education is a critical aspect of the emerging requirements of 'flexible learning environments' at every scale, blurring the boundaries between distinct contexts of learning and their activities. Amidst conditions of hybridity and flexibility higher education systems are revealed as complex and multidimensional comprising the interleaving of formal and informal social structures of learning, along with the combination of physical and digital tools mediating individuals' interaction with the world and society (Fawns et al., 2022; Goodyear, 2020). Recent 'post-digital' educational research has argued for a shift in perspective, away from viewing technologies simply as 'tools' for enhancement and toward greater recognition of the ways digital systems and infrastructures are already profoundly interleaved with the everyday activities of teaching and learning (Fawns, 2022; Jandrić et al., 2018; Knox, 2019). Fundamental to a post-digital understanding of education is an opposition to any kind of binary thinking (digital–analog, technological–non-technological, human–non-human, etc.) and a general resistance to predominant attitudes of technological instrumentalism and determinism (Fawns, 2019). As Jandrić et al. (2018) point out, in a post-digital world the 'digital technology and media is [no longer] separate, virtual, 'other', to a 'natural' human and social life' (p. 893). In seeking to describe and understand our present socio-technical reality, post-digital theory 'opens up news spaces to understand learning across wider perspectives than a simple, instrumental acquisition of skills' (Jandrić & Hayes, 2020, p. 288) and signals a critical appraisal of the assumptions embedded in a general understanding of the digital in higher education (Knox, 2019).

A post-digital outlook is core to the framing of this book, where all digitally mediated learning activity is recognised as inherently social, material, and embedded in rich and diverse contexts (Fawns, 2019; Jandrić et al., 2018). Whilst higher education has been deeply affected by the rapid expansion of digital learning technologies as an everyday feature in the learning experiences offered, such technologies are more than simply a backdrop to learning and teaching activity. We adopt a post-digital perspective in recognition that all forms of education need to account for the complex integration of digital, social, and material elements that constitute them, including the relationships, identities, practices, and mobilities that are produced, changed, and/or mediated through them (Ross, 2023). Part of a post-digital sensibility is to recognise the need to move beyond 'a tendency to understand technology in terms of tangible devices, towards a broader understanding of the socio-technical systems within which the project of education is constituted' (Knox, 2019, p. 361). Such a position takes neither technology or pedagogy as the main unit of analysis but rather a more holistic view of entangled elements and relationships which open possibilities for more meaningful investigation of learning, teaching, and assessment activity (Fawns, 2019; Jandrić et al., 2018). The decisive factor here is that digital transformation in educational settings encompasses more than just digitisation of information, tasks, and processes. It is always the sum of digital and material practices and procedures necessary to achieve a change process that enables higher education institutions to successfully leverage the use of digital technology to enhance the learning experience (Kopp et al., 2019). The integration of new technologies and related pedagogic practices into existing ecologies generates opportunities and challenges for educators. Given the widespread mainstreaming of software platforms and online teaching provision, there is a pressing need to better understand the role of digital technology across different educational settings and the complex social realities of educational practice that play out (Selwyn, 2023). Crucially, these practices are not necessarily equally accessible to all (Elkington & Chesterton, 2024; Ross, 2023). Indeed, embedded inequalities in access and engagement with digital modes of learning present an ongoing challenge for educators and higher education institutions. Today, student learning encompasses a wide diversity of practices, spaces, experiences, and outcomes, within and outside of formal educational settings that need to be recognised and accommodated for through appropriately responsive approaches to learning, teaching and assessment.

THINKING ABOUT ASSESSMENT IN POST-DIGITAL ENVIRONMENTS

Set against the backdrop of unprecedented challenge and sector uncertainty in higher education, digital skills and education technology are fundamental to the evolution of a dynamic and relevant learning environment for universities (Goodyear, 2020). When we consider this in the more defined arena of higher education assessment and feedback, it becomes clear there is considerable work that is still needed to fully grasp and understand the wide-ranging pedagogic affordances of available digital learning tools and technologies for assessment design. Universities have had to rethink how the significant resources devoted to assessment and feedback might be reconfigured for digital and physical learning environments to better support student learning across different modes of delivery (Carvalho et al., 2017; Goodyear et al., 2017; Jandrić, 2020). In this sense, assessment and feedback would appear to represent important variables in driving broader environmental changes for HE. But what sorts of assessment, and of course learning, fit with the complexities and contingencies of a post-digital world? It would seem to us a stronger awareness of who and what we assess and how we assess and value (what is done with) the artefacts produced are important considerations in developing a more critical contemporary understanding of technology in assessment and its role in supporting the student learning experience.

As noted, advancement of digital learning technologies and tools coupled with increasing diversification of learner profiles and pathways through higher education programmes has signalled a need to develop greater flexibility and responsiveness in university assessment. Here technology is, on the one hand, a key enabler for a truly personalised learning experience. On the other hand, with issues of variable access to digital technology (digital poverty) and the capacity of educators and students to effectively recognise and utilise the affordances available digital tools (digital literacy), assessment designs are increasingly needing to recognise individual differences between students for the purpose of accessibility, employing different combinations of assessment methods and support to meet the diversity of learning needs for different groups of students (Stommel, 2020). Prioritising greater flexibility in university assessment arrangements in today's post-digital educational environments means shifting our focus on to assessment approaches and designs that are sensitive to the needs and circumstances of students, giving them more control and ownership over assessment processes – with no learning deficit. Flexible, personalised assessment increases student engagement in the assessment process and is regarded as an important first step in creating a student-led pedagogy (O'Neill, 2022; Wanner et al., 2024). We argue that this transformation of assessment requires a concerted movement towards embedding more formative assessment approaches with greater input from students acting in partnership with educators. An explicit focus on formative assessment and feedback encourages an important shift in emphasis beyond assessment as a qualification system to provide universities and educators with practicable mechanisms through which to modify and improve learning and teaching processes and guide meaningful student learning development. This entails assigning greater value and importance to the active role of students in the assessment process through reinforcing and supporting their ability to manage their own learning strategies alongside their autonomy to continue learning beyond taught content and alongside wider life commitments.

At a time when the pervasiveness of technological innovation is redefining the nature and form of educational encounters for learners and practitioners alike, it has never been more important to give careful thought to the role of formative assessment and feedback and how digital learning tools and techniques might be combined and configured to provide meaningful learning opportunities for diverse groups of students. By adopting an explicit 'practice focus' this book attempts to negate and challenge the common place view of digital tools and technologies as a separate domain in assessment design. Whilst technology does have implications for assessment practice, the possibilities for any such practices are always socially and materially situated; that is, they 'relate to the traditions, practices, culture, policy, and infrastructure in which they are embedded' (Fawns, 2022, p. 715). The primary challenge is one of understanding and adapting a wider repertoire of approaches and practices in assessment to encompass new and multiple contexts that are no longer experienced as separate, virtual, or other in students' higher education experience. Indeed, the ability of universities, educators, and students to effectively navigate the digital and material domains in assessment has become of critical strategic and pedagogic importance.

ABOUT THIS BOOK

An explicit focus on formative assessment processes designed to set up and enable a post-digital sensibility offers a powerful and contrasting viewpoint from the predominant deterministic rhetoric about the role of technology in university assessment. As we interact with multiple realities, cultures, systems, spaces, and practice forms across increasingly diverse educational settings, it is our proposition in presenting this body of work that a formative outlook will be key to grasping, understanding, and sharing what our human experiences of learning mean in these contexts.

In Chapter 2, we draw upon existing and emerging research in post-digital education and assessment to present an understanding of the close, complex, and changing relationship between digital learning technology and assessment and the prospects for formative practices and processes to support truly sustainable student learning. It is generally recognised in the higher education assessment research literature that there is still a need for clarification towards digital perspectives and practices in formative assessment and feedback (Liu & Zhang, 2022; Kaya-Capocci et al., 2022). In response, this volume brings together an international collection of disciplinary case studies that exemplify effective and innovative efforts at integrated formative assessment and feedback practice in post-digital learning environments. In doing so, the volume attempts to occupy the territory between abstract theorising about issues, challenges, and technical questions related to assessment in digital education and the academic practice of effective, integrated, formative assessment processes that support flexible, timely, and accessible opportunities for student learning. The case study series itself comprises a range of different viewpoints, approaches, and scales of application that together represent a wide-ranging account of contemporary formative assessment practice spanning the disciplines and different types of higher education institutions and learning environments. The book looks to chart the changing patterns of pedagogy that accompany such diversity of practice, including the use of digital software, tools, and devices to supplement and mediate meaningful relationships between learners and teachers and to provide spaces where students can engage with a range of valid and relevant assessment tasks that enable them to demonstrate what they know, understand, and can do.

We are exceptionally grateful to the international colleagues who have contributed case study examples of formative assessment and feedback from their own practice. The collaborative spirit and ethos of this volume builds on our previous foray into exploring the state of formative assessment and feedback in higher education (Irons & Elkington 2021) and is intended to provide a practical point of reference from which educators can explore, review, consider, and potentially adopt (and adapt) the examples presented to suit their own environment and practice. Importantly, in presenting this body of work, the book does not suggest that there is a single best solution. Instead, the aim is to encourage colleagues to look again at why they are assessing, what they hope to achieve, and how they enable students to learn through the assessment approaches deployed and the feedback that is generated.

Many of the principles in formative assessment and feedback can be discussed at a generic level, and we do this in Chapter 2 (also see Irons & Elkington, 2021 for a more detailed conceptual and theoretical background). We revisit these principles again in the closing chapter of the book where they are considered alongside an analysis and synthesis of common themes, challenges, and opportunities for practice to emerge from the case studies and where certain issues are teased out and expanded upon. These include:

- the purposes and value of formative assessment and formative feedback;
- the relationship between formative assessment and student engagement in assessment processes;
- inclusive designs for creating assessment activities;
- students' ability in effectively utilising feedback for learning and improvement.

There are several recurring themes which are addressed across the case study series – no apology is made for repetition. In much the same way that students learn from feedback which reinforces a pertinent point – so we can learn from having messages reinforced as well. Themes include:

- involving students in the feedback process – one might think this is obvious, but it can be challenging to achieve in practice;
- being clear to students about what we are trying to achieve in providing feedback;
- ensuring equity in all formative activities considering the diverse student population;
- explaining to students how formative assessment activities are contributing to their learning development;
- what it means to provide timely and constructive feedback on assessment activities;
- considering the role of technology and its relationship with wider and diverse digital environments.

Through this mosaic of practice, our intention is to capture and illustrate practicable knowledge and insights into the rich digital, social, and material nature of formative assessment practice and the complex processes it involves. In doing so we draw to the fore the relevance of the particularities of formative processes and their capacity to reflect, and in many ways enrich, the human experience of learning. Inevitably, this opens up all manner of considerations as to the paths that a post-digital framing of formative assessment might follow, whether at the personal or social level and whether in formal educational spaces or beyond. What are the significant features of our changing educational contexts in which formative assessment must be worked out? And what might be the critical digital, social, and material elements in this working out? Is the practice of formative assessment better viewed from the inside, as a personal and social project, or from the outside, as a part of a still wider system? What room might there be for imagination and creativity in shaping relevant and meaningful formative processes, or are these processes fundamentally dependent on and inspired by the imagination and creativity of those involved? In the following chapters, our overarching aim is to present you, the reader, with means of grappling with the critical thrust of the post-digital as a theoretical intervention in higher education assessment. Through a consideration of diverse practice forms, we go on to consider how formative assessment might be productively thought of as a means of engaging in the building of its own technologies for learning relevant to the contingencies and complexities of a changing higher education environment.

2

FORMATIVE ASSESSMENT AND FEEDBACK IN POST-DIGITAL HIGHER EDUCATION

SAM ELKINGTON AND ALASTAIR IRONS

INTRODUCTION

Formative assessment is recognised as an integral part of the contemporary higher education learning environment, which includes both teaching practice and students' learning (Black & Wiliam, 2018; Leenknecht et al., 2021). In Irons and Elkington (2021) we define formative assessment as 'any task that is intended to provide feedback to the student such that they can improve and self-regulate their work and to the teacher so that they may adjust their teaching' (p. 9). Feedback is positioned as the active component in positioning *assessment-for-learning*; that is, providing information about student learning achievement that, in turn, allows active and student-led approaches to be adapted to respond to the changing needs of the learner and recognises the important benefit that feedback has on learning (Irons & Elkington, 2021). Carless and Boud (2018) define feedback as 'a process through which learners make sense of information from various sources and use it to enhance their work or learning strategies' (p. 1). It is well documented within the higher education (HE) assessment literature that assessment feedback is often ineffective because it is delivered too late to be useful for students for meaningful learning (Boud & Molloy, 2013); because it relates to issues, topics or tasks that are isolated (Nicol & Macfarlane-Dick, 2006); or because students do not value the information they do receive on their work and do not take action to improve their ongoing learning (Pitt & Norton, 2017; Winstone et al., 2017a). Formative feedback should endeavour to provide students with an indication of where they are in relation to achieving learning outcomes or standards, where they need to progress to, and how they will be able to reach the expected level (Black & Wiliam, 2018). For this to be effective the feedback information should be based on clear goals that the student believes are achievable and valuable (Winstone et al., 2017b). Feedback should be understandable and communicated in such a way that enables students to use the feedback to help in achieving the learning outcomes or reaching the required standard (Henderson et al., 2019a). Similarly, feedback should be framed and delivered in ways that encourage students to take actions to address any learning issues (Winstone & Boud, 2022). It follows that if feedback information delivered to students about their learning does not generate meaningful action in response, it is unlikely the feedback will impact student learning as we might intend (Carless & Boud, 2018).

In current practice, it is still the case that summative assessment – *assessment-of-learning* – tasks are typically required to carry much of the responsibility for providing feedback, often without sufficient linkage from good formative assessment (Boud et al., 2018; Elkington, 2019). Notably, recent feedback research shifts the emphasis to the role of the student in making sense of, and using, feedback, and away from inputs provided solely by the tutor (Winstone et al., 2017a; Winstone & Boud, 2022; Winstone & Carless, 2021). There is also growing research evidence demonstrating the value of using information and communication technology to support formative assessment where computer-based systems can be a source of information that stimulates the feedback process for students (Cavalcanti et al., 2021; McCallum & Milner, 2021). Despite this, there are calls (i.e., Leenknecht et al., 2021) for more research that accounts for how digital technology can used to elicit and mediate active student engagement with feedback information for the purposes of learning development. Students need to be provided with space and opportunity to act on the feedback they receive and 'close the loop' on learning tasks (Carless, 2019; Pitt & Winstone, 2020; Pitt & Norton, 2017). This is most effectively achieved, according to David Carless, when feedback is viewed as a dialogic interaction in which 'learners make sense of information from varied sources and use it to enhance the quality of their work or learning strategies' (2015, p. 192).

Such a view establishes feedback as a connected and coherent process, which needs to be designed into programmes and modules, so that students can use it in developmental ways (Dawson et al., 2019; Kruiper et al., 2022). This shifts priorities from conventional, formulaic approaches to content learning to a focus on the 'process' of student learning development. As educators we need to give careful thought to ensuring that formative assessment and feedback provide positive student learning opportunities, encourage dialogue and discourse between students and teachers, and provide motivation and impetus for students to drive their own learning (Winstone & Carless, 2019; Leenknecht et al., 2021). This is an important step in activating *assessment-as-learning* where student involvement in assessment, the effective use of feedback, participating in peer assessment, and self-monitoring of progress are positioned as key aspects of a student's long-term learning development (Jisc, 2021).

The contemporary drive to digitise student assessment raises significant opportunities for embedding formative assessment processes and devising pedagogic responses consistent with it. This, in turn, requires increasingly 'blended' approaches revolving around the combination of teacher and student perspectives, integration of available digital technologies and tools, and the range of new learning opportunities and approaches offered (Beetham & MacNeill, 2023). Such approaches foreground new flexible and inclusive spaces for assessment-for-learning. In Irons and Elkington (2021) we noted several significant pedagogic benefits for both students and educators if such arrangements can increase the amount and value of formative assessment at module and course level, including:

- Improving learner engagement by offering interactive and repeatable formative tasks with integrated feedback.
- Speedy assessment processes making assessment feedback immediate and richer through personalised feedback – through early and regular online formative tasks.
- Increasing the opportunities to act on the feedback information provided – regular culminative formative tasks capturing through an e-portfolio of reflective blogs.
- Supportive online self- and peer assessment activities to generate feedback information – encouraging online formative feedback dialogues using digital rubrics capturing assessment criteria.
- Giving students opportunities to choose how to receive, store and refer to feedback – making use of online reflective journals/blogs curated in an e-portfolio.

In digital learning environments, the imperative of securing viable summative assessment arrangements, alongside the need to provide a reliable, verifiable mark for each individual assignment, can often limit the potential of formative assessment and feedback to support student learning development (Elkington, 2019; McCallum & Milner, 2021). A post-digital view of teaching and assessment is considered a useful lens to help us examine the wide-ranging practices associated with formative assessment and feedback that incorporate combinations of digital and material approaches and activities. It sees the digital, material, and social as intrinsically connected (Fawns, 2019; Carvalho & Yeoman, 2021; Gourlay, 2021). Here, assessment practice is produced by means of a dynamic, shared relationship between the teacher, the student, the digital tools, and technologies deployed, as well as the broader context – none of which remain static, underscoring the point that students' learning activity is always epistemically, physically, and socially situated (Yeoman & Wilson, 2019). In this chapter we bring together key literature in post-digital education and assessment and feedback to construct an understanding of the close, complex, and changing relationship between digital learning technology and assessment and the prospective formative practices and processes it supports.

UNDERSTANDING FORMATIVE ASSESSMENT PRACTICE THROUGH A POST-DIGITAL LENS

It is important that we acknowledge that assessment and technology are not context neutral but rather are shaped by the circumstances of how they are used (Bearman et al., 2022; Dawson et al., 2019; Selwyn, 2023). How educators approach assessment design is at once influenced by their own disciplines and their (inter)relationships with colleagues and with the wider learning infrastructure (i.e., policies, learning management systems and campus spaces). Circumstances directly and indirectly affect how educators work with technology in their assessment designs as they weigh up students' responses alongside the desire to be innovative in their practice and how they manage logistical challenges (Bennett et al., 2017). The choices educators make regarding the use of technology in their teaching and assessment designs as it relates to task composition, preferred social configurations, and the resources required can often be restricted by perceptions of what is possible within rooted disciplinary convention relating to teaching using technology. In response, Fawns (2022) warns that 'technologies are not fixed, homogenous things with generalisable characteristics or consequences' (p. 5). In practice, he elaborates, digital technology is 'always an assembly of multiple other technologies and practices and always more than the sum of its parts' (p. 6). From this perspective, rather than focusing on certain tools, objects, or devices, it is the combination of technologies in use and their socio-material relations to the spaces, places, and contexts in which they are embedded that carry prominence (Carvalho & Yeoman, 2021). In assessment, this means moving our thinking beyond a singular focus on assessment judgements towards an understanding of assessment 'as it is practiced' (Boud et al., 2018) and a focus grounded in the shared practice realities of learners and educators and the various material, and digital resources involved (Markauskaite et al., 2023).

A post-digital view of assessment places particular significance on the relations among the formative 'in-process' interactions and material arrangements in particular environments and forms of knowing (including related knowledge artefacts, i.e., assignments) generated from these. Our pedagogical designs and arrangements enable and constrain what happens when assessments are played out in practice; they form what Kemmis (2021) terms 'conditions of possibility' for the ways that practices might unfold in a particular location and time – be it face to face, online, or hybrid. Importantly for our purposes in this chapter, such conditions are experienced formatively in the sense that they prefigure (helping to structure, inform, and shape) learning, teaching, and assessment practices; they do not predetermine them. We take the use of the term 'formative' here to describe the function that evidence generated from the act of assessment serves, rather than the assessment itself, as well as a concern with who is doing the assessment and how it is negotiated 'in practice' (Irons & Elkington, 2021). Oftentimes educators will make decisions regarding the role such evidence plays in the assessment process, but equally important is recognising the role of individual learners and their peers as active agents in making such decisions (Winstone & Carless, 2019). From this perspective, focus shifts to the resulting (inter)action(s) – what is actually done with the evidence generated through formative exercises to inform and shape subsequent (inter)action(s). The emphasis on decisions as being at the heart of formative assessment practices assists with the design of assessment processes; if formative assessments are designed with no clear decision or goal in mind, then there is a good chance that information generated from the assessment will remain unutilised, thus limiting the learning benefit for both students and the wider learning environment (Irons & Elkington, 2021). Effective formative assessment, then, involves both educators and students making incremental decisions and judgments about the quality of students' learning and using available digital tools and technology to generate actionable information to guide and improve students' understanding and skills at a practice level.

Practically speaking, formative assessment is how we shift the focus from designed teaching to the process of student learning. The choices made by educators and students with regard to the configuration of tasks, tools, and social arrangements for the purposes of formative assessment shape the ways learners are able to exercise their agency in (re)shaping what has been proposed. Goodyear and Carvalho (2014) suggest this takes place during what they have labelled 'learntime'. Learntime is conceptualised as the time when learning activity unfolds, the time when learners interact with the designed components of work set and with others. Student assessment activity at learntime is emergent and encapsulates a mutual shaping of technology, teaching methods, and contexts which are, in practice, always negotiated between educators, learners, and their environments (Fawns, 2019). Assessment practices (including their outcomes) emerge from and are contingent upon an array of complex relations and cannot, therefore, be wholly determined in advance (Boud et al., 2018). Rather, they emerge through processes of co-configuration in which students take-up, customise, and change what we as educators design and put in place for them. In this way, student assessment activity is (inter)connected with other related learning and teaching activities through different (co)configurations of digital and material tools and resources that together come to influence assessment practices and are shaped by the experiences of those individuals (learners and educators) involved. Crucially, student learning is not restricted to what happens when teachers and students come together in formally timetabled spaces and times (Gourlay & Oliver, 2018). This co-configurative work will also involve mixing aspects of practice and experience that exist as part of students' lives outside of the formal 'designed' educational environment. For instance, consider how students might combine the use of a designated virtual learning environment or set of associated learning resources with their preferred social networking applications to aid in liaising and collaborating with other students more easily for the purposes of a group-based assignment.

Student assessment activity is entangled with the dynamic spaces, places, and environments within which it occurs and inherently dependent upon the (inter)relationships of those individuals involved and the extent to which such relationships foster meaningful connections, authenticity, and responsiveness (their afforded flexibility; more on this later) in and through the learning encounters that emerge (Fawns, 2022). This foregrounds an understanding of learning activity as part of a network of multiple actors (students, educators, peers) engaged in particular ways of knowing, grounded in a range of digital and material elements (Goodyear & Carvalho, 2014). Such network learning emerges through active participation in diverse social contexts and often involves a range of activities such as reading and writing; searching, finding, and selecting topics and resources; reflecting on experiences; developing knowledge artefacts; and communicating ideas (Carvalho & Yeoman, 2021). In practice, learners will often switch between periods of individual reflection and more collaborative modes of working, along with periods of using technology individually or alongside others, often producing physical and conceptual artefacts that can take a range of forms. These might include blogs, e-portfolios, and other audio-visual tools and artefacts that enable students to engage in different ways of documenting their progress and achievements.

Engaging with ideas of emergence, connectedness, and networks to foreground an understanding of formative assessment and feedback as post-digital practice troubles the logic of predetermined assessment designs on the grounds of the many formative feedback exchanges and incremental in-the-moment adjustments and adaptations that may be required and are made by educators and learners during the assessment process for reasons beyond determining the quality of student performance. This draws attention to the multiple acts of construction that leads to what we typically identify as assessment practice (Boud et al., 2018). Perhaps more importantly, it privileges what is happening in the social and material world, rather than what an individual (educator or learner) believes should occur relative to some static criteria for performance. Also revealed is the complexity of actions, the multiplicity of demands, as well as the need for different kinds of representation in and through the assessment arrangements educators chose to implement (Elkington & Chesterton, 2023). Paying attention to formative assessment practices from this perspective helps educators not only assess and guide student performance 'in-process' but also to monitor, evaluate, and refine their own educational designs to be responsive to the multiplicity of environments in which learning occurs.

More so than ever before, we as educators must be sensitive to the wider context and account for how physical and digital environments, materials, and social arrangements are influenced not only by our educational designs but also by institutionally centralised configurations of available material and digital technologies in the form of physical spaces and virtual learning environments and platforms (Goodyear, 2020; Lamb et al., 2022). This expanded framing reveals the diversity of ways in which educators and learners engage with technology in the assessment process. Instead of assuming sameness and homogeneity in student learning experiences, assessment designs need to calibrate and set up a variety of educational options for students aligned to their needs, patterns of readiness, interests, and circumstances (Haniya & Roberts-Lieb, 2017). A post-digital view of assessment helps to highlight and understand what might be 'new' about such practices and our relationships with the digital in these designs whilst also recognising the ways that educational technology is already embedded in, and entangled with, existing assessment practices and wider systems (Dron, 2023; Fawns, 2019, 2022). A crucial element of effective technology-enabled assessment is the ability to discern and appropriately situate the affordances of specific technologies to support assessment-for-learning. Considering formative assessment activity in this post-digital practice frame provides scope for new forms of assessment work across a range of settings and environments, requiring student-centred approaches and designs that are sensitive to the learning needs and circumstances of different groups of learners, whatever their mode of study. In the remainder of this chapter, we focus on three affordances opened up by a post-digital formative assessment practice frame: embedding assessment flexibilities, activating learning processes through integrated assessment designs, and participatory multimodal assessment.

EMBEDDING ASSESSMENT FLEXIBILITIES

Advances in digital technology have revealed significant potential for flexible pedagogy, opening up the learning process, extending and expanding access, and improving inclusivity (Beetham & MacNeill, 2023). These developments have, in turn, highlighted the diversity of ways in which students perceive and understand assessment information, how they navigate assessment within different learning environments, and the ways in which they are motivated to learn and express what they know in and through different assessment arrangements (Bearman et al., 2022). Change and innovation in educational technology has facilitated a shift in expectations, practices, and discourse around how learning and assessment is situated in space and time affording the reconfiguration of different digital tools, activities, and interactions to make it possible to work with knowledge in new and engaging ways (Welch et al., 2020). Though their approaches to learning and levels of digital literacy may vary, students are using the affordances of different digital tools and platforms to discover and construct knowledge that is meaningful to their learning needs and circumstances (Goodyear, 2020). This requires increasingly blended approaches that centre on a combined appreciation of teacher and student perspectives moving us beyond the conventional view of simply providing students with a range of formative and summative tasks and the alignment of assessment tasks with learning outcomes. It is relatively straightforward to describe assessment tasks as being formative and summative in nature. However, such descriptors struggle to convey the intricacies inherent in effectively operationalising assessment and feedback processes in today's digital learning environments. It is increasingly important that assessment processes be responsive to both students' individual learning needs as well as the needs of the curriculum, accommodating students' unique patterns of readiness, interests, experiences, and related modes of learning (Beetham & MacNeill, 2023; Elkington, 2021; Elkington & Chesterton, 2024).

There is burgeoning evidence demonstrating an effective strategy to achieve this is to 'design in' greater flexibility around how students make choices about assessment methods and formats, as well as the extent to which they have an active role in shaping the assessment approaches and processes they are involved in (O'Neill, 2022). Educators might provide students opportunity for negotiated and managed choice between an accepted range of 'alternative' assessment formats (Wanner et al., 2024), make assessment strategies something students can discuss (Cowan, 2023), let students set assessment deadlines within a set timeframe, or even ask students to co-create assessment criteria (Jopp & Cohen, 2022). The research evidence tells us that flexible assessment can increase student engagement in the assessment process, positively impacting student motivation and attitudes towards learning, the exercise of choice and self-direction leading to a greater feeling of autonomy and control (O'Neill & Padden, 2021). It also represents a change in direction of knowledge flows and a redistributed model of learners as co-creators or co-designers that places particular emphasis on formative assessment processes as the locus for supporting student agency (Leenknecht et al., 2021).

In seeking to embed greater flexibility in assessment processes, educators must also consider how students see themselves as learners and the extent to which they are equipped and prepared to take responsibility for their own learning (Elkington & Chesterton, 2023). This means shifting focus onto 'learning-focused' assessment strategies and the facilitative role of formative assessment processes designed to actively involve students in assessment in ways which develop their ability to self-monitor, regulate their own learning behaviour, and act upon feedback in timely and meaningful ways (Winstone & Carless, 2019). By taking advantage of the affordances of today's digital learning environments, educators can design and implement flexible and recursive sequences of activities in which learners are actively engaged in a process of materialising their understanding in a variety of formats, constructing their learning experiences, and (re)configuring their understandings through ongoing evaluation, feedback, and reflection. Through better access to different forms of assessment information and adopting learner-focused designs that make use of a broader range of tasks, automated or speedier feedback, and timely student-student and student-staff dialogues around assessment tasks, digital learning environments that support and enable assessment flexibility offer workspaces that allow learners to bring their own interests and experiences to bear on their learning (Elkington & Chesterton, 2024).

Embedding flexibility through 'designed' formative assessment processes provides a platform for personalising student learning experiences; supporting core agendas of accessibility; and promoting independent, self-directed learning (Hanesworth et al., 2019; Nieminen, 2024). Though the form and scope of flexible assessment designs will inevitably shift and change depending on the purpose of work being undertaken, the overarching goal is always the same: designing assessments that allow for meaningful interpretation of student performance with the greatest access to information by the widest range of learners. This can, in turn, provide students with an equivalent, rather than identical, opportunity to demonstrate their understanding of the learning material (Bearman et al., 2022; Nieminen, 2022), offering examples of the kind of inclusive pedagogic reform that Cope and Kalantzis (2017) claim is needed, aligning with the affordances of new digital media to promote 'productive diversity' in higher education. At their core, such approaches are characterised as a process of seeking and selecting what Smith and Kennett (2017) have labelled 'generative constraints': those technologies, resources, and activities that an educator orchestrates to guide a student's experience and that capture creative demonstrations of associated learning. The scaffolding of student practices through a combination of flexible design and generative constraints is a key part of the effective operation of teachers across different learning environments (Fawns, 2019) and has been found to have important consequences for staff assessment orientations (Elkington & Chesterton, 2023). For such practices to be effective, staff are required to be proficient in both flexible assessment design, as well as being equally adept at the orchestration of flexible assessment practices, taking account of and being responsive to the unfolding formative assessment experiences and exchanges they share with students. Such orchestration will inevitably involve a combination of workarounds and adaptations 'in practice' as students and staff negotiate and (re)interpret assessment processes into situated practices (Elkington & Chesterton, 2023). Adopting a focus on formative assessment 'as practised' can help to avoid unproductive assumptions and generalisations about assessment design in digital learning environments recognising that 'responsibility and agency are not qualities inherent within the individual student but are relational, distributed across educators, students, and environments' (Fawns, 2019, p. 141). Such design work needs to go beyond simply setting tasks and structuring environments to include possibilities for students to configure, customise, and rehearse their own practices, as well as supporting teachers to orchestrate and activate the learning process.

These are features that can be problematic for some of the taken-for-granted assumptions underpinning wider normed approaches to assessment in HE which have resulted in a rather inflexible, excluding, one-size-fits-all curriculum that can be disabling: it does not empower all students to reach their potential (Hanesworth et al., 2019). Efforts to embed and activate such flexible assessment are often challenging and necessarily utilise a range of available digital tools and technologies to diversify how we teach and the methods by which we can evidence and enhance student learning development. Such diversification recognises that one approach does not fit all possible outcomes, with the type and form of assessment provided depending on the situation, the learning objective(s), the environment, and the student's stage of development, whilst at the same time requiring academics to think proactively about the accessibility of the assessment arrangements they choose to deploy (Elkington & Chesterton, 2023). Understood in this way, embedding flexibility in assessment becomes an important value proposition for responsive assessment design in digital environments, one grounded in a more holistic conception of individual agency and engagement – that is, viewing flexibility as an educational outcome in and of itself, emphasising the ability of learners to think, act, live, and work differently in complex and changeable scenarios.

ACTIVATING LEARNING PROCESSES THROUGH INTEGRATED ASSESSMENT DESIGNS

Working to embed greater flexibility and responsiveness in assessment processes is not an automatic feature of pedagogic strategies but holds the potential to prompt significant change in the relational dynamics of assessment design. A more 'responsive' outlook requires a shift in practice thinking that pushes beyond a 'task genre' of assessment (Bearman et al., 2022) to consider integrated assessment designs for a particular time and place, accounting for specific challenges, settings, and circumstances. Students today have the advantage of living in an age of ubiquitous learning and digitally mediated participation where emerging communication practices have created opportunities for new and varied associations and relationships among learners and wider disciplinary communities (Saichaie, 2020). This reflects the importance of using technologies to improve assessment approaches and integrate socio-technical dimensions into assessment design (Bearman et al., 2022). Educators need to consider how these designs can connect students to a digital world wherein technology is not just a tool but is deeply intertwined with social and professional practices, structures, and contexts (Fawns, 2022). These need to be supplemented by configurational strategies which consider the ways in which bundles of practices interact and interrelate, incorporating flexible and recursive assessment-for-learning opportunities to practise and rehearse, as well as test-out and hone relevant knowledge, skills, and personal qualities (Elkington & Chesterton, 2023; Irons & Elkington, 2021).

With most virtual learning environments and platforms now equipped with some form of data analytics capability coupled with the continuing proliferation of new and emerging digital learning tools and technologies, educators are presented with an array of potential mechanisms to generate and capture assessment data to help understand and scaffold for student progress. The simplest of these scaffolds tend to include regular low-stakes opportunities for feedback that seek to open up the formative plane between lower-stakes tasks and their higher-stakes (summative) counterparts (Irons & Elkington, 2021). Here, the fundamental design principle is that these exchanges provide 'developmental feedback' to students on their progress through formative activities that provide a diagnostic function, modelling and enabling deliberate practice aimed at developing student understanding and confidence relative to different assessment tasks and approaches. The aim is to gradually encourage students to adopt more participative and dialogic roles in assessment and feedback processes as they work to acquire disciplinary ways of thinking and working (Wood, 2021). This is characteristic of a learner-centred feedback paradigm (Carless, 2015; Winstone & Carless, 2019) wherein educators are positioned as just one among various potential sources of feedback in the learning process. Other sources of feedback information include peers, automated features of virtual learning platforms, and even distributed online communities.

Such varied feedback sources can be initiated either by the learner themselves or orchestrated by an educator's thoughtful design as they manipulate and facilitate the learning experience to ensure students are embedded in 'feedback-rich environments' (Esterhazy & Damşa, 2017). Feedback-rich environments provide multiple opportunities, sources, and sustained dialogic engagement around ongoing student performance. These engagements are geared towards fostering student evaluative judgement, taken here to mean the discernment of quality work (Fischer et al., 2024; Tai et al., 2018). If well designed, assessment feedback processes can act to build students' self-regulatory capacity to make judgements beyond immediate tasks or learning outcomes through creating opportunities for students to develop the capabilities to operate as judges of the work they produce (Winstone & Carless, 2019). The focus of such assessment (as-learning) is on the explicit need for learners to understand what constitutes 'good' or 'quality' in their discipline and how to make judgements about their own work, as well as that of their peers (Carless & Boud, 2018). This is a vital element of being able to work, learn, and improve in any context and foregrounds the learner's ability to actively seek, comprehend, and utilise performance data conceptualised within the assessment literature as a form of 'feedback literacy' (Carless & Boud, 2018; Gravett et al., 2020), in which learner agency is a core component (Henderson et al., 2019b).

As educators, we play a pivotal role in scaffolding and designing assessment arrangements and methods for learners to monitor and evaluate their knowledge through sequencing activities and experiences in the learning process. Designing effective formative assessment feedback sequences can be fruitfully considered the staged development of expertise in decision-making that promotes student learning (Irons & Elkington, 2021). When viewed from the perspective of effective decision-making, we can begin to understand how certain formative activities might be effectively designed and deployed in order to increase learners' autonomy and agency in the assessment process, this being contingent on their timing (the stage in the assessment process), the intended outcomes (the kinds of evidence to be produced and decisions required), and the student's circumstances. A key issue is how educators might effectively operationalise such integrated formative assessment feedback practices, through particular assemblages of resources, tools, and techniques, to enable students to make the desired progress in their learning. A review of the assessment-for-learning literature suggests three broad categories of practice are integral to effective formative assessment feedback processes: 1) preparatory feedback, 2) process feedback, and 3) performance feedback.

Preparatory feedback

Devising ways of nurturing a shared understanding of the purposes behind assessment activities early on with learners is recognised as a crucial formative step in student learning development, making transparent the criteria for evaluating their learning achievements and enabling them to have a clear overview of the aims of their work (Sadler, 2013). Clarifying key learning outcomes in this way helps to develop their 'assessment literacy', where students acquire an understanding of assessment practices, processes, criteria, and standards through open, active engagement and participation (Price et al., 2012). The contemporary assessment and feedback research suggests that students who develop a working understanding of what makes for 'quality work' are better equipped to make progress in regulating their own learning and are more likely to seek feedback on their future learning development (Carless & Boud, 2018). For example, providing regular and varied opportunities for students to actively engage with criteria for learning through analysis of comparative artefacts in the form of exemplar work can positively affect student learning by helping them to 'see' standards and work with criteria in concrete ways (Carless & Chan, 2017).

Creating time and space for meaningful dialogue around exemplar work alongside accessible assessment rubrics is a key feature in helping students understand how academic judgements are made, preparing them to transfer insights to their own work (Tai et al., 2018). Using rubrics to promote synchronous small group discussions around students' understanding of assessment criteria is an effective way of clarifying learning outcomes, particularly when utilised early on in a programme of study, stating clearly what educators are looking for (Jönsson & Panadero, 2017; Panadero et al., 2023). A progression of this approach might be to encourage students, in pairs or small groups, to agree on and sketch out the key features of assessment criteria, exploring and capturing the different ways in which they might be able to demonstrate the intended learning outcomes in practice terms. Subsequent tutor-led discussion and feedback can then draw out and address any fundamental issues regarding student interpretation of criteria, as well as providing a safe space for students to be able to voice and discuss any other issues or concerns. Clarifying, sharing, and understanding criteria for success in this way can help to foreground students developing internal standards for their work, reflect upon it, and gradually take ownership of their own learning (Carless & Boud, 2018). Whether this is mediated face to face in seminar groups or via small groups in breakout spaces online, the focus here is on eliciting student thinking and reasoning about exemplar work and providing opportunities to consider divergent viewpoints and information on what represents quality work.

Process feedback

It is generally accepted as good assessment-for-learning practice to design in opportunities for learners to practise key aspects of assessment tasks as a means of engaging them in the experience of practically doing a task and what is expected of them (Elkington, 2019; Irons & Elkington, 2021). Providing regular formative feedback on learner practice as an indication of how well they have performed prior to final summative work encourages them to appreciate the time, effort, and strategies required to successfully complete an assessment task (Blondeel et al., 2022). A relatively straightforward way of activating early feedback information and for gathering actionable data on 'real-time' student progress is to make use of live polling, quizzes, or multiple-choice questions to provide students with quick-fire consultation opportunities to gauge their understanding of topics, concepts, and criteria and to discuss progress in assessment tasks (Enders et al., 2021; Nadeem & Al Falig, 2020). Using such digital tools during face-to-face (and online) sessions can boost engagement with assessment criteria by quickly checking students' grasp of key information, promoting timely formative feedback dialogue(s). Further feedback information can also be facilitated through what has been termed 'peer instruction' (Nerantzi, 2020), where students review their respective answers in small group discussion before re-voting or contributing to a wider plenary discussion facilitated by the tutor. Carrying out such activities affords students time to practise consolidating and rehearsing subject knowledge and skills, as well as providing them with a chance to gain valuable insight into their progress, gradually building their capabilities and confidence.

Such formative exercises can be effectively operationalised in and through our everyday exchanges with students if we plan and structure our teaching in ways that guide and support students' effort in productive and appropriately challenging ways, as well as encouraging them to share their experiences with others as they progress with assessment tasks. One approach is to utilise available smart editing tools (i.e., OneNote or Padlet) to facilitate slower consultation opportunities for students and educators to monitor and evaluate learner progress over time. For example, several studies have demonstrated the utility of employing online collaborative tools like Padlet to monitor and assess students' writing performances, deliver formative feedback, and monitor interactions with feedback generated in ways that students value (see Albarqi, 2023; Jong & Tan, 2021). Collaborative smart editing tools such as these are also a useful means of encouraging spaces for peer feedback and dialogue as students progress through the assessment process, providing a non-threatening environment for different kinds of collaborative (a)synchronous exchanges. Educators need to carefully consider the kinds of feedback information they wish to generate; the forms this might take; and whether this information will be timely, relevant, and useful for students in their completion of assessment activities.

Performance feedback

In practice, the feedback students receive on their performance needs to be both specific and general, relating to the specific task or assignment, as well as identifying clear principles in practice that could be applied to future tasks (Boud & Soler, 2016). By reconceptualising feedback as repeatable opportunities to engage in dialogue about learning we can encourage active student engagement with and timely reflection on feedback information, shifting focus to the learning 'process' and the management of learning strategies rather than squarely on the quality of students' final assessed work. For example, most institutional virtual learning platforms have the functionality to provide the space for students to review and check their own performance against assessment criteria. A relatively simple way of supporting self-reflection on performance is to ask students to complete and submit an interactive top sheet alongside their assessed work (Arts et al., 2021). Students can be provided with a simple top-sheet template structured around a series of reflective questions that encourage them to generate feedback about their own work. Students can also be asked to identify how they would prefer to receive individual tutor feedback – written, audio-visual – on the top-sheet template. Encouraging self-reflection on performance can generate meaningful forms of formative (self-)feedback on summative work (Panadero et al., 2023).

When deployed as part of a distributed formative process, students can be supported to use such self-reflective activities to connect feedback on the current task to previous tasks, as well as a way of visualising progress and setting targets for future improvement. Tutors might ask students to first complete a self-assessment of their work and then produce an action plan for future work based on the insights gained. This provides a basis for comparison as students consider subsequent individual performance feedback from their tutor in relation to both their own self-reflections and the implications for future practice in relation to their action plans – all of which can be revisited. Notably, there are other ways of delivering performance feedback which are less time-intensive than providing written comments whilst also enhancing the potential accessibility of this information. For example, there is now compelling evidence pointing to the utility and value of producing screencast feedback on individual student work (Wood, 2022, 2023). Compared with written/typed feedback, audio-visual feedback is often perceived as more personal and can make students feel more connected to their tutors (Saputra et al., 2023). The audio-visual format allows tutors to convey nuances through vocal cues that promote understanding and encourage students to follow up with feedback. Crucially, these recordings do not have to be polished artefacts; indeed, students often appreciate informality when receiving personal feedback on their work (Martin, 2020). Recording a screencast of performance feedback can help students better understand tutor comments and enables connection to other relevant documents such as assignment briefs, rubrics, and lectures to explain and elaborate on feedback.

To optimise the use of feedback information, students need to possess a repertoire of strategies that they can enact confidently and productively. The variable interplay between formative activities deployed within each of the interlinking practice categories outlined previously will significantly impact the kinds of learning students derive from assessment processes. The core purpose of such integrated assessment design is to inform students' approaches to future learning, with emphasis shifting to their ability to analyse approaches to learning utilised in the process of developing certain learning artefacts. Care needs to be taken to consider the appropriate level of integrating digital technology in assessment design and practice, aligned with clearly defined criteria for student learning (the pedagogic intent) through accessible tasks that are appropriately contextualised. The differentiation inherent within these practical digital and material engagements illustrates the necessity for carefully considered formative assessment arrangements for moving between modes of attention, interaction, and agency oriented to local and individual circumstances, as well as those modes oriented to general practice as indicated in programme learning outcomes. This differentiated viewpoint provides an entry point to understanding assessment-for-learning as a series of structured opportunities where students participate in composing and reflecting multimodally throughout the learning process.

PARTICIPATORY MULTIMODAL ASSESSMENTS

Earlier sections of this chapter have considered how the now-standard integration of different technologies and multi-purpose digital devices in higher education environments has functioned to blur the boundaries between the physical and the virtual, ushering in a new orientation toward learning, teaching, and assessment that is increasingly participatory. With the staples of traditional learning and teaching no longer sufficient for leveraging new and emerging forms of knowledge production in today's post-digital educational environments, educators are turning their attention to the affordances of increasingly multimodal digital learning environments to realise a broader range of possibilities for authentic assessment feedback practices (Ross et al., 2020; Payne, 2023). The term multimodal refers to the different modes of communicative action (audio-visual, spatial, and behavioural) that work together in the expression, creation, and representation of meaning in and through the various artifacts produced by learners and educators for the purposes of learning and assessment (Varga-Atkins, 2024). Multimodal assignments are increasingly part of the learning landscape of higher education, with educators seeking to scaffold students' competence and engagement with social, visual, and interactive information and spaces into critical and creative capacities to work with and generate knowledge in different contexts (Lim & Tan-Chia, 2023; Wyosocki et al., 2019). When used in ways sensitive to context, multimodal assessment strategies can empower educators to explore new pedagogical practices, connect students with a wider range of technologies and resources, and support new forms of knowledge production (Ross et al., 2020; O'Donnell, 2020). This broader framing calls attention to the multimodal ways in which educators and learners might co-construct knowledge artefacts over time through participative assessment processes emphasising ongoing collaboration, composition, and reflection.

Designing, supporting, and assessing multimodal work and understanding and creating meaningful multimodal assessments is complex for both educators and students, with affordances and possibilities evolving alongside digital interfaces and new media to elicit changing demands, roles, and relations for each. There is increasing evidence of educators recognising the value of devising structured opportunities for students to create and share multimodal artefacts and participate in multimodal disciplinary practices as part of integrated formative assessment and feedback strategies (i.e., Hafner & Ho, 2020; Stanja et al., 2023). Assessment-for-learning opportunities can be designed intentionally to value and support iterations of students composing and interpreting material, digital, and mixed representation artefacts and performances through a focus on what Newfield (2014) has termed 'transmodal moments'. Rather than being straightforward representations of student knowledge claims, such multimodal expressions are vehicles for active knowledge construction wherein multimodal mediation and subsequent remediation not only become feasible but are well suited to framing learning as a formative process of 'coming-to-know' (Martin, 2020). For Ross et al. (2020) such an orientation is imperative if we are to support students to develop what they term 'multimodal assessment literacy', which involves 'making meaning with diverse semiotic resources, multiple modes, parsing rubrics, and criteria, understanding the assessment outcomes and how to meet them and understanding this process as a dialogue rather than a fixed and objective measure (of performance)' (p. 299). This means intentionally orienting the digital devices and platforms with which learners interact for the purposes of assessment toward viewing, composing, and revising multiple aspects of multimodal artefacts as they are mediated through online and offline iterations of integrated reading, writing, designing, discussion, composition, and reflection.

For many educators whose professional experiences with knowledge representation have been dominated by written text and the spoken word, the prospect of fostering multimodal assessment will undoubtedly challenge their established views about assessment design. To value the learning and knowing that occur within and through the multiple, multimodal, and multifaceted textual representations available to learners, educators need to devise ways of actively engaging students in productive dialogue regarding the affordances and constraints of modes, media, and tools for the purposes of learning. This means working alongside students to 'jointly construct formative and summative assessments that can capture the design process, modal choices, and meaning making' (Curwood, 2012, p. 242). This, in turn, requires technical and compositional assessment processes, learning objectives, and designs that are sensitive to and address the richness and complexity of multimodal work and the critical digital authorship it embodies (Payne, 2023; Ross et al., 2020). In the absence of assessment designs and approaches that are appropriately sympathetic to this complexity, instruction and feedback 'cannot fully support students to develop their communicative capacities for future work in digital spaces' (Ross et al., 2020, p. 291). A relatively straightforward illustration of a multimodal formative assessment arrangement might see learners tasked with representing early attempts at meaning-making in one mode or a combination of modes (such as in a reflective blog post comprising images coupled with recorded audio-visual content) before using the feedback information generated to remediate their understandings with another combination of modes in the formulation of a subsequent learning artifact (such as a piece of written work produced with accompanying illustrations and then presented verbally to tutors and peers). As learners become actively involved in assessing their own and others' multimodal representations, the ways in which they participate in disciplinary practices help to support opportunities for ongoing reflection and dialogue, facilitating what Boud and Soler (2016) call sustainable assessment or assessments that meet the specific and immediate goals of a course, as well as establishing a basis for students to undertake their own assessment activities in the future.

Facilitated by the functional and generative role that multimodal representations play in the processes of learning and assessment, e-portfolios and related smart compositional and collaborative editing tools (i.e., Miro, Microsoft OneNote, Google Sheets) can be effective vehicles for students to purposefully collect, reflect, and become participants in producing and assessing multimodal work, taking advantage of the networked, multimodal capacities of available digital spaces. E-portfolios, as communal, interactive learning spaces, offer students and educators the means to collect ongoing work and curate that work for various purposes, including ongoing formative inquiry (Lam, 2023). Students can be encouraged to stretch their learning goals across artefacts through multimodal composition processes that promote intentional reflection, revision, and dialogue; receiving feedback on several aspects of their experiences that supports their learning development, such as content, format, tools, pace of production, audience reach; and grasping and internalising the social norms of a learning community (Smith et al., 2017). Here, dispositions toward student experimentation, agency, and connection making are foregrounded in devising and sharing such multimodal representations. Collection, curation, composition, and reflection practices can be supported through the digital affordances of tools like digital portfolios, as are ongoing check-ins by tutors who are able to asynchronously comment on stages of student progress or add links out to relevant resources to help individual students navigate and enhance assessment work. Such a multimodal approach to providing formative feedback models the potential for digital media to personalise the learning process, strengthen the quality of learning artefacts, and foster an increased sense of agency and belonging for students (Lam, 2023; Yancey, 2019).

When educators rely on only one medium, such as written feedback, they can constrain or even close off a student's ability to use that feedback to continue learning. Different spaces, media, and arrangements have modal affordances that can help educators improve the clarity and utility of the feedback they provide and set up learning conversations that support personal and professional connections with students. Whether facilitated as an integrated component in a designed sequence of formative activities for an in-module assessment task or as part of an extended e-portfolio task documenting student progress over time, multimodal feedback activities are instructional design opportunities that allow educators to use sound, image, text, and animation to make material clearer and more accessible for a diverse range of students (Payne, 2023). Such feedback can come in different forms, modes, and media and at different times throughout the learning process, from a multiplicity of sources and people – tutors, peers, and students themselves. For example, using screencast technology in the form of audio-visual formative feedback is a compelling means of increasing connection and social presence in multimodal composition and construction for learning and assessment (Martin, 2020; Wilkie & Liefeith, 2022).

Audio-visual formative feedback is acknowledged as an effective multimodal tool for generating conversational feedback, providing the tutor with the ability to speak directly to students about their emerging work (Carless, 2022; Wood, 2022). The research evidence suggests that students appreciate when tutors address them by name in audio-visual feedback, helping to build meaningful connections and clarify expectations (Bjerknes et al., 2024). Nurturing such connectivity can motivate students to invest in their learning and to embrace the feedback they receive as an important learning experience (Wood, 2023). Furthermore, audio-visual formative feedback affords tutors the opportunity to use expressions and gestures as part of the feedback exchange that can significantly impact the uptake of feedback for future learning (Martin, 2020). Multimodal feedback has the power to extend the learning environment in space and time, producing feedback artefacts and experiences that provide opportunities to promote observation and reflection through repeated exchanges and viewings (Ross et al., 2020; Payne, 2023). Students can watch and review multimodal feedback as many times as might be needed – they can pause, fast-forward, rewind, and even clip feedback moments. Significantly, multimodal formative feedback also goes some way toward meeting current understanding of educational accessibility standards leveraging capabilities for close-captioning, screen-reading, and mobile viewing (Ziegenfuss & Furse, 2021).

With the growing accessibility of generative artificial intelligence (GenAI) tools such as ChatGPT, designing assessment to support multimodal learning processes involves negotiating an increasingly complex set of practices, technologies, and resources. GenAI applications, like any other technologies, have potential to significantly enhance the learning process. Whilst commentators have been quick to point out how such developments run the risk of undermining the academic integrity of our pedagogic approaches, this will only be the case if we proceed to take insufficient account of the disciplinary and situated nature of knowledge and practice which reflect the entangled relationships between people and technologies (Bearman & Ajjawi, 2023). Bearman and Ajjawi (2023) suggest that such a pedagogic outlook locates AI as another tool in a sociotechnical ensemble wherein the multimodal possibilities for designing and engaging in meaningful assessment involve students interacting with and generating valuable knowledge about themselves and their changing contexts. This has implications not only for how multimodal assessments play out in post-digital learning environments but also for teachers as assessors, especially as they invite meaningful student participation in continuous and adaptive assessment approaches (Bearman et al., 2024; Swiecki et al., 2022). Indeed, as educators experiment with new tools and socio-material assemblages, plan for multimodal instruction, determine the practices that scaffold students' agency, and engage in composition and reflection, they begin to participate in the facilitative and collaborative roles that our rapidly changing learning environments will require.

CHAPTER SUMMARY

Traditionally, when digital technology has been developed for educational purposes, it has tended to be understood as a supplement or addition applied with the intention of enhancing existing teaching and assessment practices (Knox, 2019). Adopting a post-digital view of formative assessment practice helps us, as educators, to make judgements not about assessment in general terms but about the combinations and configurations of diverse practice elements that make up the wider assessment and learning experience. By understanding how these configurations create rich and engaging assessment-for-learning opportunities, we are better positioned to see how modality of study, coupled with the increasing diversity of student cohorts, is changing the parameters and scope of assessment design and influences our capacity to respond to the situated learning practices of students in all their complexity. Emerging compositional and communicative technologies and associated sociotechnical practices have great potential for affording rich, responsive, and recursive feedback systems in our changing educational environments. These will be most effectively realised when such learning environments are intentionally designed to provide learners with a widened range of formative feedback types and sources – from tutors and peers to machines. What this means in practice can vary considerably, as we will discover in the chapters to come.

This chapter has provided a sketch of formative assessment and feedback practice from a post-digital perspective along with some of the compelling affordances for student learning development. This sketch foregrounds the collection of international disciplinary case studies that follow. Each case study offers a practical, evidence-based illustration of how digital learning tools and techniques can be combined and configured to provide impactful assessment-for-learning opportunities. Underpinned by relevant theory and practical insight, the case studies speak to the changing expectations of students in the context of an increasingly complex and shifting higher education environment, examining how technology and digital education are being used to inform innovations in the design and implementation of formative assessment and feedback.

3

CREATING A FORMATIVE-FEEDBACK TRIALOGUE BY EMBEDDING AN E-LEARNING THEORY PACKAGE INTO UNDERGRADUATE MUSIC EDUCATION

PAUL FLEET

Discipline and/or Subject/Field: Music Education

CONTEXT

The educator walks into the learning space for the first session to deliver a course designed to enable undergraduates to remember, understand, apply, analyse, evaluate, and ultimately create materials from theoretical principles (Anderson & Bloom, 2014). They plan this before the learning journey begins based upon their scholarship, pedagogical principles, and prior experience.

What is missing is the educator's awareness of the student's level of prior knowledge. Despite open days, interviews, and pre-course tests, the depth of prior experience remains a known-unknown until the dialogue begins during learning events and other means of formative feedback. This then builds into trust becoming part of the learning journey (Boud, 2010; Sadler, 2010; Irons & Elkington, 2021). For music theory courses, educators may stream before/during arrival, presume a level of knowledge from entry requirements, or choose not to teach music theory (Rogers, 2004; Cloonan & Hulstedt, 2012; Fleet, 2017). Each of these 'solutions' is problematic.

The truth is that this can never become a known-known before the learning journey begins, but that does not mean it should not be addressed quickly. Including the student in learning design principles (e.g., Structure of the Observed Learning Outcome: SOLO (Biggs & Tang, 2011), co-creation (Bovill et al., 2011), and applying authentic education (Herrington & Herrington, 2006) gives the student an active voice. However, there is also an opportunity to include a digital voice. This makes the dialogue (student and educator) a trialogue (Leganger-Krogstad, 2014) within a post-digital learning environment (Sinclair & Hayes, 2019; Rapanta et al., 2021; Lamb et al., 2022). The student, educator, and e-learning package (Musition) form a partnership where 'technology and pedagogy drive each other' (Fawns, 2019, p. 136) and become equal agents of real-time formative feedback throughout the learning journey.

STRATEGY

Koehler et al.'s technological pedagogical content knowledge (TPACK) framework is a useful model for us to consider how to embed Technology into the prior interactions between Pedagogy and Content Knowledge ((Koehler et al., 2013); previously TPCK (Mishra & Koehler, 2006)). The TPACK framework first asks the educator to consider the elements in pairs. It then asks the educator to consider a holistic blending of the content, pedagogy, and technology whilst recognising that such relationships are complex and nuanced. This is a case study, and there is not the space to delve into the mapping for each element of the course (but rest assured that this was done), so the following paragraphs outline the TPACK framework in its application through a specific element: writing four-voice harmony.

Pedagogical Knowledge (PK) is framed using authentic education principles so that the learning events are designed towards a final performance by a church choir (e.g., drafting, scoring, copy-editing, rehearsing, etc). The goal is one of professional commission rather than assessment submission, transcending any question of 'teaching to the test' (Vaughan, 2015). The Content Knowledge (CK) for an FHEQ Level 4 course is informed by its Subject Benchmark Statement (QAA, 2019), which asks the student to demonstrate an understanding of relationships between practice and theory. For a typical choir this means that students need to know which notes are physically comfortable for the singers. Putting PK and CK together moves us to considerations of Pedagogical Content Knowledge (PCK), which is informed by the prior learning journeys of students. We know from the A Level music syllabi that it is unlikely those students will have been tasked to set lyrics to their study of four-voice harmony and therefore breathing points, hyphenation, and elongation of syllables will need to be considered.

Technology Knowledge (TK) concerns the availability and accessibility of the software, which is integrated into the Virtual Learning Environment (VLE) and thereby familiar and supported in the same way as Word or Excel. Knowing what the software is capable of and what the student will have access to as they use both the tailored and pre-written tasks in the programme is the matter of Technology Content Knowledge (TCK). For Musition this meant not only integrating the musical encounters for each in-person lecture but also knowing where those encounters may lead within the pre-loaded materials. For example, the principles of writing four-voice harmony equally apply to string quartet composition, so the educator needs to be aware that the student may find themselves in that section of the software. The Technological Pedagogical Knowledge (TPK) is a critical element for the trialogue. It asks the educator to consider the capability of the technology to deliver, engage, and grade/show learning to both the student and the educator. Musition informs both the student and educator in real time as they engage with the software. Using TPACK as the strategy for inclusion provides evidence for a 'thoughtful interweaving of all three key sources of knowledge: technology, pedagogy, and content' (Mishra & Koehler, 2006, p. 1029), thereby giving structured confidence to this trialogic design.

PRACTICE

Adhering to UK HEI Quality Assurance and Standards documents (QAA, 2014, 2019), my music theory courses are weekly encounters including lecture, discussion, practical realisation, and peer-to-peer and peer-to-educator breakouts. The opening paragraph of the module handbook contains the following key sentences:

> Western European Music Theory comes from a privileged background.... As such, it should be a considered *a* theory rather than *the* theory of music.... The content of the course prepares you to consider, evaluate and compose Common Practice musical materials.... You will also undertake an e-learning journey, using the software Musition alongside the weekly lectures to enable you to practice and embed your skills outside of the immediate learning environment, monitor your own learning gain through weekly and incremental formative assessments, and to help facilitate discussions with your tutor as the course progresses.

Musition is not the only music theory e-learning programme available. There are many other music theory technologies which are designed to support 'learning processes corresponding to a rapidly changing educational space' (Goncharova & Gorbunova, 2020). However, Musition transcends many other packages by containing educational levels from beginner to advanced and from primary to tertiary, being customisable, having repeatable skill training with different sound banks in different genres, using high-quality sound files, and crucially tracking learning gain.

Musition and Auralia, its older sibling, were developed by Peter Lee (co-founder) and his peers when they were looking for practical training programmes to support their studies in the early 1990s. Their teachers used cassette tapes, but this learning only worked once; once you had the answer, the resource was spent. Musition incorporates large banks of content which explicitly link to exam boards (AMEB, ABRSM, Guildhall, LCM, etc), and it can also be modified into specific sub-packages. In each of my learning sessions there is an e-learning task that is curated from the preloaded content and explicitly linked to the Learning Skills and Outcomes. The student can also engage with the whole package to develop those skills, prepare for upcoming skills, or learn new associated skills.

For example, in week 4 students learn about the art of transposition (up and down by a tone, minor third, and perfect fifth). The theory and practical explanations for moving between key signatures and transposing instruments are given in the lecture; however, the range of prior experience will vary significantly across the cohort. A non-pitched instrumentalist may reasonably have limited theoretical knowledge, whereas an alto-sax player (whose instrument is transposing) will likely have both practical and theoretical knowledge. The cohort objective is to enable all to feel comfortable in forms of transposition, but this cannot be completed in a single lecture. This is where Musition plays a vital part in the learning journey and enters the discussion between educator and student.

The student engages with the e-learning to reinforce the Learning Skills shown in the lecture and can hear the transposition of musical examples, authenticating the theory into practice. Once complete the student can move out of that task and into the platform to engage with the linked tasks or discover related transpositional tasks that reinforce or advance their knowledge (such as moving into transposition beyond those intervallic ranges). Importantly, students can see how well they are doing in relation to the Learning Outcome instead of focusing on unhelpful comparisons with peers. As Lee says: 'they know when they need to improve, without destroying their confidence or enthusiasm through such unhelpful comparison' (2023). The educator monitors the student's engagement and can see the quality and quantity of tasks that have been completed correctly, retaken, and/or failed. From this they can monitor the student's learning gain so that they can praise, support, and/or intervene as necessary.

IMPACT

This educator-student-software trialogue has had several benefits since Musition was integrated in 2018. Qualitatively speaking, the number of tutorials being requested has not decreased, but the depth of conversation has increased in the student and educator setting and, connecting clear objectives before, during, and after the meeting due to the information from the software. Other anecdotal, qualitative evidence comes from student emails, which have typically said 'Just had a thorough session with Musition today. Loved the varied repetition, and it really makes you think' (student from 2018) or 'I have really struggled with transposition, but I've work[ed] through the specific tasks you set and managed to get 9/10 correct. I've also looked at the harder tasks which I think I can do' (student from 2020). Concerning this last quote, I checked within Musition and the student could and did do the harder tasks correctly, which I was happy to informally speak to the student about and fulfil the trialogic process.

Quantitively speaking, before Musition the average first-time pass rate was ~93% (from 2013 to 2017). This sounds like a success, but from a student perspective it meant that ~4 students failed on first attempt. After integration this figure jumped to ~98% first-time pass rate, meaning that in a cohort of ~60 students only one student failed the assessment first time. Diving deeper into this metric, it was interesting to note that such a student typically did not engage with Musition or struggled with other courses on the programme through personal external circumstances. The numerical difference is small (+3 on first-time pass rate), but the difference to those individuals is significant.

There has also been an increase in students gaining upper-second- and first-class marks. This is found in the level of detail in the answers, which since the inclusion of e-learning has moved further upwards through Bloom's taxonomy from a bulge of submissions that can remember, understand, and apply the Learning Skills to a greater number of submissions that can analyse, evaluate, and create professional musical materials from theoretical principles because the underlying theory has been significantly reinforced through connecting physical and digital encounters. In the case of transposition, the answers given in the assessments are professionally ready. They contain not only the correct sequence of notes, but they are also presented with theoretical detail such as performance directions and crisp, clean, and clear calligraphy demonstrating the authentic education principles which were designed into the curriculum.

People learn in different ways, at different paces, with different levels of engagement, and all depending on variable factors such as prior learning, interest in topic, social integration in the cohort, and student learning expectation, to name but a few. If a student feels some degree of control in their learning, through student-centred learning, then the 'responsibility for learning naturally shifts to the student' (Wright, 2011, p. 94). The aforementioned non-pitched instrumentalist who was new to the theoretical concept of transposition (and felt uncomfortable through their incorrect but impactful perception that everyone knew this skill except them) now has the opportunity to gain a greater degree of curated responsibility in their learning.

KEY LEARNING

Before the learning journey: the iGeneration have encountered e-learning alongside their in-class teaching since primary school. Examples include classroom management software, assessment software, and subject specific learning platforms (Clayton, 2023). Therefore, we must be mindful not so much of its inclusion into the higher education environment but of any unexpected absence by the student who is transitioning into higher education (Thompson et al., 2021).

During: There is the known-unknown in a student's learning experience, as they can miss (UNESCO, 2021) and misunderstand (Ashwin, 2009) Learning Skills which are too late to be addressed before reaching summative assessments. However, in this model of post-digital education it becomes a real-time known-known to both educator and student through this formative-feedback trialogue.

Ending: The trialogic model means that the responsibility of learning gain falls equally on the educator and student. Through the student's increased awareness of real-time learning gain (Hughes & Tight, 2021), the anxiety of a final summative assessment is mitigated by regular interactions without increasing the workload of an assessor (Irons & Elkington, 2021, pp. 27–29).

REFLECTION POINT

1) The TPACK framework was used to make transparent the connections between technology, pedagogy, content, and knowledge during the e-learning design. Might this framework be used retrospectively to reconsider these connections in programmes that already contain streams of e-learning?

2) Rapanta et al. state that 'flexibility, empowerment, professionalisation, and strategic decision making' (2021, p. 734) are all important considerations in the design of post-digital education. How do we ensure that e-learning is an equal voice in these and is co-owned by the student and educator?

3) Could the formative-feedback trialogue provide evidence regarding the UK OfS conditions B2: Resources, support, and student engagement and/or B4: Assessment and awards, for example, for B4.4e.i, where the reliability in the e-learning assessment could demonstrate credibility through its consistency across students over time and when compared with other providers?

4) As Adrian Hon suggests, 'the embedding of technology into a learning journey needs to be more than generic gamification, as this has the danger of 'typically involv[ing] little to no human judgements for its assessments' (2022, p. 16). Could the principles of formative-feedback trialogue be useful to humanise digital modes of assessment and feedback across curricula and other subject areas?

4

REFLECTIVE WRITING ONLINE AS A POWERFUL FORMATIVE ASSESSMENT TOOL IN TEACHER LEADERSHIP DEVELOPMENT

PHIL QUIRKE AND NADYA MOOSA

Discipline and/or Subject/Field: *Education Management and Leadership Development*

CONTEXT

This case study is set in a higher education institution in the Middle East and specifically in the teacher education faculty of the largest tertiary institution in the UAE. It investigates the impact of reflective writing assignments in an educational management and leadership professional development course, using the Notion platform, which acts as a blank canvas for participants to reflect in a range of media from text to video, images, and audio.

The DREAM Educational Management and Leadership approach is based upon ten principles, which form the course structure, with each unit requiring participants to reflect individually on the principle and underlying leadership theories and how these are applied in practice during the course (Quirke et al., 2021). The ten principles of the DREAM Management and Leadership approach are:

DEVELOP – the vision, mission, strategy, and ethos.
RECRUIT – to the team.

ENHANCE – professional development.
APPRAISE – performance looking forward.
MOTIVATE – individually and in teams by applying all the other principles.
DELEGATE – effectively with support and clarity.
RESPECT – everyone as you would like to be respected.
ENJOY – coming to work every day and show it.
ATTEND – to the details which matter to the team's daily performance.
MENTOR – the team and provide mentorship opportunities.

The case study focuses on the use of the Notion platform (Notion AI, 2023) as the medium for reflective writing and how one participant developed their educational management and leadership understanding and practice during the course. The participant in question and the tutor are the two authors of this case study, and the aim of the chapter is to encourage others to explore a similar approach and medium for teacher leadership development.

The challenges faced include the volume of reflection required, the application of a new platform, the time restraints due to workload, and above all how to generate greater depth of reflection, as detailed in the 'Key Learning' section.

STRATEGY

The formative reflective writing assignments have been part of the course since its inception, and the Notion platform empowers participants by allowing them to choose the media they believe can best deliver their reflective message. This empowerment of learners is a key factor in the social constructivist approach to formative assessment and how feedback can manage student needs (Torrance, 2012).

The formative reflective writing assignments have been continuously developed in an attempt to deepen participant reflections whilst also introducing more collaboration for the tasks. Burton's Reflective Writing Typology (2009) was applied to this development as assignments and feedback were structured to move participants from simple description to deeper theorizing over time that examines beliefs about managing and leading (see Table 4.1). It is a deceptively simple framework, which provides opportunities to create more complex reflective writing during the course.

Reflective writing has long been used as a form of formative assessment and professional development (Zeichner & Liston, 1996; Lucas et al., 2019; Ramlal & Augustin, 2020). By using guided reflective tasks and feedback, participants can be stimulated into a spiral of deepening reflection that encourages the questioning and constructive critical thinking required by education leaders today. The use of Notion as the platform for formative reflective assignments aligned to both the personalization and socialization that Burton's model encourages.

Table 4.1 Burton's Reflective Writing Typology (2009)

Type	Answering questions	Comments
1	What happens/happened?	Recording, expressing, "getting the story down"
2	How does/did it happen?	Commenting on, attempting to explain, for example, by adding more detail or approaching the Type 1 story from another perspective or question
3	Why does/did it happen? What does this mean outside the immediate context of action?	Theorizing on the story and reflection in Types 1 and 2, linking them to personal theories, for example, of language, learning, and teaching
4	Are the earlier reflections credible/reasonable? Why? Why not? What do they mean now?	A subsequent written reflection in a developing sequence of reflective writing, in which writers continue to question and maybe involve others
5	Are the earlier reflections still credible/reasonable? Why? Why not? What do they mean now in the light of subsequent experience?	After longer intervals, writers use the developing spiral of reflection (which may include other writers, e.g., as part of an interactive journal) to re-examine initial theorizing in light of intervening events that may have changed their perspectives

PRACTICE

Formative reflective writing assignments are based on the learner's experience of applying the principle under study based on a work-based task. The tutor then responds to the initial, often descriptive, post and tries to encourage deeper reflection through questioning feedback techniques (Burton et al., 2009) in a dialogue between the learner and the tutor (Mauri et al., 2016).

The tutor created a space called Our Education Faculty Dialogue Journals Café on Notion for the participants to openly discuss various topics. The tutor also posted comments to all participants and instructed them to post their first reflections in this space.

Nadya began by introducing herself and highlighting the opportunities she received at the institution under the leadership of the tutor, Phil. These opportunities include her roles as a system course team leader, teaching practicum coordinator, acting program team leader, and quality assurance manager in the Faculty of Education.

Phil then provided additional reflective writing prompts on the individual journal page in Notion. These prompts encouraged Nadya to reflect on her practice and engage in constructive critical thinking as an educational leader in today's context, moving from a Level 2 to a Level 3 depth of reflection (Burton, 2009).

The Introduction Unit post began with a prompt from the tutor asking each participant to share their personal beliefs and the theories that underpin their approach to teaching, learning, and leadership. The tutor encouraged participants by suggesting that they start with a paragraph for each aspect, regardless of length, and see where these thoughts took them. Nadya answered this initial question focusing on her current position as an education faculty member and concluded with a question to the tutor in an attempt to maintain an ongoing reflective dialogue.

There were also a range of follow-up questions from the tutor, which encouraged Nadya to provide more details while maintaining precision, allowing her to think critically. For example, when Phil asked, "How have you 'become much better at teaching and learning'?", it prompted Nadya to move beyond simple descriptions and encouraged deeper reflection, as the tutor clearly applied the Reflective Writing Typology (Burton, 2009) to guide the questioning process.

The tutor consistently concluded his formative feedback on journal entries with a positive statement, emphasizing the supportive and constructive nature of the dialogue journal. Nadya reflects now that this approach instilled confidence and encouraged her to write more openly. For example, when the tutor wrote, "Thanks a million for your detailed responses throughout, Nadya, and I am looking forward to continuing our ongoing exploration of our practice together", she felt motivated to ensure that her reflective assignments displayed an increased depth of reflection and a greater integration of theory derived from practice.

Participants were allowed to organize their individual dialogue journal pages on Notion according to their preferences. Accordingly, Nadya used color coding to differentiate her posts from the tutor's, and Phil mirrored this initiative, as both maintained the same text font color throughout. Additionally, the "toggle list" feature was used effectively to organize the posts, which reduced the need for excessive scrolling and made it easier to access the latest entries.

IMPACT

This section evaluates the impact of the Notion dialogic journals and the tutor's questioning techniques and formative feedback approach on enhancing the depth of reflective writing. The evaluation is based on text analysis and interviews with both the tutor and learners involved. Insights are drawn as to the key role of the learner as the central figure in the reflexive learning process, the power of multimedia use and the need for tutor flexibility and openness to question everything.

The centrality of the learner's role in the reflective learning process was highlighted in Nadya's reflective journal tasks as she emphasized how the core readings and the weekly collaborative discussions gave her a sense of knowledge enrichment that empowered her to comfortably share her leadership practices with more experienced colleagues. She felt this was directly linked to how her understanding developed of the way in which the theoretical content underlying the DREAM principle was applicable to her own practice. The availability of the Notion Dialogue Journal everywhere via the phone app meant that Nadya could contribute to the journal at any time, helping her reflect on her application of the DREAM principle directly in context and in action. She noted that this reflection definitely impacted her professional growth positively, as she was consciously aware of the practical and theoretical links.

It was not only the immediate availability of Notion that enhanced the dialogue journal experience but also the user freedom to structure the page as though it was a blank canvas that allowed Nadya to sequence her reflections in a way that supported the coherent dialogue. She reflected on how this created the opportunity for reflective threads to be grouped and developed in more depth, as the theme was not lost in a time sequence. She could therefore build upon her earlier thoughts and the tutor feedback, and this formative process deepened her understanding of the DREAM principles and enabled her to better discuss practical ways of implementing them. Nadya also mentioned how she saw her self-awareness enhanced and how this improved her ability to make meaningful contributions to the team. Phil notes that this clearly indicates a move from Level 3 reflections on the Typology towards Level 4, as Nadya's Dialogue Journal structure meant that she was constantly reflecting on earlier reflections. This is a powerful example of how a formative approach to reflective writing assessment can encourage greater depth of reflection.

Looking back now on the journey of reflective writing throughout the DREAM Management course over a year ago, we find ourselves moving into a Level 5 depth of reflection, and this has been one of the most beneficial aspects of writing this chapter. It is rare for us to go back to reflections after so long, and this is the time period needed to reach a Level 5 depth of reflective writing. Nadya can clearly see the positive impact the DREAM Management course, the formative approach to the reflective assignments, and the Notion Dialogue Journal have had on the quality of her work as well as her understanding of educational management and leadership. For example, when she mentioned the challenges of acting as program team leader in one of her reflective journal tasks, Phil's formative feedback prompted her to engage in deeper reflection and critical thinking as he asked, "Can you give an example of one of those decisions when you were Acting Program Coordinator? Why it was so challenging and what the outcome of your decision was". This depth of questioning naturally leads to further depth of reflection, and it is this willingness on the part of the tutor to question everything that creates the possibility to take the participants towards and beyond a Level 4 depth of reflection. The tutor must, of course, be flexible and open to all participant statements and discover ways in which each participant will open up to explore further why they do what they do and how they do it. The coherence of Nadya's journal structure around expanding themes was definitely a key feature in allowing both parties to reflect and question the ideas espoused in ever greater depth.

KEY LEARNING

Techniques to build strong connections

Nadya and Phil agreed that one of the key learning points was the need for the tutor to build a strong personal connection with the participant for depth in reflection to flourish. This connection is founded on the qualities of trust, respect, honesty, openness, and transparency, and Nadya suggests that the tutor can establish this connection by using three techniques she witnessed in Phil's practice. The first of the three techniques is rapidity of response, which makes the participant feel they are being prioritized, even if that response is only to say full comments would be provided the following weekend. The second technique is the use of praise, as it continuously motivates the participant to continue their reflections, even if the feedback is constructively critical overall. The praise is always fronted, which helps the participant feel they have done something correct and motivates them to improve the initial reflection based on the feedback. The final technique is the application of active listening principles so that the participant does not feel they are being misunderstood. The tutor constantly checks that they have read the initial reflection correctly, often using clarification questions such as "I think you mean . . ." or "That's correct, isn't it?" This leaves the participant with a sense of empowerment, as they know they will be asked to clarify and not criticized for something they did not mean to say (Andersson & Palm, 2017).

Ground reflection in practice

Once a strong connection has been established, it is easier for a greater depth of reflection to be achieved, as the tutor can begin to ground the discussion more firmly in practice and thereby constructively guide the participant from the known to the unknown (Haneda & Wells, 2000). Phil's strategy was to continuously question and probe all the participants to develop and extend their initial entries by linking descriptions of practice to theory.

Volume of reflection

Another key learning point was the need for a weekly reflective task throughout the course so that there was the opportunity to reflect at the end of every unit. Different models have been tried over the years in different courses, but Nadya was adamant that for the participant and the continuity and cohesion of the dialogue journal, the weekly reflection was essential. The regularity of feedback is a key feature of effective formative assessment (Irons & Elkington,

2021), and although it can generate a heavier workload and more time for participant and tutor, it enhances learning and the depth of reflection.

The benefits of an online platform

The opportunity to reflect in different ways should be open to each participant (Norris, 2015), and one of the greatest strengths of using Notion is that all formats of reflection are possible on the platform. Nadya used the Notion tools effectively to sequence and structure the dialogue exchanges, and she also especially liked the ease of access. Phil is keen to encourage future participants to take advantage of the blank canvas to add not only text and attachments but also audio, video and pictorial reflections. Nadya has also pointed out the potential of other features such as tables; to-do lists; web pages; bookmarks; quotes; and embedded PDFs, maps, or tweets. It is this variety of reflective formats that gives the learner the opportunity to reflect in ways that are most conducive to their learning style, making Notion such a powerful tool for reflection.

Depth of reflection

The final key learning point was that the writing of this chapter has been in itself a continual process of reflection and that the collaborative writing experience to complete the chapter has been at the Level 5 depth of reflection according to Burton's Reflective Writing Typology (2009).

The aim for future courses is to return to reflective tasks at the end of each unit, which allow different forms of reflection involving both personal and collaborative writing and give participants the opportunity to develop their reflections sequentially, building upon earlier themes and formative feedback. These can then be used to develop a final course project educational management and leadership e-portfolio.

REFLECTION POINT

We leave you with a selection of questions that will hopefully encourage further reflection on practice.

1) How would your approach to feedback and support change based on your reading of this chapter?
2) How could you use Burton's Reflective Writing Typology as a rubric to influence the structure and design of reflective writing assignments?
3) How would your approach differ to the DREAM management dialogue journals outlined in this chapter?
4) How can a platform such as Notion enhance the reflective writing process in your situation based upon your reading of its impact on the DREAM management course?

5

DEVELOPING STUDENT EMPLOYABILITY THROUGH FORMATIVE ASSESSMENT AND VIRTUAL PROJECT LEARNING IN THE SOCIAL SCIENCE CURRICULUM

JOY PERKINS AND STUART DURKIN

Discipline and/or Subject/Field: Social Sciences/Anthropology, Sociology, Politics, and International Relations

CONTEXT

The University of Aberdeen offers a 12-week, cross-disciplinary, elective 30-credit module for penultimate year undergraduate students, Employer-Led Interdisciplinary Project. The module combines employability development learning workshops with a project hosted by a micro-business, start-up organisation, or third-sector charity. This module was originally launched to deliver greater equity of access to work-integrated learning compared with other employability initiatives such as competitive year-long placements. Work-integrated learning is offered in the academic curriculum, focusing on students from non-vocational degree programmes, including anthropology, sociology, politics, and economics. This inclusive approach is designed to improve student access to quality work-integrated learning and to address the

DOI: 10.4324/9781003360254-5

growing body of research that indicates participation in this type of learning is imbalanced across student populations (Harvey et al., 2017; Jackson et al., 2023).

The move to employer-hosted 'virtual projects' rather than traditional in-person projects was necessitated by the COVID-19 pandemic. This project-based learning module has been revised, so these valuable student-employer project interactions continue remotely and digitally. The module now builds virtual project briefs into the curriculum, which provide students with real-world tasks to emulate the online workplace. Table 5.1 illustrates the variety of previous virtual projects, which typically a team of three to four third-year undergraduate students have undertaken. Undergraduate degrees in Scotland are classically four years in duration, compared to the other nations in the UK, which generally offer three-year degree programmes.

Implementing virtual projects has enabled the teaching team to broaden the range of projects available; previously projects were only sourced from local organisations based in Aberdeen and Aberdeenshire, Scotland. This approach has resulted in a wider range of geographically dispersed organisations and project types and facilitated ease of online engagement for staff, students, and external organisations alike. As a result of this new online project context, new reflective formative assessments have also been devised to underpin student learning and help reduce assessment inequities, and these have enhanced focus regarding the digital delivery of the module. The formative assessments include a group 500-word project report covering student plans, progress, and problems; a 10-minute group video progress recording; and an introductory Padlet exercise to engage students and establish a sense of community at the outset of the module. These formative assessments are designed to help facilitate module fairness by enabling all students to develop their understanding, skills, and confidence prior to the final summative assessments and grades.

Table 5.1 Examples of previous virtual projects sourced across Scotland and undertaken by students

Organisation	Location in Scotland	Project title
Nairn Spa and Lido Ltd	Nairn	Creating a Social Media Campaign for Nairn Spa and Lido
TrackGenesis Ltd	Aberdeen	Augmented Reality (AR) and Virtual Reality (VR) in Education and Industrial Training
Your Event Scotland Ltd	Edinburgh	Refreshing the Work Portfolio for 'Your Event Scotland' Post-COVID
Wester Ross Fisheries Ltd	Inverness	Wester Ross Sea Heritage Project

Students participating in externally hosted projects require support to leverage the many benefits and to address the various challenges associated with project-based learning (Rowe & Zegwaard, 2017; Vasilienė-Vasiliauskienė et al., 2016). To address this, students undertaking the module are supported by a series of in-person employability workshops to develop their digital collaborative competencies, critical thinking, and consultancy skills. In addition, the module formative assessments have also been purposely designed to incorporate reflective learning activities and use digital tools, to develop students' academic self-efficacy and self-awareness (Jackson & Trede, 2020). This case study provides a multi-modal practice view of the formative assessment and feedback in this module.

STRATEGY

A maximum of forty undergraduate students participate in the module each academic year, which facilitates students and external stakeholders to work together across subject areas, aligning with the interdisciplinary strand of the University of Aberdeen's Strategic Plan 2040 (www.abdn.ac.uk/2040/). Specifically:

> Design new modules and programmes which encourage interdisciplinary learning, and ensure that all our students can experience innovative, challenge-led education involving external stakeholders.

The Employer-Led Interdisciplinary Project module aligns with this strategic commitment and the underpinning theoretical concept of constructive alignment, where the formative (and summative) assessment tasks map alongside the intended learning outcomes for the module (Biggs, 1996).

Explicitly considering constructive alignment in the module design and planning has enabled the module formative assessments and feedback to be more transparent for the students. Module intended learning outcomes help students to develop a shared understanding of how to achieve the following intended learning outcomes on successful completion of the project-based learning module:

1. Understand the key principles of interdisciplinary project management in a professional field.
2. Understand the practical skills and concepts presented in the weekly workshops.
3. Apply the principles and concepts from workshops to group project research work.
4. Produce high-quality written communications to demonstrate learning and skills development.
5. Evaluate your own strengths and areas of development and the experience of working as a team towards solving a workplace problem.

Helping students understand the module design and the rationale for the formative assessments is important, so time is allocated during the module to explain their implementation in the module design.

Students receive feedback (no mark) for each formative assessment, and all students are expected to pass all formative and summative assessments to achieve an overall pass grade for the module. In this module, students are supported with developing their assessment and feedback literacies. Carless and Boud (2018) endorse this approach, stressing the need for students to understand and appreciate assessment and feedback processes. These areas are explored with students at the start of the module as a central element of the first teaching session. The session covers the rationale for the different types of formative assessment in the module, module feedback methods, and how to engage with and use feedback to improve academic performance. Motivating and encouraging students, often repeatedly, about formative assessments during the module has helped students understand the rationale behind their integration into the module. Allocating module time to 'assessment and feedback learning' has also resulted in strong student engagement in formative assessment activities. Students are keen to receive formative feedback from their host organisations, their peers, or the teaching team to support their ongoing learning and development. Feedback from these diverse sources is a distinctive module feature, which helps motivate students, improving their confidence, employability skills, and academic self-efficacy.

PRACTICE

Formative assessment and feedback practice in the virtual project module comprises a(n):

1. Introductory Padlet exercise with online feedback.
2. Group 500-word project report with group electronic feedback.
3. Ten-minute group video progress recording with peer feedback.

In this module, 'assessment tasks as learning tasks' are incorporated as a fundamental design feature (Carless, 2007). Formative assessment tasks are designed to engage students and build their confidence, enhance self-reflection, and most importantly facilitate student improvement in preparation for the summative assessments. These summative assessments involve devising a professional letter to the School Director of Education (20%), a group video project presentation (30%), and an individual reflective report (50%). Assessment for learning in the module and the key features regarding how this was operationalised and managed in the virtual project module are outlined in Table 5.2. These diverse practices throughout the assessment cycle, illustrated in Table 5.2, highlight how the teaching team has made various evidence-based decisions regarding managing and operationalising the module. Many of these practices exemplify how technology can transform learning.

Table 5.2 Formative assessment and feedback processes in the 30-credit module, Employer-Led Interdisciplinary Project

Assessment for learning	*Key features*
Assessment and feedback design	• Considered the assessment scheduling and order of formative assessments to avoid 'assessment bunching'. • Made all formative assessments compulsory to ensure student engagement. • Aligned formative assessments to scaffold learning, providing an opportunity to improve work before summative submission (Lynam & Moira Cachia, 2018). • Used authentic feedback approaches to provide feedback that emulates workplace feedback (Dawson et al., 2019). • Implemented tailored group learning through reflective team-based assessments. • Incorporated work-integrated formative assessments to help mitigate against plagiarism and artificial intelligence concerns (Sotiriadou et al., 2020). • Implemented authentic assessments to develop students' employability and skill sets (Sokhanvar et al., 2021).
Use of feedback methods	• Ensured feedback is returned within three weeks in line with the University's framework for the provision of feedback on assessment. • Implemented a range of traditional and technology-enabled feedback methods such as electronic, audio, peer, and class to accommodate differing cohort preferences (Knauf, 2016). • Used e-feedback to help with accessibility. • Incorporated structured feedback to support current and future student learning (Carless, 2007). • Explicitly linked formative feedback to the stated assessment criteria in the module's virtual learning environment.
Feedback dialogue	• Encouraged dialogic feedback for the formative three, video recording at a bespoke teaching session. • Invited students to comment on how they have used feedback from formative assessments in their summative assessments. • Established an open-door and/or online policy to encourage feedback discussions between all three stakeholders.
Peer feedback	• Shared the rationale with students for peer feedback and providing evaluative judgements during collaborative online learning in the formative three, video assessment (Cowan, 2010; Tan & Chen, 2022). • Outlined to students how to provide peer feedback and supplied a feedback pro forma template to standardise practice.
Creating an online learning community	• Created online meeting rooms in the Blackboard VLE for collaborative learning, peer feedback, and reflection for use by students and the external project hosts. • Used the VLE monitoring tools to monitor student engagement with the module and the assessments. • Provided learning and assessments that afford equitable learning opportunities for all (Tai et al., 2023).

IMPACT

At the start of the 30-credit third-year module, Employer-Led Interdisciplinary Project, all students undertaking the module were invited to complete a brief survey on their understanding and use of formative feedback practice. This approach helped to glean valuable insights from the student cohort, as illustrated through the following survey excerpts.

For the survey question: What do you understand by the term formative assessment? It is evident from responses across all students sampled at this stage in their academic studies that they clearly understand the term formative assessment, specifically how these assessment types are used in the module to measure student progress and learning. This is demonstrated through the following student comments:

> Non-marked assessment based on feedback rather than marks.

> I would see it as a trailer for the summative assessment to build up ideas and skills.

For the survey question: How do you think the formative assessments for the virtual project module will influence your module engagement? The survey data highlights positive student engagement terms, such as 'motivate' and 'focus', suggesting student interest and investment in their module learning, as illustrated in the following quotes:

> Some of these involve self-introduction as well as working in teams. By working with new students this will certainly boost confidence and by working on a group project, there is a common goal in mind, this will influence motivation.

> Sometimes I may be guilty of being passive in my learning when it comes to study, so this will help me maintain focus and stay engaged.

For the survey question: How do you plan to use your formative assessment feedback? The data for this question is particularly insightful and exemplifies how formative assessments support students to study with noticeable terms such as 'improve', 'reflect', and 'better' frequently featuring in student responses, as illustrated in the following student quotes:

> I am going to self-reflect and work on the areas I'm lacking and make myself more competitive in the employability market.

> Try to learn as much as I can from it and maybe also ask further questions to understand better.

> Use it to improve my summative assessments.

Overall, this survey data has helped to encourage staff self-reflection and awareness of student experiences of assessment for learning and how formative assessments can positively impact their module engagement.

KEY LEARNING

It is evident from the end-of-module feedback that students gain numerous benefits from undertaking project-based learning in the curriculum. This is illustrated via the following student quote:

> To be able to get actual work experience as part of my degree. As such I could develop skills, create a network, and improve personally and professionally.

That said, there are also challenges associated with this type of learning provision. It is important that the module co-ordinator establish effective communication channels and build professional relations with the external host organisations so they understand the module expectations and requirements. In our experience, this can help to counteract potential issues such as reputational risks and challenges like intellectual property concerns and overambitious projects. There is also a need to brief students at the start of the module regarding professionalism, such as communication, etiquette, and time-management. Again, this approach helps to lessen potential issues as expectations are highlighted explicitly in the module. Academics new to this type of teaching provision are also best mentored by a more experienced educator in work-integrated learning to help them fully understand each stakeholder and their requirements during this model of project-based learning.

Key module design and delivery learning points for individuals interested in exploring this type of teaching in their own subject area include:

- Team-based formative assessments provide an ideal opportunity for students to develop their skills and build their confidence, especially for those who are not used to collaborative learning. However, it is necessary at the start of the module to fully brief students regarding the rationale for the module and the assessment strategy.
- Video presentations provide a creative, reflective, and authentic formative assessment opportunity, which enables students in this module to showcase their digital capabilities and professional competencies to a range of stakeholders.
- Formative assessments can be valuable to improve equity and scaffold learning, especially in diverse student cohorts who typically undertake this module. For this to be effective, it is important to ensure there is protected module time to discuss 'assessment and feedback learning' to develop students' formative assessment and feedback literacies.

REFLECTION POINT

The following reflective prompt questions provide an opportunity for the reader to consider this case study and review their own teaching context:

1) In what ways do you currently use formative assessments in your teaching to support online collaborative learning? How do you know these approaches are effective to support student learning?
2) In what ways do you use technology to encourage students to engage with their formative feedback?
3) What opportunities exist for you to introduce authentic formative feedback in your teaching practice?
4) How do you persuade students to value and engage with peer feedback?
5) What approaches do you use in your teaching to devise equitable formative assessment methods?
6) How can you support external host organisations and practitioners to provide meaningful formative feedback to support student learning and development?

6

USING FORMATIVE FEEDBACK TO SCAFFOLD AND MANAGE STUDENT WELLBEING IN AN ACCELERATED ONLINE RESEARCH COURSE

NATASHA VAN ANTWERPEN, DEANNE GREEN, JOHN BARANOFF, SARA EL-KAISSI, AND ANASTASIA EJOVA

Discipline and/or Subject/Field: Psychology

CONTEXT

The graduate diploma of psychology (advanced)

Completion of a 4th (honours) year is a pre-requisite for qualifying as a psychologist in Australia. Grades received for the year and thesis component are considered by admissions panels for masters degree programs, the final hurdle to reaching professional practice. With limited places in masters available at most universities, and with admission involving an interview based on honours grades and industry experience, honours programs are competitive 'make-or-break' bottlenecks for students (Cruwys et al., 2015). In 2019, the student load for honours was equivalent to 4,137 students, and only 1,300 were extended masters places (Bond, 2021). Therefore honours (and its equivalents, including the online graduate diploma (advanced); GDPA) in psychology constitutes a critical period, with a heavy emphasis on assessment grades, particularly the final thesis or equivalent. Feedback provided prior to submitting the final thesis serves an important function in shaping and managing students' perceptions of their research work. However, within traditional honours programs, formative feedback is often at supervisor's discretion, with some courses only allowing feedback on the completed thesis.

GDPA programs bring additional unique pressures, including the completion of an individual research project and thesis-equivalent report fully online within a compressed timeline. Within our program, the research component takes place over 14 weeks, as compared to 30 weeks for on-campus honours theses. The research component must also be designed to scale – with numbers potentially reaching 200 students per iteration. Accordingly, feedback needs to be systematically built into the course itself and provided in a timely and actionable way.

Student wellbeing in the GDPA

University students form an at-risk group for psychological ill health, including depression and anxiety (Ibrahim et al., 2013; Stallman, 2010). Concerns around student wellbeing were exacerbated throughout COVID-19, with the transition to online learning contributing to student stress. This transition increased feelings of social distance from instructors and peers (Dodd et al., 2021) and impacted student motivation (Chiu et al., 2021). Because it is a graduate program, students within the GDPA tend to work part- or full-time, which creates additional work-related stress – common for online students, who frequently have reduced access to mental health resources compared to on-campus students (Chung & McKenzie, 2020; Johnson, 2015).

Extending concerns of student wellbeing are findings that 'make-or-break' periods in study impact student wellbeing (Cruwys et al., 2015). Psychology honours students have been found to report higher distress than other tertiary education populations, with 47.48% of students reporting anxiety or depression above the clinical cut-off in a recent study (Jarrad et al., 2019). With wellbeing being an outcome of importance and risk in tertiary education, particularly in the unique bottleneck of psychology honours, we designed a GDPA research project course based on considerations around not only grade maximisation but also motivation and wellbeing, with a focus on formative feedback. Formative feedback is known to improve accountability, performance, and motivation in technical subjects at the tertiary level (Leenknecht et al., 2021). Feedback, both formal and informal, therefore plays an important role in student performance and wellbeing – providing students connection to their supervisors and peers and an ongoing calibration of their grades and project work.

STRATEGY

Self-determination theory (SDT; Ryan & Deci, 2017) formed a theoretical underpinning for the course design and feedback structure. SDT posits that people have three basic psychological needs that, when fulfilled, create intrinsic motivation (the sense of engaging in an activity for the inherent satisfaction and enjoyment the activity brings rather than for external rewards or pressures). The three basic needs are autonomy, competence, and relatedness, defined in Box 6.1 alongside examples of course and feedback practices meeting these needs.

Box 6.1. Basic needs in SDT and how they were considered in course design

SDT basic needs

Autonomy

Volition and choice in one's actions. Autonomy involves experiencing independence, self-governance, and activity aligned with the self and values. We aimed to promote autonomy by encouraging student ownership of their projects by giving choice in topics, methodologies, and approaches with student understandings workshopped according to supervisor feedback. Autonomy was also enhanced by self-reflection and student-directed feedback.

Competence

Feeling capable and effective in one's activities. Competence involves developing skills, achieving goals, and experiencing mastery. We aimed to enhance competence by providing students with the necessary resources and guidance to develop their research skills and knowledge. These resources were combined with regular feedback, formal and informal, on student progress and skill development.

Relatedness

Feeling connected and experiencing belongingness with others. Relatedness involves having positive and meaningful relationships, feeling understood, and being part of a community. We fostered relatedness by encouraging synchronous and asynchronous peer and supervisor interactions in sessions and via group messages and channels, including informal feedback from all members of the research group.

To meet the basic needs, our course was structured around providing different types of feedback – student-directed formative, other-directed formative, and summative – described in the 'Practice' section. Student-directed formative feedback is carried out by students themselves and involves reflecting on performance, identifying areas for improvement, and setting learning goals. Other-directed formative feedback is carried out by the instructor or computer software and is more closely tied to whether learning outcomes are being met (Klute et al., 2017). Summative feedback contributes directly to students' grades, including numerical ratings of performance on assessments.

Link between need satisfaction and wellbeing

A fundamental premise of SDT is that fulfilment of basic needs while pursuing meaningful goals will improve wellbeing. Multiple studies have shown a relationship between need fulfilment and wellbeing (Howell & Demuynck, 2023). A further proposed key mechanism underlying the relationship is the sense of purpose and meaningfulness associated with completing a task while taking ownership (i.e., personal responsibility; Hanauer & Dolan, 2013). In designing the course, we expected the combination of project ownership and optimal challenge – the extent to which a task is neither too difficult nor too easy – would increase need fulfilment and intrinsic motivation, in turn improving wellbeing – as long as our feedback – both summative and formative – was structured to enhance competence. We detail the process of integrating this feedback into the course structure in the following.

PRACTICE

Student-directed formative: modularised course content encouraging outlining prior to drafting

The course consists of weekly modules and features fortnightly summative assessments. The modules contain online content and videos. Each pair of modules supports an assessment, with the first module of each fortnight stepping students through outlining (i.e., dot-pointing) their assessment in line with requirements. Each second week, students are supported through drafting and editing. The requirements for most assessments are based on the Journal Article Reporting Standards (JARS) specified by the American Psychological Association (2020). As an example, the course structure and JARS standards for the introduction are presented in Figure 6.1.

Other-directed formative: weekly group or individual tutorials

Supervisors oversee groups of ten students working on separate but related research questions. Each week, supervisors conduct 90-minute Zoom group meetings or 20-minute individual meetings. Both meeting types enable

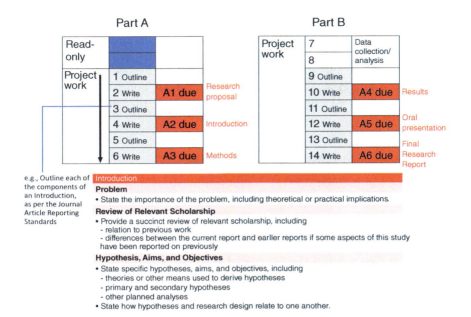

Figure 6.1 The weeks (numbered) and assessment due dates in Parts A and B of the research project course. A1, A2, and so on correspond to Assessment 1, Assessment 2, and so on, due at the end of each second week.

feedback centred on learning outcomes and assessment requirements. For example, before the introduction assessment, students meet as a group to discuss the introduction structure in a relevant journal article, then meet with their supervisors individually to discuss thoughts and concerns around the structure of their introduction.

Other-directed formative: scaffolded summative assessments

Supervisors mark and provide comments on the first five assessments, three of which – the introduction, method, and results – constitute sections of a final research report marked by external markers. The first assessment, a research proposal, provides feedback on overall project understanding and logistics, while the fifth, an oral presentation, provides feedback on the study narrative. Students are consistently reminded about the connections between assessments and are provided with guidance on understanding how markers' feedback will assist them in writing a higher quality final research report. Figure 6.2 shows a module content page describing the connection between the research proposal assessment and feedback with the introduction, which is being finalised that week.

> ### Week 4: Responding to research proposal feedback
>
> By now, you will also have feedback from your supervisor on your Assessment 1: Research Proposal. As you go through and edit your introduction, this is also a good time to go over your research proposal in light of your supervisor's feedback.
>
> Keep an eye out for any areas where the feedback from your research proposal may be useful. This may include feedback on certain details of your project or on elements of your writing.
>
> Remember that writing is an iterative process. As you progress through this course and continue to receive feedback on your work, try to adjust your work in response to it. This will help you continue to improve as a student, researcher, and writer, and will make for a stronger final assessment at the end of the capstone: **Assessment 6: Final Research Report**, which is due at the end of Week 14.
>
> You may also find it helpful to revise the content in **Week 1 on receiving and responding to feedback effectively**. Remember, your supervisor has made these comments to help you improve your work; try to see them as a helpful colleague, rather than as punitive or antagonistic.

Figure 6.2 A module content page providing guidance on assessment scaffolding and responding to marker feedback.

Student-directed formative: Conference-style feedback on the oral presentation

Student-directed formative feedback includes the processes of providing and receiving peer feedback (Klute et al., 2017). Our course encourages peer feedback through whole-group meetings and through pre-recorded oral presentations organised into online conference day sessions. Students are encouraged to view and respond to other students' presentations.

Summative: final research report

While the first five assessments have weightings between 20 and 40% of the course, the final research report carries a particularly high weighting, being 60% of the grade in Research Project B. Masters admissions committees often ask specifically about the honours thesis grade in lieu of overall honours GPA. Thus, it is not only in weighting but in subjective status that the final research report grade provides a summary evaluation (i.e., final assessment) of a student's performance.

IMPACT

To evaluate our course's impact on students' basic needs, intrinsic motivation, project ownership, and wellbeing, we conducted a longitudinal survey with four waves of data collection spaced evenly at the 1st, 5th, 10th, and

15th weeks of the course. As data collection is ongoing, here we present pilot data. Out of 85 students participating in the last 10 months, 13 completed the relevant measures in Waves 1 and 4 – the waves of primary focus in the pilot. We recruited students through course-wide announcements and messages from an academic unaffiliated with the course, and we incentivised participation with a chance to win a $50 gift card for completing all four waves.

Each survey consisted of a measure of basic needs, challenge, project ownership, and intrinsic motivation and multiple measures of wellbeing (cognitive, physical, and emotional wellbeing). The measures are described and referenced online in Open Science Framework (OSF; https://osf.io/5cs7p/). Participants were given the option to provide a free-text response in each wave and responded to demographic questions in the first wave they completed.

We calculated changes from Wave 1 to Wave 4 using the Reliable Change Index (RCI) for each variable of interest using the ClinicalSig package in R (Jacobson & Truax, 1991). Further detail on this process and graphs of trajectories are available on the OSF (https://osf.io/5cs7p/). RCI represents the degree of change over and above measurement error. Figure 6.4 shows results in terms of direction of change and significance of change, also explained in the following. Significant changes (exceeding measurement error) are represented by coloured (as opposed to grey) cells.

	Participant												
	1	2	3	4	5	6	7	8	9	10	11	12	13
Challenge	–	–		–		–		–					
Project ownership								+	+			+	
IM: To know													+
IM: Accomplishment			–		+								
IM. Stimulation			–		+								
IM: Total			–		+								
IM: Simplex			–						–			–	–
Satisfied basic needs: Autonomy		+		+	+			+	–	–	+	+	
Satisfied basic needs: Competence	+		–				+			+		+	+
Satisfied basic needs: Relatedness													+
Life satisfaction													
Quality of life		+							–	–			–
Physical health		+							–				
Positive affect	–	+							–				
Negative affect		–					+		+				
Distress (K10)													+

+/–: Direction of change

Variable type:

- Higher scores indicate better state
- Higher scores indicate worse state

RCI indicates that change is:

- statistically significantly for the better assuming alpha of .05
- statistically significantly for the better assuming alpha of .10
- statistically significantly for the worse assuming alpha of .05
- statistically significantly for the worse assuming alpha of .10
- statistically significant assuming alpha of .05
- statistically significant assuming alpha of .10
- not statistically significant

Figure 6.3 RCIs for each participant who completed Waves 1 and 4 for challenge, intrinsic motivation (IM), project ownership, basic needs, and wellbeing measures.

Of the 13 participants examined, 3 – Participants 3, 9, and 10 – reported significant change in a direction indicating decreased motivation and wellbeing as measured by negative effect. Four participants (2, 5, 8, and 12) reported mostly improvements in these elements, including increased positive affect, quality of life, project ownership, and autonomy, and decreased negative effect. One (Participant 13) reported a mixture of decrements and improvements (increased relatedness and competence but also distress and reduced quality of life). Four or more participants reported significant changes in challenge, intrinsic motivation (simplex – a score reflecting a person's position on a continuum from external reward-driven to intrinsic motivation, with more positive scores indicating higher intrinsic motivation), autonomy, competence, and quality of life. The changes in competence were in the positive direction for all but one participant with significant changes.

While our pilot sample is too small to draw larger inferences, these initial findings suggest students increased in competence and experienced few negative changes in wellbeing, despite the high stress of the course. Thus, our pilot data suggests providing a structured environment with consistent feedback and goals can assist students in navigating stressful course and research experiences without incurring negative effects on student wellbeing.

KEY LEARNINGS

Initially, we began this study aiming for our course to improve student motivation and wellbeing. However, when reviewing our results, we realised this aim was inconsistent with the course's broader aim – to teach research skills and assist students in completing their honours-equivalent reports. Accordingly, a 'harm reduction' approach may be better suited to similar aims among other educators – considering how practice can reduce stress and negative impacts on wellbeing. In this respect, the course appears to have performed well. Despite the expedited timeline and challenges of completing study online, few participants reported a negative change in wellbeing. We suggest providing students with a clear sense of structure, supervision support, and consistent feedback – rather than the traditional thesis model, which only provides formal (graded) feedback at the course's conclusion – may help to reduce negative impacts on wellbeing and foster an increased sense of competency and project ownership throughout the course.

We suggest structuring the research experience around feedback: giving students regular and formal feedback on sections of their work leading up to the final product. Similarly, having regularly structured communication points, such as supervision meetings, can help students to feel supported and to receive informal feedback encouraging their sense of competence during their project. However, when structuring assessments and feedback this way, educators should be conscious that students may pay greater attention to the grade as feedback and presume their final product will receive similar grades without alterations. Educators using this approach should therefore work with supervisors to encourage students to reflect on and integrate feedback into their final written pieces.

Additionally, as noted in the results, when calculating intrinsic motivation using the simplex calculation, one student's scores demonstrated a decrease. While scaffolding the students may assist their stress and wellbeing, finding ways of enabling students to maintain autonomy and intrinsic motivation throughout this process is important. We suggest providing research projects and questions with scope for students to extend themselves if they choose to may be one approach to this challenge. This approach enables students who are more motivated to take greater ownership of their projects, while those students who desire more structure can work within narrower constraints.

REFLECTION POINT

1) Consider the key formative and summative assessment activities for a course you teach. How do these activities align with providing optimal challenge for your students?
2) Motivation is multidimensional and unique to individuals, including intrinsic and extrinsic incentives. What key motivational factors are most relevant to your student cohort? How can your course design harness these factors?
3) How does your feedback process, including type and frequency, facilitate students taking ownership of their learning?
4) Consider your learning environment; does your setup satisfy students' needs in relation to the three components of the basic needs of self-determination theory (autonomy, competence, and relatedness)?
5) Outline the factors that might support wellbeing and the factors that might thwart wellbeing among your students.

7

PROMOTING SITUATED CHANGE TOWARDS SUSTAINABILITY AND CLIMATE ACTION THROUGH POST-DIGITAL ONLINE DISTANCE LEARNING PEDAGOGY

ANNABEL DE FRECE AND ROS TAPLIN

Discipline and/or Subject/Field: Development Studies/Sustainable Development and Climate Change.

CONTEXT

This case study captures pedagogic innovation in assessment that led to action-oriented and values-driven learning. This intervention was introduced in postgraduate online distance learning (ODL) programmes at the Centre for Development, Environment and Policy (CeDEP), SOAS University of London (School of Oriental and African Studies).

CeDEP has been offering ODL programmes since its inception at the former Wye College in the 1990s. It currently has around 800 students enrolled in its MSc Climate Change and Development and MSc Sustainable Development. Students can study from anywhere in the world, and enrolled students reside in over 100 countries. Most are mid-career professionals. Challenges with online learning for CeDEP students include multiple time zones and cultural nuances of learning.

Demand for ODL has been a growing market since the global pandemic in 2019. Analysing figures from global online learning platform Coursera, the World Economic Forum finds that between 2020 and 2021 online course enrolments grew from around 71 million to 189 million (Wood, 2022). Much of this growth comes from emerging economies such as Paraguay, Lebanon, Philippines, Guyana, Indonesia, Kenya, and Ethiopia (Wood, 2022). Distance learning provides global access to education and flexible learning and facilitates skill building; cross-sectorial, interdisciplinary learning; and collaboration.

STRATEGY

CeDEP's change in practice emerged from a desire to transform learning from a didactic distance learning approach incorporating only summative feedback to an action-oriented and values-driven approach to include formative feedback from tutors and peers. The aim was to redesign the pedagogy and delivery, including assessment to meet the specific needs of students of sustainable development and climate change.

The first core driver for transformation concerned the urgency of the climate change and sustainability crises, which require action-oriented changes to conventional teaching approaches. While all online and distance learning should be active and student centred, there are particular challenges raised by the complexity, interdisciplinarity, and urgency of sustainable development and climate change. Learning should result in graduate outcomes which directly impact the ability of students to engage critically, creatively, and collaboratively in the fields of sustainability and climate change.

To implement the first core driver, we embedded ESD principles (QAA/Advance HE, 2021), centring on competencies developed through active and participatory learning, collaboration and dialogue, critical and creative thinking, and interdisciplinary and systemic thinking within teaching and learning practice.

As detailed in UNESCO (2017), learning objectives for ESD are cognitive (e.g., knowledge of relationships between sustainable development and climate change, colonialism, industrialisation, and international and local governance), socio-emotional (e.g., ability to collaborate on sustainability and climate strategies), and behavioural (e.g., ability to speak and act in favour of people threatened by degraded environments).

Assessment is conceptualised as "for learning", "of learning", and "as learning", where ESD competencies from formative assessment are developed (QAA/AdvanceHE, 2021, p. 34) (see Figure 7.1). Theoretical approaches to formative assessment adopted for CeDEP's transformation in approach stem from the work of Black and Wiliam (1998) and Irons and Elkington (2021).

Understanding the context and needs of CeDEP students was a second driver. We wanted to better support our students, who are globally located mature students with diverse experiences of student-situated learning

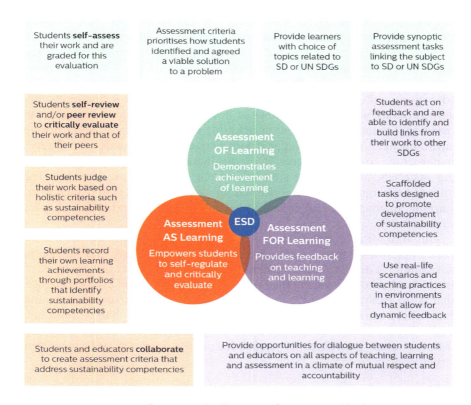

Figure 7.1 Assessment for, as, and of learning for sustainable development.
Source: QAA/AdvanceHE (2021, p. 35)

practices. They are professional, multi-sectoral, and interdisciplinary in background. In addition, they are remote but increasingly want to be connected and experience a sense of community. Therefore, we aimed to transform our support for our students in a manner aligned with the critical post-digital thinking of Fawns (2019, p. 143), who argues "all forms of education must account for a complex integration of digital, social and material elements"; they suggest that the "'online' is a place where meaningful relationships, based on trust, can develop" and "challenge the perception that the experiences of online learners are limited by distance or technology".

PRACTICE

The focus of changes to pedagogy and assessment by CeDEP has been to refashion online programmes to promote situated change towards sustainability and climate action among its learners via active learning and critical thinking. In practice, this involved the redesign of our two postgraduate taught programmes (MSc Sustainable Development and MSc Climate Change and Development) and the transformation of their assessment structures to formative and connected. Online programmes are delivered via the Bloomsbury Learning Environment (BLE) based on the Moodle learning management system. The BLE is a digital education partnership of higher education institutions in Bloomsbury, London. Teaching is predominantly asynchronous, with a small number of live webinars offered at key points in the study session, and focused on orienting students to the digital learning environment and providing support with assessments. In practice, the changes implemented comprised a redesign of: the digital space, the delivery of teaching materials, and the way student learning outcomes are assessed. The intended outcomes of this transformation were to foster greater student-led learning, interactivity, and enhanced presence in the context of learning for sustainability.

Our aims for assessment design were to provide varied and authentic connected assessment, formative feedback from tutors and peers, and support in navigating the distance learning format. We wanted students to have space to interact, reflect on, and share their professional and personal lived experience, that is, to facilitate globally situated learners within their own values and experiences, learning together and developing tools for personal, professional, and collective action. To achieve these aims, we identified the following key features which needed to be embedded in the learning and assessment structure:

- Fostering a learning community.
- Building digital skills for learning.
- Scaffolding skills and learning.
- Combination of formative and summative assessments.
- Combination of low- and higher-stakes tasks.
- Combination of peer and tutor feedback.
- Varied skills and competencies embedded in teaching resources and assessments.
- Varied learning resources (academic, non-academic published works, multimedia).

Core modules in the programmes are Understanding Sustainable Development and Climate Change and Development. Students also take three elective modules as the 'taught' components of their programmes. The changes made to module assessment involved the design of six connected assessments or 'e-tivities' (E1–E6) for each of the modules delivered on the Moodle platform. The first five e-tivities are formative and positioned in the first eight weeks of the session, with the final summative assessment positioned at the end of the session. The forms and functions of the e-tivities that students engage with in each module are as follows.

E1 online participation

This e-tivity combines weekly learning tasks and participation in a weekly discussion forum. A form of the just-in-time teaching process (Novak, 2011) is used. Weekly study materials engage students in learning tasks which variously require students to read and critically respond to literature, analyse data, and answer prompt questions on the week's topic. Students then respond in the weekly discussion forum, receiving informal feedback from their peers and the tutor who collates responses and provides feedback. This also enables tutors to adjust teaching strategies, clarifying or extending learning as students' needs become apparent. The tasks and forum provide students with a space to reflect on their learning and engage with their peers, sharing different perspectives on the topic and how others apply ideas to their own interests and varied contexts. This includes being able to reflect on their positionality and personal and professional experience and contributes to online community building. Ongoing formative interaction is critical for teaching in the digital space, allowing the tutor to monitor students' understanding and application of the learning materials.

E2 library retrieval

The key learning outcomes of this formative assessment are for students to be able to navigate the online digital learning space, build skills in research, and share resources with peers. Students are guided in accessing online library and electronic databases and are tasked with identifying, accessing, and evaluating appropriate academic journal articles for a relevant topic and presenting their findings in an accurately formatted bibliography which is shared in a dedicated discussion forum. This formative assessment is vital for grounding students in the digital learning environment and for building initial skills in research for subsequent assessments, along with creating a sharing environment and community building. Tutors are able to give feedback to individuals privately in the forum to correct errors and support as well as responding to the whole group in the forum.

E3 critical commentary

The first written assessment is a critical commentary on a journal article. Posts are made to a dedicated discussion forum for the students' critical commentaries. In the forum, they can read all the work of their peers. Feedback is provided to the student via peer review and personal tutor feedback. Students are provided with marking criteria when the task is set so that they understand the learning objectives of the assessment. As the first piece of writing students submit, this is worth 5% of the overall grade and therefore a key low-stakes assessment aimed at building confidence and scaffolding skills in critical reading and writing to enable students to do well in their final summative assessment. Peer-to-peer feedback enables students to develop online communication skills and an opportunity to view the work under study through others' eyes, thereby gaining more than one perspective.

E4 essay plan

The second written assessment consists of an outline plan for the final summative assessment. In this formative assessment, students are expected to acquire academic skills. Students provide an outline of the debates, theories, frameworks, and arguments and identify relevant literature for their essay. By receiving feedback early on, they gain confidence in their approach as well as being able to act on feedback to improve their work.

E5 blog

This assessment is a blog written by students for an audience of their choice. The objectives of this low-stakes task are to provide students with an opportunity to produce a piece of non-academic writing. The topic must be aligned to the chosen topic for the final assessment. The aim of this assessment is to give students the opportunity to explore the topic from a different perspective and to write for a lay audience.

E6 essay

The continuum of five connected formative assessments scaffolds learning and skills toward this final summative assessment worth 60%.

Learning and assessment are constructively aligned and follow a pattern which is aimed at building and developing knowledge through a range of learning resources which engage multiple learning needs and preferences of students (see Figure 7.2). Different skills are developed through scaffolding of learning activities and assessments which elicit formal and informal, formative, and summative feedback. The combination of these activities across the learning journey enables students to build skills with their learning as well as to become reflective and active learners (see Figure 7.3).

IMPACT

The transformation process was evaluated through student feedback and critical reflection among staff and external examiners. Feedback from students who had completed both the old module format and the new format was sought via an online survey in January 2023. Twenty-two students responded to 20 questions (Q1–20) (multiple choice and open-ended) about their experience. Four students volunteered to participate in a focus group designed with the SOAS Learning and Teaching Enhancement team. The evaluations demonstrate that it is the combination of changes made to the module format and

PROMOTING SITUATED CHANGE TOWARDS SUSTAINABILITY 65

WEEKLY GUIDE	VIDEO INTRODUCTION	READING LIST	LEARNING EXERCISES	ONLINE FORUM	6 PERIODIC E-TIVITIES
Overview Aims Learning outcomes	Introduces weekly topics Summarises key concepts, themes, literature and research	2-3 Core texts Multi-media (podcasts, videos, reports, interactive data sets) Further readings list	Conceptual and empirical Based on multi-media resources Reflective learning Research skills Feeds into weekly online forum posts	Comments on readings Reflections on personal and professional experience relevant to the weekly topic Responding to learning exercises Responding and interacting with peers	Online forum Library exercise Critical Commentary Formative essay plan Blog writing Summative essay

Figure 7.2 Learning design: resources, activities, and assessments.

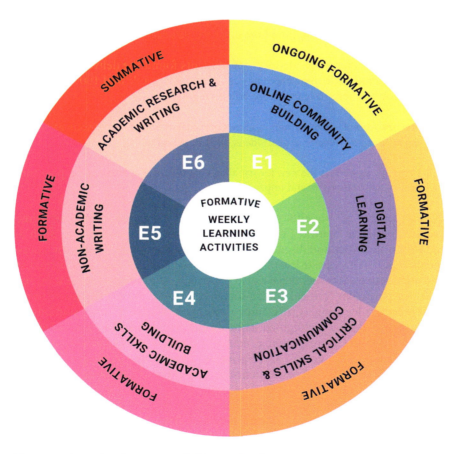

Figure 7.3 Learning journey: activities and outcomes.

the assessment structure that has resulted in students being more successful in meeting the learning outcomes. The transformation has significantly enhanced student interaction, engagement, and development of a variety of key skills and competencies, as well as supporting progression.

Weekly engagement on our online forums now averages almost 90% of students compared to only 25% before the new approach. The weekly discussion forum provides students with the time to reflect on the content and its relevance for their lives.

> What's most interesting is to read how other people take that weekly material and how they've applied it in their own work life . . . which I think is great about this course.

> The weekly discussion and activities keep me on track with university work as well as networking with peers that have same interests.

> [In the new format] . . . it's been . . . how you can apply this or how does this work in terms of a country or place that you're familiar with. So, it's much easier to write. I feel like we can actually learn from other people's experience.

Our evaluations have revealed 91% of students found the delivery of content on the new module format more engaging and accessible and 100% reporting that it allowed them to learn more effectively (Q5).

> The new format is more dynamic, allows me to learn from different sources (including articles, of course, but also videos, platforms and tools).

> I strongly agree that the new format allows for distance learning to be more comprehensive, interactive and impactful.

Ninety percent of students responded that they 'strongly agree' or 'agree' (10% responding 'neutral') that the ongoing formative assessments such as the weekly activities and discussion forum better prepared students for assessments (Q19). The varied learning activities, weekly exercises, and formative and summative assessments have also contributed to the development of new skills, in particular 'critical skills', 'communication', 'research and writing', and 'reflective learning' (Q10). Improvements in students' understanding of the subject was also highlighted as being positively linked to assessment by 95% of students (5% responding 'neutral') (Q14). Further, 86% of students 'strongly agreed' or 'agreed' (9% responding 'neutral' and 5% responding 'disagree') that the variety of assessments enabled them to articulate their understanding in different ways (Q16).

Alongside the range of connected assessments, students responded positively to formative feedback as beneficial. Responses to Q17 on the impacts of E-tivity 4 feedback perceived by students included:

> The assessments encourage me to dig deeper into the topics of the module and explore different styles of writing. The individual feedback from my tutor on the

E-tivity 4 is very helpful, particularly as it highlights the parts which are at fault, rather than just general comments.

The assessments provide me an opportunity to review, assess and research (as needed) topics to become more familiar with the subject matter.

They (formative assessments) enable me to apply concepts from various units . . . to allow me to really understand the context in specific places through using case studies. The assessed plan is really useful to get specific feedback and ensure I have both the topic and academic skills (e.g. understanding the reasons behind food insecurity and understanding how to critically evaluate evidence for these).

Overall, the most cited benefits of formative feedback were 'constructive guidance', 'improved academic achievement', and 'personalised engagement'.

Key insights gained from the process of transforming formative assessment and feedback on ODL programmes through a post-digital lens are:

- Students are remote geographically but want to learn together.
- Connected formative feedback from tutors and peers enhances learning outcomes and progression.
- Formative assessment, activities, and learning resources require alignment, both constructively and in time, to facilitate a scaffolded learning journey over the study session.
- Student interaction and critical engagement online promote development of diverse key skills and competencies.
- Students are more satisfied engaging in a post-digital environment but find the process more challenging and time consuming, as it requires their continual focus and intellectual energy throughout the session.

KEY LEARNING

Key learning from delivery of formative assessment and feedback approaches on CeDEP MSc programmes has included that formative feedback and connected assessment improve the quality of critical appraisal of materials referred to by students in summative assessment. This is particularly important for climate change and sustainable development topics and has longer-term associated policy ramifications, as many of our students become policy advisors in international and national arenas.

Students being spread across the world in different localities, cultures, and professional settings is the bonus of post-digital distance learning as they share their perceptions about sustainable development and climate change and development challenges experienced directly by them. Students learn through comparisons and contrasts of their learning and with their own situations. Relatedly, students dedicating time for engagement and interaction and reflection on formative guidance is integral – and their motivation to do that is a key to their learning. In addition, with students sharing their own insights via peer commentary and assessment, they contribute valuable learning to the whole group, going beyond the resources and guidance provided by academic staff.

Our experience emphasises that the broader learning and teaching approach that we transformed to requires ample time and resources for staff, in particular, to dedicate to formative assessment design and feedback, which is essential.

REFLECTION POINT

1) How can the post-digital online distance environment be a better learning space for climate change and development and sustainable development students than a face-to-face learning environment?
2) What are the advantages of greater assessment weighting being given to formative rather than summative assessment in the ODL environment?
3) What benefits for online distance students may be derived from summative assessment in other media beyond just text based?
4) What types of formative or summative assessment could be peer reviewed by online distance students? Would peer review facilitate better final outcomes and holistic learning?
5) What are the opportunities and barriers in the online distance environment for enhancement of delivery and formative feedback to achieve ESD's cognitive, socio-emotional, and behavioural learning objectives?

ACKNOWLEDGEMENTS

We wish to gratefully acknowledge our Centre for Development, Environment and Policy academic colleagues, Tom Tanner, Giuseppina Siciliano, and Jon Phillips, together with Victoria Hart, SOAS Learning and Teaching Enhancement, whose ideas and practices are reflected in the design of the MSc programmes discussed in this paper.

8

CONVERSATIONS IN CONTEXT

REFRAMING ASSESSMENT FOR INTERNATIONAL TRAINEE TEACHERS

ALISON MCMASTER

Discipline and/or Subject/Field: *Education/Teacher Training*

CONTEXT

This case study demonstrates the way in which a small but dynamic team of early career researchers employed by a teaching-intensive institution in the northeast of England sought to transform the existing assessment of international trainee teachers into a more authentic and meaningful experience for both trainees and assessors. The basis of all communication on the suite of international Postgraduate Certificate in Education (PGCE) distance education programmes is, for many trainees, wholly virtual and originally existed only via the university virtual learning environment (VLE) and email exchange.

The paradigm shift away from teaching to an emphasis on learning aligns itself to the widespread growth of 'student-centred learning' as an alternative approach. For the small PGCE Early Years Teaching (EYT) team, and subsequently the PGCE iQTS team, this collective philosophy was a vital driver in achieving high impact and sustainable change to the existing assessment model. The longer-term aim of this action research was to direct learning beyond the competencies of the mandated Teachers' Standards (DfE, 2011, 2021) moving towards the acquisition of pragmatic professional skills through praxis (Bracken & Novak, 2019). Trainees demonstrated basic Teachers' Standards via a pass/fail assessment. However, a necessary reconsideration aimed to prioritise additional skills essential for success in today's global, technology-centric 21st-century society.

Being responsive to the enabled voice of participants (trainees and assessors) is a crucial component of action research; therefore, the process was emergent, evolving to reflect participant perspectives with a willingness of the researchers to take new thinking into action (Costley & Fulton, 2019).

STRATEGY

In 2019, the School of Education inherited the PGCE EYT distance learning programme. A thorough revalidation, responding to trainee and academic feedback and considering innovations in assessment practices, ensued. Trainees sought an early-years–informed pedagogical approach, aligning with the team's desire to provide a programme balancing opportunities for structure and spontaneity, replicating the holistic approach advocated within the early years.

Traditionally, the assessment process for the International Initial Teacher Training (IITT) programmes was characterised by the signature pedagogies of practical lesson observations (Shulman, 2005), often conducted by a third party, and the collation of a portfolio of digital evidence documenting practice meeting the relevant, criterion-referenced Teachers' Standards. When graduates were asked for advice they would offer future trainees one specific response regarding the practical teaching module particularly resonated:

> Be prepared for the amount of paperwork; it nearly killed me!
> (International PGCE EYT trainee, 2019)

This provoked an uneasy professional dilemma within the team and a shared consensus that there must be a better way to quantify effectiveness as a practitioner. The feedback was the stimulus for a thorough review of content and assessment strategies, aiming to realign the programme with contemporary thinking and enhance trainee experience through a more pragmatic, reflective, and meaningful approach (Irons, 2008; Sambell et al., 2013). We knew that simply having vague ideas alone around enhancements was insufficient, and without research and analysis, a stagnant state was likely; thus, we found ourselves stepping into the role of change agents, seeking richer interactions with trainees, and championing 'the very essence of practice research – awareness of a need for change and desire for impact' (Costley & Fulton, 2019, p. 43).

PRACTICE

Assessment can showcase student learning and progress positively. However, initial action research data, including focus groups, questionnaires, and anecdote circle data, exposed a paradox within existing practices: existing assessment methods led to trainees' and assessors' apathy and resentment, with most expressing the view that the focus prioritised quantity of evidence over quality.

The influential, experiential knowledge which frames professional identity was not being accurately captured through the detached and dispassionate digital portfolio, and, while the premise behind the evidence portfolio bore echoes of a patchwork text portfolio, the crucial, reflexive component advocated by Winter (2003) was ineffective in demonstrating synthesis of theory and practice. The portfolio's superficial nature diminished the value, and its remote assessment eliminated the opportunity for trainees to articulate their understanding and tacit knowledge.

Casting our own minds back to our own teacher training assessment experiences, it transpired that each of the team holds negative memories, having gained little from the process of presenting our 'evidence' of meeting the standards, aside from a passing grade. Once again, we found ourselves thinking there had to be a better way.

Continuous reflection was already taking place with the team, viewing the revalidation as an opportunity to take a step back and systematically reflect on our own professional practice: What do we consider the indicators of quality teaching and learning, and moreover, how can we best provide opportunities for trainees to develop these, reflecting the inexplicable entwinement of experiences and knowledge within the learning process?

Practicalities of distance learning

The innate logistical and practical challenges of distance learning simply reinforce perceptions of its interpersonal inadequacies. Over three decades ago, Postman (1992) predicted challenges in being able to effectively construct meaningful relationships via a digital space. For a team of social constructivists working on a distance learning programme with the underpinning belief that knowledge is co-constructed through social interactions, to say this was a bleak forecast would be an understatement!

Although the concept of online learning was not new to the international team, the rapid evolution of communication channels in response to the worldwide COVID-19 crisis evoked a potential positive of the pandemic, progressing remote communication to real-time collaboration and exchange via Microsoft Teams. This inclusive communication platform expanded the previously restrictive boundaries of distance learning and reimagined the virtual dialogic space (Wegerif, 2011), increasing potential for collaboration, shared thinking, and co-constructing new knowledge across the 62 countries in which our international trainees are based.

Importance of building relationships

Although hugely beneficial, the extraordinary advancements in technology do not eliminate the additional layer of challenge distance learning carries when seeking to personalise the trainee experience. The instrumental value and impact of trainee and assessor relationships is prevalent throughout the literature (Pilkington, 2018; Gravett et al., 2021; Wegerif, 2011), and graduate trainee feedback leaves no doubt of its contextual significance.

> my PAT [personal academic tutor] was crucial for me . . . the relentless support really helped throughout the course. I'd have quit a thousand times if it wasn't for her support, and I'll be forever grateful.
>
> (PGCE iQTS trainee, 2023)

The connotations of this relationship extend to the dialogic exchange: for this to be equitable, mutual respect must exist, with all contributions valid and the value of experiential knowledge appreciated (Lea et al., 2003). Trainees should be seen as active participants rather than simply objects of assessment, a theory which Buber (2003) referred to through his exploration of human relationships, summarising this as reciprocal, authentic, interpersonal, and complementary to one another.

Consideration of Buber's theory suggests that online learning platforms result in the disappearance of relations and the authenticity of emotions and feelings. However, data collated by the researcher counters this cynicism and concludes that successful and genuine relationships can be established through a holistic approach, resulting in not only authentic but also empowering exchanges.

> It (the dialogic assessment) allowed me to have more confidence in my abilities . . . reminding myself of how much I really do know and how much progress I made during the year. In a way, I surprised myself with my ability to talk of my practice. It was like having a professional conversation with a really smart friend who was genuinely interested in what I do and the impact I've had.
>
> (PGCE iQTS trainee, 2023)

In terms of competent, rigorous, and robust assessment, assessors familiar with the relevant Teachers' Standards and the programme content have capacity to offer comparable experience. However, disparity occurs when an assessor approaches the dialogic exchange as 'traditional assessment', a 'test' of the trainee's ability to meet the criterion-referenced standards. In the role of assessor, this is adequate in that it affords opportunity for trainees to demonstrate knowledge competence but significantly reduces, if not completely removes, the golden thread through this research: the uniqueness, the transparency, and the authenticity of the experience.

Similarly, this has implications when considering the differing motivations of trainees. Consider this – we have trainees who, upon enrolment, objectify the opportunity, viewing it as no more than a qualification. The findings of the action research produced data supporting the assertion that a positive learning experience has the capacity to evoke the intrinsic motivation of trainees to immerse themselves in all aspects of a cohesive and holistic programme (Irons, 2008):

> My employer told me I needed this qualification which is why I joined the programme . . . over time, I saw how my philosophy of teaching changed. I went for an interview, and they offered me the lowest pay-scale. . . . I called back to say I recognise my value and I am worth more. . . . I know what I have to offer thanks to this programme.
>
> (International PGCE EYT trainee, May 2023)

This trainee's meta-reflection supports the notion that motivation is not a prerequisite but can, in fact, be a product of effective teaching, with social motivation evoking feelings of 'ownership' (Biggs et al., 2022), further emphasising the significance of passionate and inspirational teachers.

Perceptions of assessment

Trainees were continuously involved in designing an assessment model to 'measure what matters,' ensuring that the assessment process is done with instead of to them.

Naturally occurring data gathered by the team exposed dissonance in perceptions – to be expected within the communicative space of authentic action research (Kemmis, 2006). For some trainees, the dialogic assessment was approached with scepticism and viewed as:

- less valid than a high-stakes written submission to validate competency.
- high pressured and inequitable in terms of parity of experience.
- vague and lacking in structure, with the recommendation that a pre-prepared list of questions to be asked would be useful.
- a test of what is known.

There was some reluctance from the wider team to move away from a definitive summative assessment and place more emphasis on formative assessment, more specifically one conducted dialogically. This was largely due to concern about the accuracy and rigour involved; many academics were concerned about the additional workload a dialogic assessment may induce, and a number were simply reluctant to move away from the status quo.

Some aversion from both trainees and assessors regarding the 'live' nature of the dialogic assessment and the anxiety the circumstances may cause to both parties was shared, and the request for a pre-determined dialogic assessment 'guide' recurred in assessors' responses. Assurance was given that a balance of both formative and summative assessments would still be in existence, but the revalidation had allowed for the programme to be viewed as a whole, with all assessments forming a cohesive, developmental pathway, rather than existing discretely, each with their own assessment agenda. Although the dialogic assessment model exhibits traits of being summative in nature, it is not intended to determine the overall practical module outcome in isolation.

Concerns were voiced around standardisation and moderation of the assessment. This has been accounted for through joint observation of dialogic assessments, both live and recorded, which determined consistency, further verified by the programme's external examiner. It is acknowledged that this outcome may have been affected by researcher bias and, prior to any dissemination, broader inter-rater testing is essential.

In traditional discourse, the role of early childhood practitioners has been viewed through a reductionist lens, persistently seen as less, when evidence suggests this approach to be so much more. The PGCE EYT team faced stereotypical views of early-years practitioners, though our fundamental principles are simply an extension of the level of care and empathy we would show in the classroom, challenging the dismissive discourse of a holistic pedagogical approach and instead championing its power and potential, which our international trainees benefit from.

As advocated in any pedagogical approach, we constantly role model good practice, giving serious regard to trainee voices and encouraging trainees to have strength in their convictions. The merits of the approach were visible, evidenced through increased confidence in trainee disposition and their willingness to challenge and be open to challenge, as well as through incidental programme feedback, focus group sessions, and questionnaires – this positivity stimulated us to continue.

The data suggests that the transparency displayed by the team gives surety that there is no hidden agenda and no pre-conceived expectation of the way in which trainees meet the relevant standards, simply that they demonstrate doing so in their own style. The proposal for changes made during the revalidation process was based on theoretical evidence and presented in person, with the team believing this opportunity would enable us to:

- articulate prior knowledge in our own terms.
- respond and elaborate where necessary to provide clarity.
- justify decisions we had made grounded in theory and contextualise these to demonstrate consideration of the diverse needs of our trainees.
- engage in the sharing of our own lived experiences in a supportive space with a like-minded, student-centred other.
- reflect collaboratively, showing vulnerability in not having all answers but demonstrating we have the tools, knowledge, and resources available to us to determine ways forward.
- demonstrate ourselves to be responsive and reflexive practitioners, open to being guided by new and contradictory evidence which the research may reveal.
- show the 'gatekeeper' (in this case, our associate head of school) the passion, enthusiasm, and commitment we were investing, which the factual evidence alone could not convey.

The process outlined here encapsulates the fundamental nature and purpose of the dialogic assessment as designed and demonstrates the possibilities of a 're-culture' in assessment practices as well as highlighting benefits for all in adopting a holistic pedagogical approach . . . even in higher education!

IMPACT

This research suggests that the overall dialogic assessment is fundamentally transferrable as a robust model to assess trainee competence against the appropriate Teachers' Standards.

Findings endorse the hypothesis that there is potential for all stakeholders to profit from moving to a dialogic form of assessment, and key themes emerging from the data have included, but are not limited to:

1) empowerment – a recognition of trainees' tacit knowledge, value, and self-worth, particularly in regard to the positive impact on pupils' learning and progress.
2) enjoyment – a surprisingly pleasurable opportunity for both trainee and assessor to reflect on progress made across the duration of the programme, a celebration of strengths and achievements.
3) increased levels of self-confidence – not only in the ability to articulate their practice but also in justifying decisions and making valuable contributions to professional discussion.
4) improved ability to make connections between theory and practice, reflecting and responding in a reflexive manner which positively impacts professional growth.
5) positive perceptions of assessment and an appreciation of the significant impact and purpose of timely formative feedback, which gives more credence to the process rather than the outcome and values experiential knowledge born of lived experience.
6) recognition that developing trainees' holistic competencies or 'soft skills' and providing opportunities for these to be demonstrated through innovative forms of assessment is possible without compromising professionalism or competence.

Thematic analysis of the data illuminates that, while dialogic assessment alone has capacity to modernise assessment practices, the value of the exchange itself is determined by the effective integration of a holistic pedagogical approach and how this is implemented in relation to sincerity, sustainability, and scalability. This highlights the following as areas calling for further exploration: the merit of adopting holistic pedagogy in higher education and the relationship between trainee and assessor. Careful strategic consideration of both is required, specific to context, in order to achieve positive outcomes for all stakeholders which have been evidenced in the primary research study on the International PGCE EYT and PGCE iQTS programmes.

KEY LEARNING

In independent distance learning teacher training, co-constructed insights through collaborative dialogues become key, with foundational relationships between students and assessors as the catalyst for transformative learning (Wegerif, 2011). This shared space shifts the balance of power from academics to a partnership, fostering new knowledge and elevating the effectiveness of portfolio-based assessment. Such interactive discourse benefits educators and learners, highlighting the value of integrating dialogic assessment to enrich educational practices and aspiring teachers' journeys.

REFLECTION POINT

This case study aims to provide insights into the complexity of trainee teacher assessment in one specific HEI, though it is anticipated that there will be resonance beyond this particular context, and the following points are for consideration:

1) How is or can the dialogic approach be implemented to further authenticate assessment practices in your institution?
2) To what extent is the premise of 'power with the learners' endorsed through assessment practices?
3) How closely does the ethos of the staffing team align with the values embedded in provision? Consider the strengths and tensions arising from aligned and contrasting motivations.

9

FORMATIVE AND SUMMATIVE ASSESSMENT RUBRICS FOR A UK POSTGRADUATE TAUGHT EDUCATION STUDIES MODULE

ANDREW HOLMES AND PAUL HOPKINS

Discipline and/or Subject/Field: Education Studies

CONTEXT

Hull University was founded in 1927, and the programmes offered by the School of Education include a masters in education (MA[Ed]), which attracts a significant number of international students, mainly from West Africa. In 2021 the university made a strategic decision to lower its fees for international students; as a result, the number of students on the masters has grown considerably: 70 (20/21), 150 in (21/22), and 250 (22/23). In recent years we have also seen a growth in plagiarism, including contract plagiarism. The Contemporary and Critical Perspectives in Education module is mandatory for all students in the programme, which includes three different MA pathways: early childhood studies, education studies, and education and social inclusion. Most students work as teachers in their home countries, and for the majority English is a second language, albeit, for many, one learnt from childhood; hence the standard of written and spoken English is mostly comparable to that of UK students. The module is taught in the first trimester, when most students are new to the UK. In 2020–22 two staff, Holmes and Hopkins,

DOI: 10.4324/9781003360254-9

delivered and assessed the module; in 2021–22 they were supported by four staff in marking and feedback, and in 2022–23 they delivered and a further eight staff provided supporting tutorial workshops, with all ten staff assessing student work. A large group face-to-face lecture was followed by smaller-group (25 students each) lecturer-facilitated workshops. All course materials are provided through the university's digital virtual learning environment (VLE), Canvas, with assessments submitted online and feedback provided online via Canvas Speedgrader, along with one-to-one feedback tutorials at the request of each student. All assignments are automatically run through a plagiarism checker, Turnitin (an online originality checking and plagiarism prevention service that checks work for citation mistakes or copying), and where similarity scores of >20% are identified, the student is directed to take an online course on understanding academic misconduct (plagiarism).

STRATEGY

The rapid growth in student numbers has posed a number of interesting teaching and assessment challenges, particularly:

- plagiarism and developing international students' understandings of what plagiarism or 'academic misconduct' means in a UK context (Medway et al., 2018; Lancaster, 2020),
- embedding authentic formative assessment that also acts as assessment as learning (Yan & Boud, 2022),
- developing students' understanding of formative assessment (most students have previously been assessed by formal examinations and have little experience of formative assessment),
- changing the previous video-blog formative assessment process to allow for larger student cohorts,
- standardising the marking and feedback process across a large tutor team to ensure equity and fairness for all students (Broadbent et al., 2018).

Previously students had produced a short video and a blog on critical reflection for the summative assessment. With larger numbers the combination of technical issues and the low levels of students' digital literacy (Gilster, 1997; JISC, 2014) made this unmanageable.

We wanted to place greater emphasis on formative assessment because many of the international students are not used to studying within the UK higher education system and thus may not be used to writing critically, nor reflectively (essential requirements in the field of education studies). We wanted to counter contract plagiarism through an authentic assignment that would be very difficult for an 'essay mill' to write (Lancaster, 2020). We wanted an authentic assessment (i.e., one with real-world relevance that tested students' knowledge and understanding) that would act both as assessment *for* learning (Wiliam, 2011), assessment *as* learning (Yan & Boud, 2022), and learning-oriented assessment (Carless et al., 2006; Carless, 2007) which required students to learn new knowledge from their engagement with the assessment task itself as well as the accompanying assessment processes. Yan and Boud (2022) identify that assessment as learning is a learning strategy that 'requires students to learn from engagement with the assessment task itself' (Yan & Boud, 2022, p. 13) and 'necessarily generates opportunities for students through their active engagement in seeking, interpreting, and using evidence' (Yan & Boud, 2022, p. 13).

We wanted to try to standardise the amount, quality, and type of feedback provided by the ten different tutors involved in marking work and help develop both students' assessment literacy and feedback literacy (Price et al., 2012; Carless & Boud, 2018; Malecka et al., 2020; Pitt & Winstone, 2023). We recognised that feedback practices are essential components of students' learning, personal development, and the development of confidence (Pitt & Winstone, 2023). For assessment literacy we refer to Smith et al.'s (2013) definition, 'Students' understanding of the rules surrounding assessment in their course context, their use of assessment tasks to monitor or further their learning, and their ability to work with the guidelines on standards in their context to produce work of a predictable standard' (pp. 45–46). This comprises three elements: First, students need to understand the purpose of assessment and how it connects with their learning trajectory. Second, they need to be aware of the processes of assessment and how they might affect their capacity to submit responses that are on task, on time, and completed with appropriate academic integrity. Third, opportunities for them to practise judging their own responses to assessment tasks need to be provided so that students can learn to identify what is good about their work and what could be improved.

A well-designed assessment and feedback process supports the development of student's assessment literacy (Boud & Molloy, 2013) and helps reduce awarding gaps. Exemplars have been identified as being an important element of developing students' feedback literacy (Carless & Boud, 2018), and to facilitate this our digital VLE had a range of exemplars provided within different grade boundaries (i.e., clear fails under 45%, marginal fails 45–49%, passes 50–60%, good passes 60–69%, and very good passes 70% and above. Although, due to teaching time constraints, we did not spend classroom time working with the exemplars, as good practice would suggest (Smith et al., 2013), all students were directed and encouraged to read them.

PRACTICE

Development of a formative assessment rubric

To help develop students' understanding and ensure marker consistency, the two module co-leaders developed a specific formative assessment rubric, or 'analytic rubric' (Ragupathi & Lee, 2020). There is a growing body of evidence suggesting that rubrics support learning and development and assessment feedback consistency (Carless & Boud, 2018; Panadero & Jonsson, 2013; Ragupathi & Lee, 2020; Bearman & Ajjawi, 2021) and may help reduce student anxiety about assessment through making the assessment process more transparent (Mansi, 2021). They also reduce inequalities from the 'hidden curriculum' (Hincliffe, 2020).

In developing the formative rubric, we focused on providing students with key 'essential' information they would need to be able to improve their work, along with weblinks to additional 'study skill' learning resources. The focus was on development, not grading (Bearman & Ajjawi, 2021) and as such could be identified as being a holistic rubric (Ragupathi & Lee, 2020). We recognise that, by definition, this may not be a 'rubric', as it is unweighted (Reddy & Andrade, 2009) and is not used for grading purposes.

A video explanation supported students before they produced their formative work, a critique of a published academic research paper chosen from a range provided aligned to the different topics delivered in the taught sessions, allowing them some choice in the assessment topic (Morris et al., 2019). This 1400-word critical reflection was submitted at the midpoint of the course (week 6 from 12) allowing staff two weeks to provide formative, developmental, and constructive feedback in line with good practice (Carless & Boud, 2018; Mansi, 2021; Dawson et al., 2021; Carless, 2022) and giving sufficient time for the students to engage with it before commencing their summative work; a 1400-word critical reflection (60%) on a different peer-reviewed research paper and a 1200-word critical commentary on critical practice and the nature of criticality in education (40%).

Development of summative assessment rubrics

Two rubrics were developed using digital collaboration tools (Google Docs) among the small team of academics/developers and operationalised following existing good practice (Ragupathi & Lee, 2020) via the virtual learning environment. Both facilitated assessment-as-learning and explained how work was graded. The mark scheme on the rubric was aligned with the module's learning outcomes. A pilot of the rubric indicated we misjudged the weightings, as a substantial number of students were gaining marks of 80+. We amended by allowing some flexibility in the rubric weighting boxes, what we identify as a 'flexed rubric', allowing for greater marker academic judgement, and re-marked prior to releasing grades to students. As Banerjee et al. (2015) suggest, rubrics require regular review and revision if they are to be effective assessment tools. With hindsight we recognise that the lower-end descriptors were not as developmental as they needed to be, an aspect that is recognised with the research literature on rubrics (Tierney & Simon, 2004).

IMPACT

An online survey tool (JISC Online Surveys; www.onlinesurveys.ac.uk/) was used to survey students about the rubrics and their use and effectiveness. We surveyed students after they had received their grade and summative assessment feedback after they had completed the module.

Research sample size. The research sample was from four of the ten tutor groups. From the 98 students in these groups, 45 (46%) responded. The majority of these (93%) were from the overseas students (the majority of the cohort). Significant numbers of the students had previously been assessed by essay methods (71%) or examination (76%), and just under half (43%) had some experience of feedback using what they considered a 'rubric'.

Students previous experience of assessment rubrics

The majority of the students used the rubric before writing their assignment (82%), during writing (79%), or before submitting (74%), with only a small minority (15%) saying they did not look at the rubric at all. Student qualitative comments were mostly positive, some more 'low key', such as 'It gives guidelines to improving on my assignment', or 'It was quite helpful', and some more enthusiastic, such as 'It was really useful. I tried to pay attention to the different areas pointed out in the rubric', 'It was so useful in a great way', and 'It helped me in arranging and adjusting and writing well'.

Rubrics helping students understand assessment feedback

When asked about how the rubric helped with feedback, the vast majority of the students (95%) said they looked at the rubric to help understand their grade and feedback, and when the comments were graded from 1 = not helpful to 4 = very helpful, there was an average score of 2.8. Again, student qualitative comments were mostly positive. Overall, the comments were very positive: 'It was very useful. I understood why I got what I got, as opposed to what happened with the other course', 'It highlighted my strong and weak points that will make my next assignment attain earn higher points', and 'The feedback I received within the rubric was a kind of measure of the level of my critical thinking ability'. However, there were some negative comments, such as 'My feedback was poor in detail' and 'It is not really explaining in detail feedback I can understand'.

When asked about the usefulness of the rubric to help improve their work, again the tone is generally very positive that the feedback gives a good indication of how to improve: 'definitely, the feedback will help me prepare for the next assignments', 'The focused feedback saved me a lot of time', though there was some more tentative usefulness: 'I could understand where I lost the mark. However, feedback is quite challenging to understand' (here we believe this may be attributed to how our VLE displays rubric feedback).

KEY LEARNING

Although the introduction of rubrics was very successful, particularly in helping students understand what was required and in standardising feedback from multiple tutors, there was one particular issue that arose, which we feel is important to bring to the reader's attention: that of some of the international students' misunderstanding of the provision of formative feedback.

Although very satisfied with the feedback in terms of it helping them to reflect on and improve future work prior to submitting their summatively assessed assignment (Fisher, 2003), some students were concerned about not receiving a grade for their formatively assessed piece. Although one of the taught sessions was about assessment practices, and the concepts of formative and summative assessment were clearly explained, students still wanted and expected to receive a percentage grade/mark for the formatively assessed work.

Many international students had little experience of formative assessment, and, while they understood that its purpose was to provide a low-stakes assessment from which they received developmental feedback, they could not understand why they did not also receive a grade. In their previous pre-UK university experience, all work they produced had been graded. In one-to-one tutorials students sometimes expressed feelings of dismay and disappointment that they had 'failed' the formative assessment because the feedback indicated areas they needed to improve, even though at the same time they recognised that they could not fail, because it was a formative, ungraded assignment. One student specifically articulated during a tutorial that, whilst they understood the formative assignment was ungraded, their (correct) interpretation was that it indicated that they would have failed the assignment had it been a summative assessment. It was explained that they had not failed because a formative assignment could not be failed, and though they acknowledged that they *already* recognised this, what they experienced would seem to be a form of cognitive dissonance (Festinger, 1962). This illustrates the need to more clearly explain to international students that formatively assessed work is ungraded and that, whilst the rubric feedback may give an indication of what grade would have been achieved, the work cannot be 'failed'. Western academics need to recognise that there are cultural differences in students' assessment literacy.

REFLECTION POINT

1) How can you ensure international students' understandings of assessment processes and formative assessment/feedback if they are different from those in their home country where this practice is uncommon and where use of technology may be less common?
2) How can you ensure consistency of the volume, type, and quality/nature of formative and summative digitally provided assessment feedback when a large team of tutors is involved?

3) How can you embed authentic, realistic real-world formative assessment into a module that caters for a diverse student body of learners used to revising for high-stakes formal examinations whilst ensuring any hidden curriculum elements are removed/minimised/explained?
4) How can you effectively explain to students how they will be assessed, why the assignments have been chosen, and how they will receive feedback when this may be different to their pre-UK university experiences?
5) How do you ensure 'accurate' weighting of rubrics when they are first implemented?

Note: Copies of the rubrics can be obtained from the authors. Please contact Andrew Holmes via email: A.G.Holmes@hull.ac.uk.

10

IMPLEMENTING IPSATIVE FEEDBACK THROUGH INTERCONNECTED TASKS AND COMPARISON PROCESSES IN A DIRECT-ENTRY PROGRAM

BIANKA MALECKA

Discipline and/or Subject/Field: English as a Second Language

CONTEXT

Learner-centred approaches to education focus on exploring the potential of feedback to direct student learning. Feedback is no longer understood as a one-way transmission of information from teacher to student (Boud & Molloy, 2013) but a process with shared responsibilities of students and educators (Carless, 2020). Such feedback has been linked to the concepts of self-regulation, which refers to the self-generated, reflective and strategic engagement in academic tasks (Zimmerman, 2000); evaluative judgement understood as students' capability to make decisions about the quality of own work (Tai et al., 2017); and student agency conceptualised as a psychological process aimed to implement learning and studying strategies (Winstone et al., 2017a). All these concepts are important for students' academic success in higher education (HE), where they are required to take increased responsibility for their own learning, and feedback plays a role in fostering these capabilities.

Yet despite the contention that students must develop capabilities to act on feedback and judge the quality of their own work, there has been insufficient consideration of how such opportunities can be created, especially in the post-digital reality for HE. This case study explores how material and digital resources were configured to create opportunities for ipsative feedback processes to promote learners' engagement with feedback. Ipsative feedback is a learner-centred feedback process organised across consecutive tasks with similar learning outcomes (Malecka & Boud, 2021). The study was guided by the following question: how can ipsative feedback design improve student action on feedback?

This case study was conducted with direct-entry program students (DEP) at an English language centre affiliated with a large university in Australia. DEP students are international students who have received a conditional offer from the university but do not yet meet English language entry requirements to commence studies. Most students at this centre come from mainland China, followed by Saudi Arabia, Thailand and Vietnam. The direct-entry program is a 10–20-week course focused on academic writing, reading, speaking and independent learning skills. The duration of the course is determined by students' current English level as reflected in international English language competency tests such as International English Language Testing System (IELTS), Test of English as a Foreign Language (TOEFL) or Pearson Test of English (PTE). DEP has a weekly class time of 20 hours and students learn skills such as giving academic presentations, facilitating and contributing to class discussions, reading university-level academic texts and conducting academic research. Developing students' writing skills is an important focus of the course, with 6 hours of weekly writing lessons, including analysing various written academic texts; composing paragraphs, essays and research reports; and class workshops where students analyse their own and peers' writing. Students also have weekly one-on-one consultations with teachers where they discuss the quality of their writing. All course content is on the Moodle and OpenLearning platforms. The first 10 weeks of the course include formative assessment tasks, whereas summative assessments are conducted in the remaining part of the course. Upon successful completion of DEP, students progress to diploma, undergraduate or postgraduate degrees of their choice at the university.

The practice reported in this case study took place over three 5-week cycles in 2020. The class size in each cycle was 18 students, with a total of 54 students participating in the intervention. The study involved 10 participants who were on the pathway to postgraduate (9 participants) and undergraduate (1 participant) studies in a variety of disciplines at the university. At the beginning of the second cycle the mode of course delivery changed due to the COVID-19 pandemic, and the course was fully online.

STRATEGY

To effectively support students' learning, teachers need to design and orchestrate feedback opportunities irrespective of the format or environment in which they are situated (Fawns, 2019). Boud and Molloy (2013) advocate a curriculum approach to feedback with multiple and nested tasks so that students can apply comments received to their future work. Nash and Winstone (2017) emphasise the importance of shared responsibility between educators and students. Teachers need to foster students' awareness of the importance of feedback and cognisance of strategies to implement it, while students are responsible for taking productive action upon feedback. Henderson et al. (2019b) identify four conditions for successful design for feedback. Alongside the importance of aligning learning outcomes of multiple tasks and the variety of sources and modes of feedback, the authors emphasise tailoring feedback to meet learners' individual needs through delivering personalised and meaningful feedback information which monitors learners' progress.

In a program which includes interconnected tasks there is an opportunity for the implementation of ipsative feedback. Such feedback requires two necessary conditions: the presence of iterative tasks in the curriculum as well as students' and teachers' access to students' past work via online systems. It therefore emphasises the significance of careful planning and design (Malecka & Boud, 2021). Of course, as already mentioned, design is paramount to all feedback interactions; yet, as ipsative processes involve explicit comparisons of two or more samples of students' work, they demand clear links between tasks to communicate information about progress or lack of it. If the curriculum includes a series of one-off tasks with different learning outcomes and assessment criteria, such comparison would not be possible.

E-portfolios are effective tools to implement ipsative feedback processes. They can be designed to promote a variety of learning activities: revising and improving students' work before submission, discussing feedback from teachers or peers (Steen-Utheim & Hopfenbeck, 2019) or incorporating programmatic assessment (Fung, 2016). E-portfolios can also be used to synthesise information from multiple sources and monitor students' progress towards learning goals (Winstone, 2019). To facilitate ipsative feedback processes, e-portfolios need to be designed to allow both teachers and students easy access to students' past work and feedback comments (Malecka & Boud, 2021). The inclusion of learning outcomes for particular tasks is also recommended to assist teachers in framing comparisons of student effort to communicate a message about progress or its lack.

As a teacher at the aforementioned English language centre since 2013, I had a thorough understanding of the course, its formative assessments and requirements and believed that it constituted a promising context for research on the role of ipsative design on student action from feedback. Moreover, having participated in the curriculum writing, I saw it as a feedback-rich environment with many similar writing tasks, thus allowing for the implementation of the ipsative feedback intervention.

PRACTICE

The e-portfolio used in this research consisted of five parts corresponding to 5 weeks of study. The writing tasks which students practiced included essay introduction, body paragraphs, full essay and data commentary. Apart from ipsative features of the design, the e-portfolio included various activities to promote student engagement with feedback such as goal setting, reflection and action planning. Each part included three pages:

1. Writing page – personal goals, writing task and reflection (completed by student)
2. Feedback page – teacher's feedback comments and student reflection on feedback (completed by teacher and student)
3. Action page – rewrite and action log (completed by student)

At the start of each course, the teacher explained how to form learning goals for writing tasks, reflect on task completion and interpret feedback comments. Students were asked to complete the e-portfolio tasks on a regular basis.

To provide ipsative feedback, that is, comments on a student's improvement or its lack between tasks, the teacher had to read the student's current and past work. Student goals and reflection constituted additional referents for comparison. Teacher's comments were, therefore, guided not only by the requirements of the task but also learners' individual goals, capturing the similarities and differences between tasks more clearly than comments only on the task at hand.

The e-portfolios were initially designed in Microsoft Word, and students were asked to post them weekly on the Moodle Discussion Board. However, Microsoft Word proved too cumbersome, as students had to scroll down the document to locate current work. This resulted in some students completing tasks in the wrong sections of the document or missing feedback comments from past weeks. Sometimes students were also posting work in the wrong threads on the Moodle Discussion Board. That is why GoogleDocs was used in subsequent cycles, as it allowed easier collaboration, sharing and storage. Both Moodle and GoogleDocs were used as open access platforms to enable collaboration and facilitate multi-source feedback.

IMPACT

The ipsative design of feedback processes influenced student action by facilitating a variety of comparison processes. First, the comparative nature of ipsative processes directed students' attention to the improvements and inefficiencies of their work. As the DEP course is focused on enhancing students' academic writing skills, improvement was framed through a comparison of grammatical ('I made fewer mistakes in the week four writing practice compared with the week one or week two') and lexical performance ('the number of WW [Wrong Word] errors reduced, and I used more academic words'). Second, learners reported rereading of their own as well as peers' past work and feedback, which helped them re-examine strategies and generate new insight on their own work. These comparisons impacted students' own thinking and planning and were future oriented – 'before I need to write down this whole essay [in week four] I was looking for feedback in week three and I can find out what's wrong in my body paragraph and introduction in week two.' Third, learning goals, which students were encouraged to formulate before writing, were also a common referent for comparison, especially during the production and revision of written work – 'After I set these goals, I will remember and pay more attention to these points when I was writing.'

Two participants reported continuing with the beneficial feedback practices learnt during the ipsative feedback intervention when they moved to subsequent courses. These practices included formulation of learning goals prior to completing a task, rewriting work as well as using GoogleDocs to give and receive peer feedback. None of these practices were included in the course that students progressed to, yet students were keen to incorporate them into their independent learning. Ipsative feedback design has, therefore, motivated students to engage with feedback beyond requirements through revisiting previous work and feedback, revising current tasks and transferring beneficial practices to other learning contexts. These processes build students' ability to regulate their learning through such cognitive and behavioural actions as self-monitoring of work, evaluating feedback messages and acting on them.

Moreover, teacher comments on student progress, rather than only performance at a current task, were seen as a reflection of care and vested interest in students' learning. Establishing strong mutual relations based on trust and mutual valuing are salient in feedback interactions (Telio et al., 2015), and ipsative feedback processes contribute to forming them.

Finally, students appreciated the affordances of e-portfolios to store all their work in one place – 'it is stable, useful and convenient . . . as I can review my work very fast as it is in one document.' In the case of ipsative feedback design then, digital tools such as an e-portfolio can foreground feedback practice by archiving traces of student work (Fawns, 2019) and opening opportunities of learning through comparison making, rewriting or reflection.

KEY LEARNING

The implementation of ipsative feedback processes in an appropriate e-portfolio provides important insights into the benefits of scaffolding feedback practices in post-digital environments. Decisions about feedback design need to be made at the same time as decisions about learning objectives of particular tasks. This view implies arranging course elements in sequences and with sufficient alignment in task requirements and objectives to facilitate learners' acting on feedback information as well as support the generation of internal comparisons. Staged tasks, interactive cover sheets and e-portfolios are effective tools to promote students' engagement and provide teachers with a clear picture of students' progress, facilitating the ipsative focus of their comments. Initially, teachers may find formulating such comments time consuming, yet, as both teachers and students gain proficiency with these processes, teachers' inputs can be minimised in favour of peer feedback and self-comparisons.

When ipsative feedback processes are implemented in the early stages of students' tertiary education, for example, in diplomas or first year courses, they enhance the repertoire of feedback strategies that students may be able to use later. Using ipsative feedback processes in direct-entry programs has an additional advantage of familiarising international students with an array of feedback practices that they may be unfamiliar with. Overall, the rich feedback encounters inherent in ipsative processes equip learners with tools which may be useful in feedback-deficient settings and provide learners with skills to create their own opportunities for learning through establishing informal peer feedback networks or applying feedback practices considered successful in past contexts.

A key point about the ipsative feedback practice reported in this case study is that, in the move online due to COVID-19, the practice hardly changed. Technology undoubtedly facilitates the implementation of ipsative feedback processes, as all records of student and teacher work and feedback are stored conveniently in one place with easy access. Yet it is crucial to think about learning activities and their design and practice, 'whether they involve microchips – or not' (Fawns, 2019, p. 142). Moreover, in the post-digital environment, it is also important to consider the meld between digital affordances and relational factors. Student interactions with digital technology need to be accompanied by affective and social experiences with teachers and peers. Educators need to monitor learners' engagement with ipsative processes and augment the effects of digital tools by providing personalised feedback comments which can offer additional affective support. Similarly, situated feedback practices with peers can enhance students' learning and facilitate idiosyncratic configurations of feedback practices.

REFLECTION POINT

Based on the content of this case study, here are some questions that educators wanting to implement ipsative feedback processes should consider:

1. Does my program/course/unit include interconnected tasks which test similar learning outcomes?
2. Do I have access to digital tools that will enable access and storage of student and teacher work and feedback?
3. How can I support students to make comparisons of their own work to identify progress?

For educators wishing to review the ipsative feedback practice, here are some possible research directions:

1. How do teachers engage with standards to map learners' trajectories with regard to meeting learning outcomes for specific tasks?
2. How do different levels of teacher feedback literacy impact the implementation of ipsative feedback processes?
3. What other digital tools can be effective in supporting students' engagement with ipsative feedback processes?

11

AN ONLINE PEER ASSESSMENT TOOL FOR EMBEDDING AUTHENTIC FEEDBACK LITERACY IN STUDENTS STUDYING CREATIVE SUBJECTS

DAVID ANTHONY PARKINSON AND MICHAEL EDWARD PARKER

Discipline and/or Subject/Field: *Creative Subjects/Design*

CONTEXT

This case study introduces a method for creating online peer assessment and feedback exercises that are designed to embed authentic feedback literacy in undergraduate level-six students studying creative subjects. It was developed to help address student criticism of assessment and feedback in creative subjects, as publicised in measures such as the National Student Survey in the United Kingdom. Student involvement in and experience of assessment and feedback processes are a critical component of their learning experience at university, and they can be used to actively promote attributes that are valuable to the world of work (Carless & Boud, 2018; Dawson et al., 2021).

There is a growing field of research supporting the view that interventions can be designed to deliver authentic experiences and enhance student assessment and feedback literacy (Carless & Boud, 2018; Dawson et al., 2020). However, ensuring quality assessment and feedback processes in a

DOI: 10.4324/9781003360254-11

post-digital environment poses unique disciplinary challenges for creative subjects. Subjectivity is central to creative processes; being able to make judgements about the intent, ambitions, and objectives of an assessor are regarded as critical skills (Baynes, 2010); therefore, it is critical to consider how we might incorporate these activities into online assessment and feedback exercises to maintain engagement and offer flexibility of access.

STRATEGY

In recent years, both feedback literacy and authentic feedback have emerged as areas of research within pedagogy. In this case study, leading theoretical frameworks from these fields are adapted and combined to establish a new framework for designing an online peer assessment and feedback exercise, aimed specifically at developing authentic feedback literacy in students studying creative subjects.

Feedback literacy developed as an emerging theme from established research into assessment literacy. Predominantly, within the field of assessment literacy, research has attempted to understand students' conceptions of how and why they are assessed to try to develop their engagement in the process (Smith et al., 2013). Developing this further, Carless and Boud (2018) propose that we should also try to understand how and why students appreciate the value and importance of feedback and the active role they play in this process. They have consolidated their research through the following model, which suggests that feedback literacy has four elements: the ability to appreciate feedback, make judgements, manage affect, and through these take action (see Figure 11.1).

These features have been identified in other empirical studies on feedback literacy (Molloy et al., 2020). However, they focus on generic rather than specific disciplinary contexts in the application of feedback literacy.

Authentic feedback can be viewed as a progression of feedback literacy that includes consideration of how academic feedback practices relate to a subject's professional context (Dawson et al., 2020). Considering the context in which assessment and feedback take place, the field of authentic feedback is predominantly concerned with:

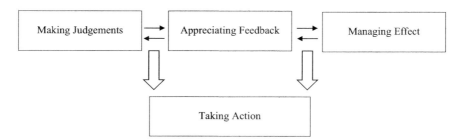

Figure 11.1 Features of student feedback literacy (Carless & Boud, 2018, p. 1319).

teaching and learning taking place within the subject and the recognition of the types of practice that may be unique or more relevant to that subject [and] the professional or work context of the discipline and the extent to which they emulate the professional environment.

(Parker & Parkinson, 2022)

The underpinning principle is that for assessment and feedback to be authentic, it should establish a quantifiable connection between the academic and professional contexts to bolster students' learning. As such, Dawson et al. (2020) establish five principles for embedding authenticity into feedback:

1. **Realism**: that the feedback is authentic to and represents the reality of the life graduates of the discipline will face and prepares the students accordingly.
2. **Cognitive Challenge**: that the feedback supports engagement with high-order thinking, problem-solving, and decision-making.
3. **Affective Challenge**: that the feedback promotes engagement with challenging and potentially critical responses to work, recognising the occurrence of such practices in the workplace.
4. **Evaluative Judgement**: that the feedback supports the development of capabilities to make decisions about the quality of your own, or other peoples', work.
5. **Enactment of Feedback**: that the feedback is engaged with constructively to support development or either the object of feedback, future approaches to work, or both.

Through combining the theory in this and Carless and Boud's (2018) frameworks, whilst considering the creative disciplinary context, we have developed a framework for embedding authentic feedback literacies (Figure 11.2) to guide the design of online peer assessment and feedback exercises.

The framework focuses on appreciating feedback, making judgements, managing affects, taking action, and realism as skills. A series of corresponding behaviours in students are proposed for each of these skills. Finally, a series of corresponding design principles are recommended for encouraging these behaviours in students through the exercise. The design principles include guidance on the practicalities of delivering this experience online to support a post-digital formative experience in the creative subject context. For example, the theme appreciating feedback proposes: 1a) that students should be able to understand and appreciate the role of feedback in improving work and the active learner role in these processes. The design principle for the peer assessment intervention that correlates to this suggests introducing the peer assessment and feedback exercise by the educator, with clear reference to criteria and overview of the relevance of the formative exercise to improving work. We have established several propositions and correlating design principles for each theme in the framework, building a strategy for delivering an online peer assessment exercise.

94 FORMATIVE ASSESSMENT AND FEEDBACK IN POST-DIGITAL LEARNING ENVIRONMENTS

	APPRECIATING FEEDBACK	MAKING JUDGEMENTS	MANAGING AFFECT	TAKING ACTION	REALISM
QUALITIES	**1a.** Students are able to understand and appreciate the role of feedback in improving work and the active learner role in these processes. **1b.** Students recognise that feedback information comes in different forms and from different sources.	**2a.** Students can develop capacities to make sound academic judgements about their own work and the work of others. **2b.** Students participate productively in peer feedback processes. **2c.** Students refine self-evaluative capacities over time in order to make more robust judgements.	**3a.** Students maintain emotional equilibrium and avoid defensiveness when receiving critical feedback. **3b.** Students are proactive in eliciting suggestions from peers or teachers and continuing dialogue. **3c.** Students develop habits of striving for continuous improvement on the basis of internal and external feedback.	**4a.** Students are aware of the imperative to take action in response to feedback information. **4b.** Students can draw inferences from a range of feedback experiences for the purpose of continual improvement. **4c.** Students develop a repertoire of strategies for acting on feedback.	**5a.** Students engage in the tasks and social and physical context of feedback in the discipline or profession.
EXERCISE DESIGN PRINCIPLES	**1a.** Introduction of the peer-assessment and feedback exercise by the teacher, with clear reference to criteria and overview of the relevance of the formative exercise to improving work. [Shared screen presentation with visual aids to all participants]. Engage in peer discussion to reach a consensus on grading and feedback points. [Use breakout room function if number of participants is greater than ten]. **1b.** Students undertake independent evaluations. [Away from screen]. Students then engage in peer discussion to reach a consensus on grading and feedback points. [Use breakout room function if number of participants is greater than ten]. Teacher then discusses similarities and differences across groups with the class in the context of actual feedback given by the teacher. [Presenting to all participants].	**2a.** Individual grading of 3 exemplar projects, before mediating through peer discussion and agreement. [Share files and then use breakout room function if number of participants is greater than ten]. Relating individual and group feedback to actual teacher feedback to improve understanding. [Shared screen presentation with visual aids to all participants]. **2b.** Individual grading of 3 exemplar projects, before mediating through peer discussion and agreement. Requires all students to engage in the process. [Share files and then use breakout room function if number of participants is greater than ten]. Students prompted in the questionnaire to identify areas for improvement in their own work to encourage students to relate judgements to action. [Post exercise]. **2c.** Individual grading of 3 exemplar projects, before mediating through peer discussion and agreement. [Share files and then use breakout room function if number of participants is greater than ten]. Relating individual and group feedback to actual teacher feedback to improve understanding. [Shared screen presentation with visual aids to all participants].	**3a.** Students assess anonymised, exemplar projects to mitigate against emotional reactions to the assessment and feedback process. [Share files and then use breakout room function if number of participants is greater than ten]. Individual grading of 3 exemplar projects, before mediating through peer discussion and agreement. [Share files and then use breakout room function if number of participants is greater than ten]. **3b.** Individual grading of 3 exemplar projects, before mediating through peer discussion and agreement. [Share files and then use breakout room function if number of participants is greater than ten]. Teacher shares feedback at the end of the exercise and discusses similarities and differences, teacher reinforces value of the seeking feedback. [Shared screen presentation with visual aids to all participants]. **3c.** Students prompted to consider actions for applying learning to their own development as part of the questionnaire. [Post exercise].	**4a.** Students prompted to highlight one area of learning to take from the exercise to apply to own projects. [Led by teacher during final discussion with all participants]. **4b.** Individual grading of 3 exemplar projects, before mediating through peer discussion and agreement. [Share files and then use breakout room function if number of participants is greater than ten]. Teacher shares feedback at the end of the exercise and discusses similarities and differences. [Shared screen presentation with visual aids to all participants]. Students prompted to highlight one area of learning to take from the exercise to apply to own projects. [Led by teacher During final discussion with all participants]. **4c.** Students prompted to highlight one area of learning to take from the exercise to apply to own projects. [Led by teacher During final discussion with all participants].	**5a.** Introduction of the peer-assessment and feedback exercise by the teacher, with clear reference to criteria and overview of the relevance of the exercise to improving work. [Shared screen presentation with visual aids to all participants]. Introduction includes clear reference to the specific context of design as a profession and the importance of peer review and feedback. Reference is made to the exercise supporting specific projects, but also having value in developing feedback skills critical to the profession. [Shared screen presentation with visual aids to all participants]. Individual grading of 3 exemplar projects, before mediating through peer discussion and agreement to simulate design briefing sessions with colleagues and clients. [Share files and then use breakout room function if number of participants is greater than ten].

Figure 11.2 Framework for embedding authentic feedback literacies.

PRACTICE

To test this framework, we used it to guide an online peer assessment and feedback exercise with 30 level-six undergraduate students studying design.

To begin, a short presentation was delivered to the students by the educator leading the exercise (approximately 15 minutes). The presentation gave an overview of the assessment and feedback exercise and discussed the criteria that were used in the assessment of the work examples that would later be disseminated to students. The assessment criteria were then shared digitally with the students for their reference throughout the exercise.

After this, the students were given access to three examples of work. They were asked to consider marks and feedback independently as the call was paused (approximately 15 minutes). After this, they were split into six groups of five using a breakout rooms function. In groups, they had to discuss their thoughts with one another and agree on marks and feedback (approximately 30 minutes).

Following this, students were brought back from their breakout rooms, and each group presented their agreed-upon marks and feedback to the entire cohort (approximately 5 minutes per group, 30 minutes in total). The educator leading the exercise contrasted and compared the student marks and feedback in a group discussion before presenting the assessment that was carried out by the original assessor (approximately 30 minutes). Questions were invited before ending the exercise.

For quantitative data, a questionnaire was used that adapted the propositions from the second row of the framework into 'to what extent'–style questions, requiring student responses on a Likert scale of 1–5. For example, proposition 1a was translated as follows:

> To what extent do you feel the peer assessment exercise helped you to understand and appreciate the role of feedback in improving work?

In addition to this, qualitative feedback was collected through the questionnaire using free text options, a recording of the peer assessment and feedback exercise, and semi-structured interviews with a sample of participants. This mixed-methods approach mitigated against over-reliance on one type of data set and is evidence of a more robust use of case study methodology (Rashid et al., 2019).

IMPACT

Aggregated statistics were generated from the propositions set out in the questionnaire, and a thematic analysis was carried out on the qualitative data sets. Thematic analysis of transcripts is an appropriate tool in case study methodologies where a conceptual framework has been created that includes a series of propositions for testing (Gerring, 2006; Rashid et al., 2019).

When observing the quantitative data set, across all thematic areas and propositions, results were consistently between 4 and 5 on the Likert scale (slightly agree to strongly agree) with very little variation. These results can be regarded as emphatic and indicate that student self-perception of the development of literacies was significant.

When compared to qualitative data analysis, there is significant corroboration between the data sets. The qualitative data also provides insights into how and why students arrived at their self-perceptions, contributing a deeper understanding of how effective the exercise was. The following sections discuss the findings against each emergent theme.

Appreciating feedback

Student perception was that the exercise helped them to understand and appreciate the role of feedback in improving work and to understand the feedback of others and how this relates to their own work. Against these two propositions, the quantitative data set showed mean scores of 4.75 and 4.67, respectively, in student responses to the Likert scale of 1–5. This showed that students strongly agreed with the effectiveness of the exercise in helping them achieve these propositions.

Emergent themes in the qualitative data sets relating to appreciating feedback included students placing greater emphasis on the importance of feedback as a skill required in their subject and students reflecting on their views of each feedback source, their value, and how they relate to one another. These themes demonstrate that an online peer assessment exercise that embeds authentic feedback literacy is useful for helping students to understand criteria in relation to the quality of work.

Making judgements

Student perception was that the exercise helped them to form opinions about their own work and the work of others, encouraged them to interact with fellow students to make judgments about work, and informed how they will give feedback in the future. Against these three propositions, the quantitative data set showed mean scores of 4.5, 4.58, and 4.33, respectively, indicating significant agreement from the students on the effectiveness of the exercise.

Emergent themes in the qualitative data sets relating to making judgements included students feeling more confident in their assessments through triangulating and refining views and a reiteration of the feeling of encouragement in interacting with fellow students to make judgments about their work. The lack of discussion around the third proposition (the exercise's effectiveness in informing how they will give feedback in the future) is possibly due to the future-facing nature of the question, as it requires students to imagine how their learning may change in the future as opposed to allowing them to reflect on current experiences. These themes demonstrate that the exercise was useful for helping students to feel more confident in discussing their work with others and building opinions of their own work and others. However, to truly gauge effectiveness of longer-term impact, it may be necessary to re-deliver the peer assessment exercise to the same group of students later and then ask them to reflect on their learning journey between each exercise.

Managing effect

Student perception was that the exercise helped them feel comfortable giving or listening to critical feedback, feel comfortable asking for suggestions from fellow students about their work, and to seek ways to improve approaches to feedback. Against these three propositions, the quantitative data set showed mean scores of 4.58, 4.17, and 4, respectively. This showed that students strongly agreed with the exercise's effectiveness in helping them achieve these propositions.

Emergent themes in the qualitative data sets relating to managing effect included students stating that they found it easier to speak critically about other people's work as opposed to their own; a reiteration of their increased comfort in seeking feedback from fellow students; and declarations that, irrespective of the exercise, they always seek ways to improve their work. These themes demonstrate that the exercise was useful for helping students to feel more confident in critiquing the work of others and seeking critique in return but that it supports, as opposed to establishes, a desire to seek ways of improving their own work.

Taking action

Student perception was that the exercise helped them to use feedback from the exercise to inform their own work, to consider the role of feedback in the professional world of design, and to understand how to act on feedback. Against these three propositions, the quantitative data set showed mean scores of 4.33, 4.33, and 4.17, respectively. This showed that students strongly agreed with the effectiveness of the exercise in helping them achieve these propositions.

Emergent themes in the qualitative data sets relating to taking action included students developing a deeper understanding of inadequacies in their own work, better distinguishment between alternative sources of feedback, and a clearer method for improving their own work. These themes demonstrate that the exercise was useful for helping students to understand how various forms of feedback can be used to identify areas and methods of improvement.

Realism

Realism was explored in the qualitative data sets of this research. It was found that students were able to speak confidently about the connection between peer feedback and its relationship to professional design practice post-exercise. Many regarded the peer-feedback exercise as a 'way to actually be a designer'. Two dimensions of realism became present in the thematic analysis: the first was the acknowledgment of authenticity in the peer-assessment exercise and the second acknowledging that giving and receiving feedback is an intrinsic quality of a 'good designer'. These themes resonate with the sociocultural perspective of this research: that authenticity relates to how individual identity is formed (Gipps, 2002; Mercer & Howe, 2012). This demonstrates that the exercise was inherently viewed as authentic due to the students' ability to identify this type of activity as synonymous with their profession and an understanding that these skills are what you need to identify as a designer.

KEY LEARNING

The case study work presented here has demonstrated that this online peer assessment and feedback exercise allows students to develop skills and attributes broadly accepted as being inherent to authentic feedback literacy and to be critically conscious of their own development.

A set of practical recommendations also emerged from the qualitative analysis to develop the exercise:

- Educators should consider creating multiple opportunities for students to engage in peer-assessment and feedback exercises over time, reinforcing skills and attributes, particularly those related to making judgement and taking action. Facilitating this through online environments allows for flexible access to the exercises, recording interactions, and easier reflection.
- An iterative approach to peer-assessment and feedback exercises can effectively simulate the iterative process of design, encouraging the development of appreciating feedback and reinforcing realism.
- Educators should progress from using anonymised exemplars to using students' own work to develop behaviours of emotional equilibrium associated with managing affect.
- Educators should actively prompt and check how students take action following the exercise. This could be linked to taking an iterative approach to the exercise or linking formative assessment and feedback exercises to summative exercises.

REFLECTION POINT

To reflect on and develop your own approach to delivering online peer-assessment and feedback exercises, it is important to ask yourself the following questions.

1) What feedback processes are authentic to the professions that relate to your subject area, and how might you embed them in the exercise?
2) Do you have examples of past work that relate to current student work to use in your first iterations of online peer assessment?
3) What functionality does your online platform offer for supporting engagement and managing interactions between students, and how can they be used to ensure inclusivity?
4) What are the various sources of feedback your students can draw upon?
5) How might you find out how students take action following delivery of exercises?
6) How will you keep track of peer-assessment exercises run with different cohorts of students, and how might you build on subsequent iterations (e.g., moving from anonymised examples of past work to current student work)?

Whilst developed with the context of creative subjects as a focus, the principles underpinning this online peer assessment and feedback exercise are transferrable. Testing these principles in other disciplinary contexts is actively encouraged to promote the development of authentic feedback literacies in students, which is an increasingly important part of the broader student learning experience.

12

INTEGRATING SCAFFOLDING INSTRUCTIONAL STRATEGY THROUGH DIGITAL TOOLS FOR IMPROVING ACADEMIC PERFORMANCE AMONG UNDERGRADUATE FINANCE STUDENTS

SANDAR WIN, ELIANA LAURETTA, TASNEEM JOOSUB, AND JAYNE REVILL

Discipline and/or Subject/Field: Business/Finance

CONTEXT

In business schools, accounting and finance courses have distinctive characteristics compared to other disciplines because they are predominantly numeracy based. The widening participation objectives of universities have also created a need to enhance students' numeracy, critical thinking, and academic writing skills. Hence, students often face challenges at the start of their Year 1. Likewise, tutors teaching these courses must put significant effort and identify innovative teaching practices to support their students. Moreover, in 2020, the global pandemic has led many universities to transition to remote teaching. Despite the challenges, the event provided a unique opportunity to develop new and innovative tools to support students.

DOI: 10.4324/9781003360254-12

One of the modules in Year 1 at Coventry University (CU) for undergraduate accounting and finance courses is Introduction to Finance. It introduces students to the basic concepts of finance. The module content is fundamental for students to critically understand more complex theories and calculations to progress and complete their studies successfully. Some areas for improvement, especially in students' engagements within the module, were identified. Therefore, the teaching strategy adopted in the module has been reviewed. During the pandemic, we adopted Microsoft Forms in this module. It is one of the most readily accessible digital tools to students and tutors as it is part of Microsoft Office 365, which is the most subscribed software package among the UK universities.

Improvements in students' progressions and their engagements in online lectures and seminars were found. Hence, though Microsoft Forms was initially used to only facilitate remote teaching, its use was continued after on-campus teaching was resumed in 2021. In the following sections, more details will be provided on how was introduced during the pandemic and continues to be adopted to enhance the student learning curve.

STRATEGY

Traditionally, the CU accounting and finance modules are designed based on active learning (Corbett & Spinello, 2020; Meyers & Jones, 1993) and scaffolding instructional strategy, which implies that students' learning starts from understanding simple concepts, which would allow them to gradually develop more critical thinking and a better understanding of more complex concepts (Jaramillo, 1996; Marginson & Dang, 2017). The Introduction to Finance module is delivered over 11 weeks in which every lecture will be followed by a seminar. During each seminar, students would solve finance-related problems and apply mathematical formulas using the examples provided by tutors during the lectures. Gradually, students would be introduced to more advanced finance concepts and complex mathematical formulas. In other words, for students to understand the lecture contents in week 11, they must actively engage with the module tutors and develop a good understanding of the lecture contents from week 1 onwards.

The first step to successfully implementing scaffolding strategy in a module requires us to understand every student's existing knowledge of the subject and their learning readiness to implement targeted interventions. In practice, embedding this teaching strategy for a large number of students is challenging. For instance, the average number of students enrolled in the Introduction to Finance module is between 200 to 300 every academic year, creating difficulties in understanding every student's learning progress prior to their completion of summative assessments. As the university promotes widening participation, establishing a non-hierarchical, democratic, and inclusive environment in a class by ensuring that learning resources used are accessible to all students, is crucial. Furthermore, no less important is the promotion of students' reflective thinking, which could assist students in taking responsibility for their own learning journey and seek support from tutors when necessary.

The decision to adopt Microsoft Forms as a tool to conduct formative assessments came after the module team took into careful account all the aforementioned considerations discussed earlier in this section. Thanks to the use of Microsoft Forms, the teaching team could understand and keep track of students' learning progress and their knowledge gaps and design effective interventions to help them successfully complete not only the module but also the course. Last but not least, formative assessments could support students in developing reflective skills which they could continue to use as part of their learning journey.

PRACTICE

The primary goal of formative assessment is to acquire an understanding of what students know (and don't know) to make changes in teaching and learning strategies and techniques beyond conventional summative assessment strategies such as exams and coursework (Pryor & Crossouard, 2008). Originally, in the Introduction to Finance module, lectures were primarily designed to provide basic core theory and knowledge, including introducing students to the basic calculations in finance. Seminars were calculation based. The module leader used to design seminar activities for every teaching week, which were related to the module contents. Often, these activities mainly focused on supporting students with acquiring the knowledge required to complete their assessments within this module. These seminar activities were taken the form of formative assessment, as students would practice those calculations and tutors would give feedback during seminars. Through exercises and case studies, the students were invited to revise, critically discuss, and expand the main concepts learned during the main lectures. At the same time, they were provided with formative feedback and feedforward which was delivered in the form of a shared and critical discussion on the conducted weekly activities. Nonetheless, this feedback was not explicitly formative as such. The adopted teaching approach was aligned to how finance and accounting modules were traditionally (pre-pandemic) delivered to students.

Unlike the traditional approach, the adoption during the pandemic of Microsoft Forms allowed students to engage in seminar activities prior to the actual seminars, enabling the module team to understand the knowledge acquired by students and track it over time, identify their learning needs, and adapt and redesign seminar activities to address students' needs. A typical example of how this is operationalised can be summarised in the following steps:

1) Initially, students are exposed to the new topic during the main lecture. They are then invited to critically think to some aspect of the topic via questions during class (online or on-campus) and virtual learning platform.

2) Students are provided with seminar activities which they need to complete before attending each weekly seminar session. The aim of these activities is primarily designed to revise and practise the financial calculations related to the lecture topic and develop logical, problem-solving, and analytical thinking skills.
3) For each seminar activity a Microsoft Forms link is provided to the students. Students can submit their answers on each seminar activity by clicking on these links. These activities were initially designed as multiple-choice questions (see Figure 12.1).
4) The module team review the answers submitted by students before the seminar. These answers downloaded in an Excel spreadsheet are compared, and students' learning journeys is monitored over the course of the module.
5) Furthermore, students are also provided with real-time feedback on the submitted answers as part of the seminar session. Also, if required, tutors develop additional seminar activities based on the submitted answers to help students understand key concepts and theories.

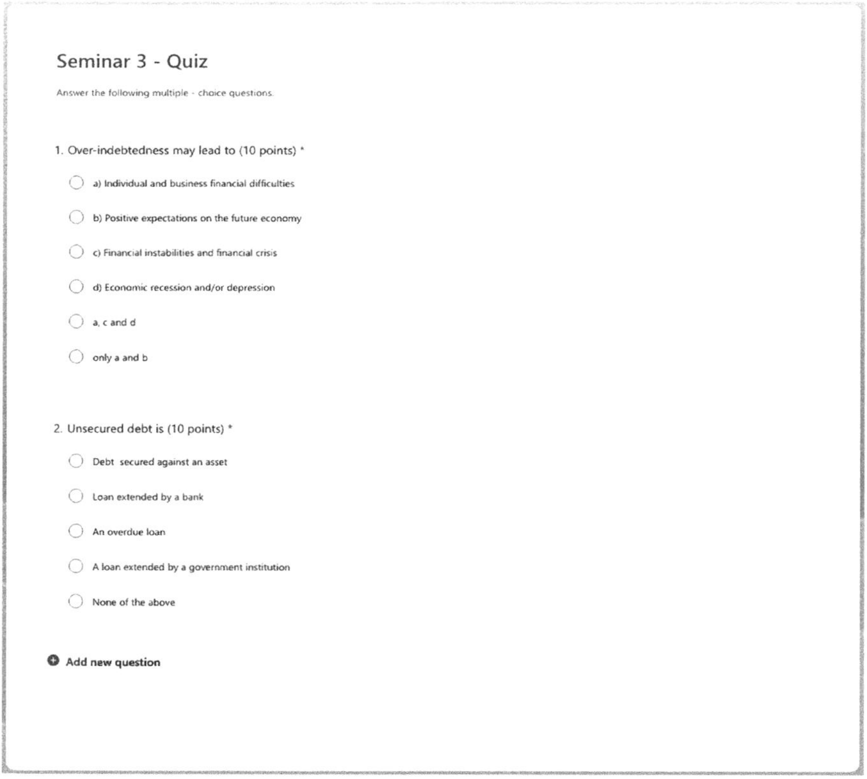
Seminar 3 - Quiz

Answer the following multiple - choice questions.

1. Over-indebtedness may lead to (10 points) *

a) Individual and business financial difficulties

b) Positive expectations on the future economy

c) Financial instabilities and financial crisis

d) Economic recession and/or depression

a, c and d

only a and b

2. Unsecured debt is (10 points) *

Debt secured against an asset

Loan extended by a bank

An overdue loan

A loan extended by a government institution

None of the above

Add new question

Figure 12.1 An example of the practical application of Microsoft Forms.

6) The seminar tutors guide students through analysing their answers and encouraging critical discussions in class about the submitted answers while developing students' reflective thinking. Consequently, students became aware of the rationale for applying different formulas to do financial calculations.

Evolution of the practice

In order to continue to integrate digital tools as part of pedagogy strategy, the module team referred back to the module and course descriptors to identify skills needed for students to support their learning journey.

Introduction to Finance as a module is organised into two assessment components, a coursework, and an exam which focuses on calculations. Through reviewing the students' academic performance in the module, we observed that their ability to apply theoretical knowledge and numeracy skills improved. However, there was a need to improve their academic writing skills for the coursework assessment component of the module. Hence, the teaching team explored how Microsoft Forms could be used to this aim. Microsoft Forms is a real-time quite intuitive and easy-to-use instrument which can be used for not only multiple-choice quizzes but also allows to integrate open-ended styled questions. To develop students' academic writing skills, research skills, and critical thinking skills, we integrated open-ended questions and tasks, which required students to conduct research on the finance topics (see Figures 12.2 and 12.3).

By integrating open-ended questions and tasks that required students to conduct research, we were able to provide students with opportunities to prepare themselves from year one onwards for more advanced tasks,

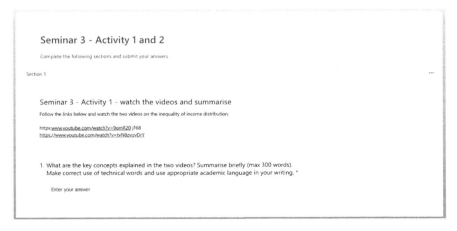

Figure 12.2 An example of integrating open-ended questions in Microsoft Forms.

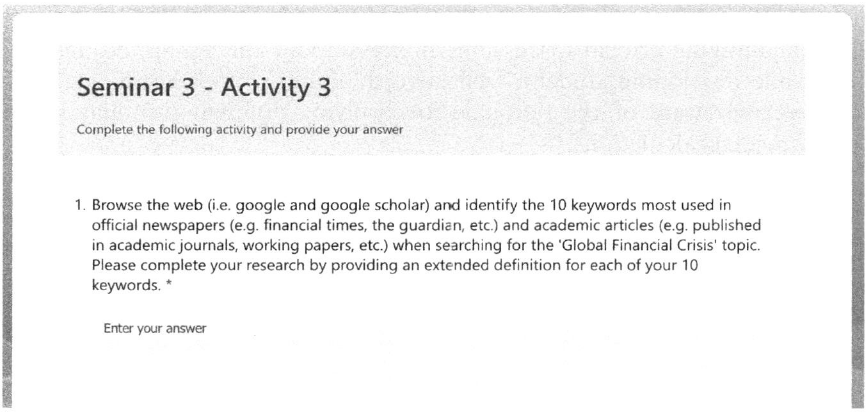

104   FORMATIVE ASSESSMENT AND FEEDBACK IN POST-DIGITAL LEARNING ENVIRONMENTS

> **Seminar 3 - Activity 3**
> Complete the following activity and provide your answer
>
> 1. Browse the web (i.e. google and google scholar) and identify the 10 keywords most used in official newspapers (e.g. financial times, the guardian, etc.) and academic articles (e.g. published in academic journals, working papers, etc.) when searching for the 'Global Financial Crisis' topic. Please complete your research by providing an extended definition for each of your 10 keywords. *
>
> Enter your answer

Figure 12.3 An example of integrating research-based questions in Microsoft Forms.

such as completing their dissertation in their final year of studies. In a way, over time, we not only integrated scaffolding teaching strategy but also research-led teaching, thereby further developing students' critical and analytical skills.

IMPACT

Microsoft Forms, as the digital tool adopted, allows the module team to identify learning issues and provide formative feedback and feedforwards. It is especially important in applying early interventions such as targeted academic support, encouraging students to seek help from the module team or direct them to learning and resource support centres (e.g., library supports for developing numeracy skills, academic writing support, etc.). Also, the module team consider a dynamic teaching strategy by considering applying changes to the teaching plan whenever necessary or assessed to be beneficial to students' learning experience (e.g., inviting guest speakers to provide students with more real-world examples, involving students in solving real-world case study, among other possible options). As the module is delivered as part of a team, other tutors would adopt Microsoft Forms in their respective teaching practice.

During the pandemic, the use of Microsoft Forms for online classes encouraged the progress of the students' learning journey beyond the module learning objective (e.g., developing academic writing skills and research skills). Moreover, students could collaborate online by sharing their Microsoft Forms experience. When returned to the on-campus classes, the tool has proved to greatly increase students' engagement when combined with the face-to-face interaction for the weekly seminar sessions. Subsequently, this has improved students' experience and their overall academic performances, measured through summative assessments. In numbers, with respect to the pre-pandemic teaching approach (academic year 2019–2020), the module recorded an increase in the overall students' satisfaction of approximately 11%. Furthermore, an increase was seen in the average coursework and exam marks of approximately 14% and 12%, respectively. Further, in academic year 2020–2021 we observed enhanced coursework and exam pass rates of approximately 7% and 6%, respectively. However, the latter has recently registered a decline in percentage variation, positively reflecting a more intellectually challenging module structure and a more discriminatory and well-distributed marking approach.

KEY LEARNING

One of the key lessons that we acquired from integrating Microsoft Forms in the Introduction to Finance module is the importance of educators remaining 'flexible' and 'open-minded' when designing their teaching and assessments. It is widely recognised in UK business schools that accounting and finance educators face unique challenges; that is, they are constrained by professional accreditations which require them to integrate exams as part of the summative assessments in their modules (Willcoxson et al., 2010). As a result, many educators were mostly focused on developing exams as part of their assessment strategies. And yet very few of them were aware of how to support students in completing these accredited exams. This has drastically changed now, and the pandemic provided the opportunity to explore the 'uncharted waters' of innovative teaching digital tools that can address this challenge.

Furthermore, some of the accounting and finance modules which received professional accreditation are taught to business school students. They could be studying non-accounting and finance courses such as BA (hons) international business and BA (hons) business and management. Hence, educators have to address the learning needs of students with varying and particularly challenging differentiated levels of accounting and finance knowledge given that most introductory modules such as Introduction to Finance take place in year one. In other words, a key learning point for educators is the need to move away from 'one size fits all' schemes to design business school curricula.

Approaching the Introduction to Finance teaching and assessments by being flexible and open-minded in designing the module's curriculum and strategy has enabled the module team to successfully integrate digital tools to support more effectively and efficiently the students' learning curve and overall learning experience.

REFLECTION POINT

When implementing new digital tools in courses that are traditionally exam based with a focus on developing students' numeracy skills, it is important for educators to ask the following questions:

1) Are there better and more effective digital tools available to facilitate scaffolding of the learning process? It is important to recognise that technology is ever changing, implying that we should explore new technologies that can improve students' learning experiences. Likewise, when delivering large modules, it is often inevitable that we have to work with module teams with different levels of digital literacy. Hence, it is important for educators to use simple tools that are accessible not only by students but also by other educators.
2) How do you set realistic expectations from students in terms of learning objectives? It is important to know students' prior subject knowledge and digital literacy before implementing new digital tools. Otherwise, digital tools may not facilitate students' learning. Instead, they can hinder their learning process.
3) What are the measures available to assess the impact of the digital tools on students' performance? It is important for educators to be aware of measures or mechanisms in which they can assess the impact of digital tools on students to improve their teaching strategies. The main objective of digital tools is to implement early interventions. Without appropriate measures to assess their impacts, it will be difficult for educators to improve students' learning.
4) Have you set clear expectations for other educators in the module? It is inevitable that educator must change or add seminar questions depending on students' performances in the module. Hence, it is important to inform other educators in the module team that seminar questions can be changed based on the students' performance to facilitate early interventions.
5) How can you explore other new ideas in collaboration with students to improve their learning journey? It is important for educators to be aware that there are other digital tools which can be more easily accessible and efficient compared to Microsoft Form. Even within the existing digital tools, there can be other functions that they have not explored before. Thus, it is important for educators to remain flexible and explore new ideas in collaboration with students to improve their learning experiences and support their learning journey.

13

DEVELOPING AN EXPERIENTIAL FORMATIVE ASSESSMENT ACTIVITY WITH THE GIST FRAMEWORK

YUSUF OC

Discipline and/or Subject/Field: Business Studies/Marketing

CONTEXT

This case study outlines a small simulation initiative developed at King's College London's Business School. During their tenure as lecturers in marketing education, marketing academics are expected to navigate the intersection of academia and real-world business, furthering the practical implementation of theoretical knowledge. This is particularly true for certain modules such as Marketing Communication, where the expectation is to delve deeper into industry dynamics, including agencies and their working models. Teaching these marketing modules becomes even more challenging in an online environment due to the reduced contact time. This case utilizes the Marketing Communication module in the online marketing MSc programme to illustrate the benefits of employing a small case study as an experiential learning activity. Teaching the module involved developing asynchronous module content and providing weekly synchronous sessions. The module itself, an advanced marketing component, is a crucial part of the curriculum, offering students insights into the complex world of communication strategies by introducing important concepts such as communication agency selection and budget allocation. Being an online module, it was challenging to prepare academic content that would hold students' attention without making it monotonous. This is because, unlike in a traditional classroom setting, you don't receive immediate feedback from students regarding the material.

There was a recurring problem during teaching this module. Many students struggled to grasp the complexities of these concepts, frequently finding it difficult to connect the academic material with real-world application. This was reflected in classroom discussions, assignments, and formative assessments, where students showed a noticeable difficulty in understanding and applying these marketing procedures. At first glance, the concepts may appear straightforward since they are related to social aspects of the lives such as advertising or marketing spending, but students are required to think critically about their actions and plan their next steps accordingly. Therefore, they need to grasp the importance of the process.

Furthering the challenge was the diverse student body at King's College. The students, hailing from various educational and cultural backgrounds, displayed a wide array of learning presences. The traditional content based, lecture-centric teaching method was often insufficient to cater to this diversity, particularly for intricate processes like agency selection and budget allocation. There was a clear need for an innovative teaching approach that could offer a more interactive, hands-on learning experience.

In response to this challenge, a simulation game was developed to serve as an experiential learning platform. In collaboration with King's Online instructional designers, the lecturer designed the game to simulate the real-world processes of agency selection and budget allocation in marketing communication campaigns. The intent was to use experiential learning to help students relate the theoretical knowledge with its practical application, creating a more holistic understanding of the subject matter (Morris, 2020).

The game was initially introduced to online marketing MSc students as part of their formative assessment. The decision to begin with the online students was strategic, as remote learning often presents unique challenges in engagement and understanding (Lockee, 2021). The simulation game was seen as a way to offer an immersive and engaging learning experience, despite the physical distance. The game's success with the online students and the positive impact on their learning outcomes prompted its incorporation into the on-campus modules as well. The game was implemented in two on-campus MSc-level Marketing Communication modules and one Executive MSc International Marketing module, receiving a lot of positive feedback.

STRATEGY

The genesis of the marketing simulation game was inspired by the recognized need for a more immersive, dynamic learning environment for teaching multifaceted marketing concepts (Kolb, 2014). The motivation stemmed from a dual observation: the pedagogical need to better equip students with a practical understanding of agency selection and budget allocation, and the broader trend in education toward innovative, engaging teaching methodologies (McCallum & Milner, 2021). The lecturer developed the simulation based on the gamification, instructing, sharing, tracking (GIST) framework (Oc & Plangger, 2022).

The increasingly digital learning environment, hastened by trends towards online education, has emphasized the value of adaptive teaching strategies that go beyond traditional lecture-style instruction (Bates, 2015). Experiential learning, by offering a more interactive and engaging experience, emerged as a critical driver behind the development of the simulation game (Kolb, 2014). It was designed not merely as a theoretical exercise but as a tool to foster an engaging and realistic learning environment, mirroring the challenges and tasks professionals face in the marketing field (Knight & Yorke, 2003). One of the core objectives of the simulation game was to encourage active learning and critical thinking, essential skills for future marketers. By immersing students in simulated scenarios, the game aimed to provoke strategic decision-making, compelling students to apply theoretical concepts to practical tasks, thus fostering a deeper comprehension of the subject (Chernikova et al., 2020). Gamified features can transform into a sustained learning environment if they are bolstered by sharing (enabling students to share their results with peers), instructing (guiding students to follow specific scenarios), and tracking (monitoring students' actions and providing them with feedback) components (Oc & Plangger, 2022).

This strategy is firmly anchored in the principles of formative assessment, which posits that learning is best facilitated through active engagement, immediate feedback, and the iterative process of trial and error (Tapingkae et al., 2020). Research shows that such an approach not only enhances understanding but also builds resilience and problem-solving skills, as students learn to navigate challenges and adapt their strategies based on the feedback received (Moss & Brookhart, 2019). In sum, the simulation game was developed as a strategic response to the evolving needs of the students and the wider trends in the education sector. By aligning with contemporary pedagogical approaches, the game represents an innovative step towards experiential learning; formative assessment; and an immersive, engaging learning experience.

PRACTICE

Based on the GIST framework (Oc & Plangger, 2022), the lecturer and game designers created a game-like environment, showing students whether they reached the targets and allowing them to compete with their peers (gamification). Students are briefed on the case study and objectives (instructing). They then share their results and strategies on an online forum or a Padlet page where all the other students in the class can see them (sharing), allowing the students to track their performance and receive immediate feedback on their results (tracking).

The primary objective was to create an engaging learning environment where students could apply theoretical knowledge, make decisions, and receive instant feedback in a safe and controlled setting. To initiate the process, the lecturer constructed the logical backbone of the game in an Excel sheet. This involved defining rules and consequences (see Appendix A in the supplementary document file, accessible via the QR code in Figure 13.1), along with providing basic information about agency types and their services (see Appendix B in the supplementary document file, accessible via the QR code in Figure 13.1). The structure of the game involved various marketing agencies and services, encouraging students to deliberate on choosing the appropriate agency based on their specific services and budget constraints. This design aspect reflects the essence of situated learning, where learning occurs in a context or situation similar to its application in real life (Lave & Wenger, 1991).

King's Online game developers brought the concept to life, creating an intuitive and interactive digital interface based on the small case provided by the lecturer (see Appendix C in the supplementary document file). This interface included features to present the assessment brief, interact with the game, and instantaneously visualize feedback on campaign results, promoting immediate learning and fostering adaptability (see Appendix D in the supplementary document file for a few examples of the screens). This aligns with the principles of formative assessment, enabling students to adapt their strategies based on feedback, thus enhancing their learning experience (Shute, 2008). In the online learning setting, a competitive environment was nurtured by having students share their game strategies and results on a dedicated discussion forum. This interactive approach echoes the gamification concept, where elements typical of game playing are applied in non-gaming contexts to enhance user engagement and group collaboration (Oc & Plangger, 2022).

In on-campus classes, the game was implemented as a group activity, promoting peer learning and fostering cooperative problem-solving skills

Figure 13.1 The QR code to access the developed simulation game.

(Du et al., 2023). During gameplay, students were encouraged to discuss their strategies, critique their approaches, and collectively seek effective solutions, reinforcing the constructivist approach to learning where knowledge is built through social interaction.

The game itself can be found on the following URL in the QR code for all lecturers to use it in their own classes.

IMPACT

The game's impact was assessed using a multi-faceted evaluation approach, employing both quantitative and qualitative measures. Quantitative data was collected from student performance on assessments, both related to the game and subsequent assignments, while qualitative data was gathered through student feedback and short interviews discussing their experience with the simulation game. A significant uplift in student engagement and motivation was observed, reflecting the principles of game-based learning and gamification where learning becomes an active, enjoyable process. The game also facilitated an improved understanding of the subject matter, as students could implement the theoretical concepts in a practical setting, allowing for more profound and lasting comprehension.

Furthermore, students compared their experience with longer-term simulations, commonly implemented over several weeks, and expressed a preference for this short, topic-specific simulation game. This feedback was in line with the concept of microlearning, where complex ideas are broken down into digestible, focused learning experiences (Leong et al., 2021). It also aligns with cognitive load theory, which posits that reducing cognitive load through bite-sized learning experiences leads to enhanced understanding and retention of complex subjects (Sweller, 1994). The experiential learning aspect, combined with the instant feedback system embedded in the game, empowered students to learn from their mistakes, adjust their strategies, and develop a problem-solving mindset (Woitt et al., 2023). The game's formative assessment nature allowed students to grasp the agency selection and budget allocation concepts through an iterative process, making the learning experience more engaging, challenging, and, ultimately, more effective (Leenknecht et al., 2021).

KEY LEARNING

The development and implementation of the marketing simulation game yielded several critical insights. A pivotal lesson is the necessity of taking into account diverse learning needs of students when designing educational resources. The small simulation catered to this diversity by providing an interactive and experiential learning environment, enhancing the educational experience for students based on the GIST framework (Oc & Plangger, 2022). This is in line with theories of differentiated instruction, which emphasize the importance of adaptability in teaching methods to cater to a broad range of learning preferences. In addition, the game demonstrated how the experiential learning approach, grounded in Kolb's experiential learning theory (1984), could effectively facilitate students' understanding of complex concepts. Initially, students encounter a Concrete Experience by navigating a simulated marketing scenario in the game. Post-gameplay reflections and discussions align with Kolb's Reflective Observation stage, enabling students to analyse their actions and the ensuing outcomes. This reflection propels them into the Abstract Conceptualization stage, where they develop a deeper understanding of marketing concepts through the practical lens the game provides. Last, armed with new insights, students revisit the game to try different strategies, embodying Kolb's Active Experimentation stage. This cyclical journey facilitated by the game helps bridge theoretical knowledge with practical application, thus significantly enhancing the students' grasp of complex marketing concepts (Kemp et al., 2019; Kolb, 2014).

The game's implementation illuminated the invaluable role of formative e-assessments in nurturing a conducive learning environment. Specifically, the game heightened student engagement by immersing them in real-world simulated scenarios, making learning interactive and enjoyable. The immediate feedback feature within the game allowed students to promptly gauge their understanding and adjust their strategies, contributing to a more adaptive learning experience. Furthermore, this immediate feedback mechanism provided an avenue for early intervention by the instructor, enabling timely identification and addressal of learning gaps, thus promoting a more tailored and effective learning journey (McCallum & Milner, 2021). This finding aligns with the work of Cavalcanti et al. (2021), who argue for the positive effects of automatic feedback in formative assessments on learning outcomes. However, the successful implementation of such innovative teaching methods also requires careful planning to mitigate potential risks. Ensuring technological compatibility, addressing issues related to digital literacy, and making sure that the assessment accurately measures intended learning outcomes are some key considerations to be kept in mind.

These insights can be useful for educators and instructional designers in creating other innovative educational resources, ensuring they are engaging, relevant, and effective in enhancing student learning.

REFLECTION POINT

1) How does experiential learning contribute to the comprehension of complex concepts within your field of study?
2) In what ways can frameworks like GIST enhance the learning experience and engagement for students?
3) How can formative assessments be utilized to promote active learning and provide immediate feedback in your teaching practice?

4) How does taking into account individual student needs influence the design of educational resources in your domain?
5) What are the potential benefits and challenges of incorporating e-assessments in higher education?

SUPPLEMENTARY MATERIALS

You can access basic game mechanics and an explanations document from the following QR code.

Figure 13.2 QR code to access the supplementary material.

14

FORMATIVE FEEDBACK FOR INTERNATIONAL SUPPLY CHAIN POST-GRADUATE STUDENTS COMBINING DIGITAL AND FACE-TO-FACE FORMATS TO ENHANCE ENGAGEMENT AND CRITICALITY

REBECCA PAGE-TICKELL AND RICHARD ADDO-TENKORANG

Discipline and/or Subject/Field: Business Management/Supply chain management

CONTEXT

The context of this case study is a post-92, city-based school of business and law with a large international postgraduate taught (PGT) student body undertaking professionally focused studies in supply chain management with a strong focus on employability and criticality for this diverse group. The large international cohort is supported through multiple interventions, including peer mentoring, language support, and extensive induction processes to ensure that students are supported to access the curricula. Challenges experienced from students focus on the depth of language competence as well as difficulties in engaging with the course related to culture shock, previous more didactic ways of learning, and difficulties such as distance travelled for commuter students. In terms of pedagogy, the cohort is divided into smaller groups which are taught in a large lecture and smaller seminars. The intervention described here was delivered in small seminar groups where space and time are available for high levels of interaction between academics and students. Additionally, peer-to-peer group pedagogy is utilised to encourage engagement in the form of:

- discussion of the case
- dialogic formative feedback practices, both peer to peer and tutor to peer group
- application of theories and models
- critical review through case study.

This case study centres on the use of OneNote in these seminar classes to provide spaced iterative feedback in the seminar, individualised to small groups and followed up through face-to-face discussion within the peer groups as well as more directly with the seminar tutor. This aims to facilitate a community of inquiry (Arbaugh et al., 2008; Shea & Bidjerano, 2009) where ongoing engagement would continue in a blended format across the life of the course and, it is hoped, through community building into the students' professional lives.

STRATEGY

International students come from diverse educational backgrounds with a strong emphasis on recall through exams. This primes students to focus on the production of facts under pressure. The focus on critical thinking, evaluation, and synthesis through the teaching of case studies can be difficult for students to perceive as a valid and useful way of learning. The aims of this practice are to use feedback intervention theory (Alder, 2007) as well as to infuse the findings of (Carless & Boud, 2018) from their study on "the development of student feedback literacy: enabling uptake of feedback." Carless and Boud (2018) note that students' feedback literacy shows the understandings, capacities, and dispositions needed to make sense of information and use it to enhance work or learning strategies.

The seminar design aimed to provide a space for reification through ongoing iterative formative feedback drip fed across the semester to small groups of students. This enabled feedback on nested activities, which were then structured to support the development of increasingly complex concepts in terms of the content as well as skill development. The "timely and convenient" (Carless & Boud, 2018, p. 1317) mode of feedback being shared through a conversation brought shared engagement with the feedback so that students moved from an often-naïve understanding of feedback as being focused simply on the mark through to appreciating feedback not as a form of telling but as a shared exploration of possible explanations and solutions to complex business problems in an ambiguous world. This then allowed the development of processes for modelling engagement with feedback to develop an understanding of how to use feedback in both formative and summative assignments. This also allowed a modelling of the need to take action following an understanding of the feedback. As students debated the feedback and worked out how to respond to it, they could try a response which the tutor would rapidly engage with, both through online comments on OneNote as well as in discussion face to face. This helped students to hone their response to the questions and clearly modelled how to take action to make the best use of feedback. Development of the capacity to make judgements around their learning and its presentation is particularly key for these students, whose previous educational experiences were typically related to exams in which they demonstrated a repetition of knowledge rather than application, evaluation, and synthesis, which are required to do well in this course.

Each feedback event was designed to specifically incorporate the application and evaluation of theories and models alongside formative assessment to the group on their case study work during and around seminars. We found that there was a need to ensure that this was administered with a captivating and engaging approach. This was particularly important to manage the students' affect around the feedback. Through modelling a supportive, non-challenging, but clear and detailed mode of feedback, the risk and negativity around feedback were reduced, and students in fact became eager to hear the feedback offered – discussing it in detail to ensure that they understood it fully and could go on to apply it.

The approach taken was to scaffold the feedback, with student student-centred focus, using feedback intervention theory (FIT) (King, 2016) while also considering the findings in Carless and Boud's (2018) feedback literacy study. This proposes that feedback efficacy is related to three primary constructs. First and foremost is message cues (locus of attention). In this case study, this would be the applied business case studies that students are tasked to find feasible solutions to by applying business theories, concepts, and models. Second are the assessment traits, in terms of the nature of the task to be learned, and, finally, the near-real-time impact of the formative feedback (Wood, 2021), employing the educational technology platform OneNote (www.microsoft.com/en-gb/microsoft-365/onenote/digital-note-taking-app). Students receive real-time feedback during the seminar from their group work both face to face as well as via OneNote in a near-real-time feedback. The tutor floats in the class during the seminar to give additional formative feedback where needed. Students submit a final summary submission of their group work, which also receives feedback via OneNote.

PRACTICE

A case study with stimulus questions in used across seminars to small groups of students, who together applied theory and models to respond to the stimulus questions. A common seminar group OneNote channel is created for the module seminar sessions. Students use this to write up their answers contemporaneously for rapid formative feedback given in OneNote and accompanied by supportive small group discussion offered by the lecturer who 'floated'. This ensured understanding of the feedback and allowed for a permanent record of the feedback to be used by the students as a support for preparation of their summative assignment.

An applied real-life seminar case study task is assigned to students in small groups where they discuss and brainstorm to together apply the theories, concepts, frameworks, and strategic decision-making matrices they might have been introduced to during their lecture sessions. Students are given a seminar briefing at the beginning of the seminar session to introduce the tasks and what is required of them by the end of the seminar session. Students are then fully engaged interactively by the seminar tutor, who floats among the small students' groups, giving direct monitoring, guidance, and formative feedback as well as indirectly via near-real-time OneNote formative feedback (Van Wyk & Haffejee, 2017; Gebre, 2013; Henderson et al., 2017, 2019a; Wood, 2021). At the end of every seminar session, the small students' groups are then expected to submit for assessment and formative feedback consolidating their assimilation and understanding of how the various theories, concepts, frameworks, and/or matrices are expected to be feasibly applied within their summative group coursework. A range of formats in which student groups could submit their final summary submissions to OneNote were selected. These included both narrative explanations and the use of charts and data. This allowed an opportunity for students to think through how best to communicate their ideas and could be reviewed once uploaded during the seminar session. The final formative submission could also be reviewed following the seminar.

IMPACT

This real-time formative feedback strategy was evaluated on two fronts: at the department level via student voice surveys and at the school level using module evaluation data. This dual-level evaluation process gives the module leader student insights and constructive criticism. Students' good performance on summary submissions had a positive impact on their learning outcomes. Students were also more likely to complete the module evaluation questionnaires with an increased opportunity to exercise their voice. This allows the student's voice to be heard clearly. Students indicated a very clear positive response to the ongoing feedback.

We have found that, at the beginning of the academic year, because most of the students are international students, they are preoccupied with basic settling-in needs like GP, bank, accommodation, and even student registration processing which affects their attendance. Therefore, not many of them take part in the formative feedback process, although this helps LTA methods make sense of feedback material (Carless & Boud, 2018; Henderson et al.,

2019a). This confirms the fundamental difficulties and complexity in students' feedback literacy uptake and not entirely fulfilling the need of able to significantly influence students' learning (Carless & Boud, 2018; Boud & Molloy, 2013; Evans, 2013). By the start of the next semester, most of the students had settled in well and had managed to overcome most of the challenges they had in SEM A, so they were able to engage properly and take up feedback quite well. However, SEM C is when there are very few students left on campus, mostly students returning from placement and some retakers, so the number of student responses and/or uptake to feedback is usually quite low (Carless & Boud, 2018).

Therefore, these initial challenges of developing effective and engaging formative feedback in higher education could not be achieved without directing the discussions and applications around technology-enabled LTA designs for formative feedback engagement and dialogue (Winstone et al., 2017b; Molloy et al., 2020). Therefore, a learner-centric view of formative feedback emphasises the learner's involvement in engaging with formative feedback, using it, and managing emotions (Carless & Boud, 2018; Wood, 2021; Winstone & Carless, 2019).

KEY LEARNING

Given the remarkably diverse international group, additional support was needed in how to engage with one another in seminar groups as well as how to shape good questions. In addition to the soft skills listed previously, the key learning outcomes for students needed to be gradually developed over the semester. The interactive, real-time feedback enhanced learning, but some students needed additional encouragement to engage fully. Integrated language development was important in the learning, teaching, and assessment environment to enable students to fully engage. The rich contemporaneous feedback enabled students to move past performativity to gain real value from the seminars (Macfarlane, 2015). Over the years there has been a need to be innovative and creative with the traditional learning, teaching, and assessment approach in higher education (HE) delivery with the aid of educational technology enabler software or platforms. The key learning approach demonstrated in this process is to effectively connect theory learnt during lecturer sessions with case study practice during seminar (Blicker, 2005; Brodie & Irving, 2007; Klein & Riordan, 2011; Okoli et al., 2019; Rossatto & Dickerson, 2019; Treleaven & Voola, 2008). In other words, this approach, also known as experiential learning (EL), has received increased attention by educators (Blicker, 2005; Brodie & Irving, 2007; Rossatto & Dickerson, 2019), as it allows students to be equipped with a specific, employer-relevant skillset and, most importantly, provides a more engaging experience for students.

Figure 14.1 illustrates the key learning cycle approach for the experiential learning process adapted for effective and efficient LTA delivery (Kolb & Kolb, 2017). The process begins with connecting with the students by

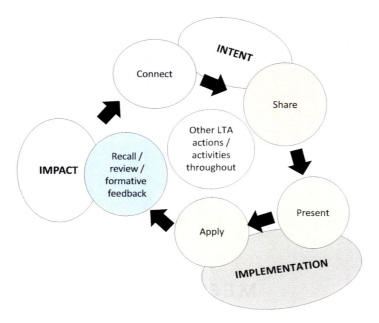

Figure 14.1 Key learning cycle approach for experiential learning.

recapping theories and concepts during the lecture session and connecting them to the case study introduction presentation for the seminar session. The process follows through to the review and recall, which are done via OneNote and/or floating among students' groups to give them real-time formative feedback.

REFLECTION POINT

1) How do I build opportunities for iterative formative feedback to support skill development among students?
2) How can I help students to unpack and explore their formative feedback?
3) What are the earlier education experiences of students that I should consider in designing the learning journey?
4) Where can a post-digital human and technology approach enhance learning in my modules?
5) What evaluation of the learning journey will be the most useful to understand how to improve both the learning experience but also the quality of work produced by students?
6) What are the blockers and enablers to my incorporating a post-digital human approach in learning–teaching I deliver?

15

MEET ZARA

AN AI-GENERATED TEACHING ASSISTANT FOR ENHANCING FORMATIVE ASSESSMENT AND SELF-REGULATED LEARNING

BRONWYN EAGER

Discipline and/or Subject/Field: Business Management/Entrepreneurship

CONTEXT

This case study presents an initiative that leveraged the capabilities of artificial intelligence (AI) text-to-video technology to facilitate formative development and enhance learning experiences for students enrolled in a third-year undergraduate module, Freelancing and Small Business, in a bachelor of business program at an Australian university.

The initiative involved creating videos featuring an AI-generated teaching assistant named Zara, who offered students instruction on weekly learning content and reflections on how she might apply learnings from the content to her (fictional) journey of becoming a freelancer. Following Brookhart's (2013) concept of 'forward moving' formative assessment design, Zara's narrative was purposefully crafted to propel students forward in their learning journey, serving to encourage self-regulated task engagement and enhance students' comprehension of how they might apply the module content to advance completion of graded assessment tasks. In essence, Zara's narrative acted as a guiding point, facilitating students' active participation and fostering a deeper understanding of the practical application of the module content.

DOI: 10.4324/9781003360254-15

Additionally, the videos acted as a dialogical springboard with the potential to positively influence discourse and discussion (Irons & Elkington, 2021) within online and offline learning environments through self, peer, and student-educator interactions.

Through this case study, I aim to contribute to the ever-evolving knowledge base regarding applications of AI technologies in educational settings (see Bozkurt et al., 2021). Specifically, I seek to offer practical and applied guidance and insights for educators interested in adopting AI-generated content in their teaching practice.

AI has garnered significant recognition as a transformative force in higher education (Bates et al., 2020; Hodgson et al., 2021; Eager & Brunton, 2023). Integrating AI into educational settings equips educators with powerful tools to facilitate skill development and nurture self-reflection among their students (Lameras & Arnab, 2021; Chang et al., 2022). Across various educational activities, AI applications have been leveraged, offering compelling examples that provide practical insights for those looking to embrace AI within higher education environments (Adams & Chuah, 2022).

One noteworthy example is Jill Watson, an AI chatbot integrated into a college course at the Georgia Institute of Technology that provided round-the-clock access to formative feedback (Ahmad et al., 2020). Other examples of text-to-speech and face animations can be found in the design of massive open online courses (Dao et al., 2021). Regarding AI text-to-video functionality, which is the focus of this case, well over a decade before the recent surge in AI capability, Falloon (2009) explored the possibility of leveraging avatars (i.e., digital representations of humans, simulating human-like behaviours akin to Zara) in educational environments. Falloon's exploration revealed the unique potential of integrating avatars in education to enhance learner engagement and motivation. At the time, significant challenges, including access to technology, costs, and digital literacy, posed barriers to educators wishing to explore and/or adopt AI. Yet many of these roadblocks to AI adoption have been removed with recent advances in generative AI technologies and the accompanying explosive growth in the consumer-based AI tools market, culminating in new opportunities and greater levels of adoption by educators (Dogan et al., 2023).

AI technologies have additionally brought opportunities for enhancing formative assessment design. Khan Academy arguably leads the field in adopting a formative approach to leveraging newfound AI capabilities. Their product, Khanmigo (www.khanacademy.org/khan-labs), provides students with personalised learning pathways scaffolded by AI-informed feedback mechanisms. The success of Khan Academy's product no doubt sets a precedent for education providers aspiring to unlock similar benefits for their learners through the integration of AI. This approach brings new possibilities to the well-documented advantages of 'feedforward' assessment design, as articulated by Irons and Elkington (2021).

STRATEGY

In this case, the inherent formative potential of all assessments involving interactions between students and educators (Irons & Elkington, 2021) is extended to silicon-based actors, with focus given to elucidating two elements: AI-generated video as an innovative modality for nurturing self-regulated learning and facilitating meaningful dialogue.

The case revolves around an educator-AI-student paradigm. In this scenario, the author played the educator role, Zara the AI, and the student cohort included both on-campus and online enrolments. On-campus students engaged with the module in a flipped classroom environment, with content delivered via an online learning management system. Off-campus students completed the module entirely online.

Creating captivating learning materials that foster student engagement can be challenging in online environments. The content creation process may require educators to possess diverse skill sets spanning proficiency in using recording equipment, knowledge of video and audio editing software, and storytelling techniques. Shortcomings in any of these domains can produce low-quality content, resulting in learning materials with questionable attraction (i.e., utility) for captivating student audiences whose expectations may be prefaced on video content like that produced by 'influencers' on popular social media platforms (e.g., YouTube). AI text-to-video technology offers promise in addressing such challenges due to removing many in-person videography requirements (e.g., camera equipment, good lighting, and confidence and skill in being in front of a camera) and the relative ease of production afforded by consumer-based AI tools.

Integrating AI-generated videos in the module delivery was initially a strategy motivated by a desire to explore how AI technologies could alleviate the performative demands of on-camera delivery. Moreover, it was employed to explore how the novelty of AI, which was gaining increasing media attention at the time, could be leveraged to attract students to engage with learning content. The strategy was achieved by blending digital and human elements, creating an immersive formative assessment experience for the student cohort.

The decision was made to imbue Zara's avatar with a human-like narrative and pedagogical rigour to transition the videos beyond merely being an AI novelty (i.e., gimmick). This was achieved through a storytelling approach, wherein the script for Zara included her shared reflections on how the module content aided her in planning a freelance career. The narrative was strategically motivated by the pedagogical insight that students are likely to be predisposed to engage more with learning content when it is interwoven in a context that holds relatable significance. Zara's shared experiences offered reflection points for students similarly tasked with designing freelance careers. The narrative was designed to resonate while empowering students to recognise and reflect on learning content for their academic and professional advancement.

In summary, the strategy behind using AI-generated videos was grounded in educator-led enthusiasm for experimenting with novel technologies but, more importantly, as a way of addressing the challenges of engaging and motivating students within online learning environments. The initiative harnessed the innovative appeal of AI avatars, using them as a modality to deliver a dynamic narrative that elucidated learning content and its practical application in both academic and professional contexts. Efforts to achieve this involved employing a range of formative mechanisms, including the delivery of thought-provoking content to stimulate active engagement. The strategy also involved positioning students as active participants in their learning journey, made possible when students are provided with reflective touchpoints, discussion opportunities, and engaging activities (Irons & Elkington, 2021). These elements were designed to enhance students' progress and provide feedforward opportunities for students as they worked towards completing their assessment tasks.

PRACTICE

The Zara video series leveraged AI text-to-video technology to convert written lecture scripts into dynamic video content. Tools such as Synthesia (www.synthesia.io) and Elai (https://elai.io/) can be used to facilitate this process. For a practical demonstration, an example video is available to view via the following link: https://bit.ly/BMA357-ZARA-AI-Video.

The scripts for the Zara videos were developed through a human-AI partnership, with ChatGPT assigned to the role of AI collaborator. This iterative process focused on generating and refining text-based scripts, wherein ChatGPT was guided to produce initial draft scripts that were mindful of aspects such as the duration of the videos and stylistic tone. Additionally, entrepreneurship concepts, such as overcoming the hurdles inherent in startups and the art of rapid prototyping for career exploration, were woven into the script narratives, and these were further tailored to align with the educational objectives of the curriculum, ensuring their relevance to the weekly themes and related assessments.

Throughout the series, Zara embodies an emergent entrepreneur, contemplating the development of a business concept and her career trajectory. Zara's entrepreneurial journey is interwoven with the course content, providing students with relatable, real-world scenarios and common challenges faced by entrepreneurs (which students may also be facing when contemplating their entrance into entrepreneurial career pathways). This approach not only offers the potential for engaging learning materials but also serves as a mirror for students to reflect on their entrepreneurial aspirations and strategies, which is an approach that draws on the influential role of relatable role models in nurturing entrepreneurial intentions (Abbasianchavari & Moritz, 2020).

Formative assessment activities were embedded in the videos, designed to foster self-regulated learning. These activities encourage students to apply the concepts discussed in the videos to their entrepreneurial ideas, promoting a deeper understanding of the material and its practical application in the real world. The integration of AI technology in this manner aligns with the principles of formative assessment, emphasising continuous feedback and self-assessment opportunities for students.

IMPACT

Conversations were conducted with students during the scheduled class time to gauge the initiative's impact. These further offered activity-based reflective opportunities wherein students could reflect on the learning content and feed information gained through discussion into their assessment tasks. The process encouraged sustained communication and contemplation throughout a student's learning journey. In addition, an invitation was extended to students to anonymously contribute their perspectives on the initiative via an online survey midway through the semester. This survey was designed to elicit student feedback, unfettered by inhibitions regarding verbal participation in class while adding a layer of anonymity to garner responses. Findings from the survey were fed forward, such that they aided ongoing module development, highlighting the benefits of formative assessment for students and as a mechanism for educators to achieve module enhancements (Irons & Elkington, 2021).

Feedback revealed that AI-driven videos were generally received enthusiastically, regarded as engaging and instrumental in facilitating comprehension and reflection of weekly content. This suggests that the initiative achieved the goals of bolstering student engagement and enhancing learning outcomes. Furthermore, the novelty of AI-generated video content appeared to engage student curiosity, leading to learning content engagement. This corroborates the proposition that the novel allure of AI avatars shows promise for enhancing student attention and engagement. However, it is not known for how long such novelty will be sustained.

One of the perceived strengths of the initiative is the ability to employ AI text-to-video functionalities without necessitating an in-depth comprehension of AI technologies. This quality renders the approach accessible to a wide spectrum of educators, including those whose expertise may not traditionally encompass AI or technological domains. However, one limitation of these technologies relates to financial cost. At the time of writing, AI text-to-video tools are available via limited free trials or paid subscriptions.

Upon reflection, incorporating AI appears to bridge the gap between traditional in-person education and the rapidly evolving (and increasingly AI-augmented) digital education environments. This amalgamation of AI with conventional teaching methods may culminate in a hybrid (AI-human) model of education, which could benefit the varied learning preferences and needs of a diverse student body. While the use of AI in education is still nascent, this case study points to the potential that lies in the synergy of AI technology and educator enthusiasm to trial these technologies in their teaching practice.

KEY LEARNINGS

The initiative presented in this case yielded several key points of learning relating to the practical implementation of generative AI technologies.

Personalised learning experiences

The rapid generative properties of text-to-video AI tools (e.g., the ability to transform a written lecture into a video in minutes) make it possible for educators to mould and adapt multiple variations of learning materials catered to students' unique needs. For example, content could be adjusted across various aspects, such as pace and tone, and translated into multiple languages. Additionally, AI technologies enable the customisation of the avatar's appearance, such as age, gender, ethnicity, and attire. These abilities afford the potential for students to one day enjoy the freedom to choose an avatar they can connect with and for learning content to be generated accordingly, thus further personalising a student's learning journey.

Taking personalisation one step further, additional AI technologies, such as AI chatbots, could be integrated with AI text-to-video functionality to create multifaceted and interactive learning experiences. Such an approach could allow students to engage actively with materials by asking questions and obtaining customised real-time feedback. Moreover, chatbots represent more than just a communication tool for student interaction; they serve as data collectors, gathering valuable information on student engagement and comprehension. Analysing this data may provide educators with valuable insights into what students find confusing or intriguing, enabling educators to adjust their content accordingly. This feedback loop, where data informs content, could ensure a continuously improving and highly personalised learning experience tailored to the needs and preferences of each student.

Blurring the digital-human divide

Using AI-generated teaching assistants to narrate human stories to illustrate learning content presents an innovative approach to blurring the boundary between digital and human interactions. This fusion of the digital and human realms could potentially lead to more immersive and authentic learning experiences for students, thereby enhancing the effectiveness of online learning environments.

In the context of formative assessment, this blurring of the digital-human divide can have significant implications. AI-generated teaching assistants, such as Zara, offer affordances for replicating many aspects of human interaction within digital environments. For example, AI-generated teaching assistants can create a more human-like formative assessment experience by providing personalised feedback and narrating human stories.

This alignment with dispersed assessment and feedback within a post-digital reality creates opportunities for innovative teaching and formative assessment practices. For example, the AI-generated teaching assistant can provide immediate feedback on assessment tasks, thereby supporting self-regulated learning. This immediate feedback can help students identify areas of strength and weakness, adjust their learning strategies, and improve their understanding of the subject matter.

Blurring the digital-human divide with AI-generated teaching assistants offers a promising approach to enhancing the effectiveness of formative assessment and self-regulated learning in online learning environments. This is enabled through harnessing the potential of AI technologies, wherein educators can create engaging and effective learning experiences that blur the boundary between digital and human interactions.

Positive impact on self-regulated learning

Using AI-generated video lessons in higher education, as demonstrated in this case, highlights the potential for technology to assist and enhance traditional teaching methods, ultimately offering opportunities for improving student learning outcomes. As the role of human instructors evolves to accommodate AI instructors in online education, it is crucial to understand how to create effective AI instructors that can be well-received and understood by students.

In conclusion, the key learnings from this initiative suggest that using AI-generated video content in formative assessment offers a promising approach to enhancing student engagement and learning outcomes in online learning environments. However, while exploring these opportunities, we should not lose sight of the ethical considerations and concerns surrounding AI in education, such as data privacy, bias, and learner autonomy (Chen et al., 2020). Going forward, further exploration and development of this innovative modality are required.

REFLECTION POINT

1) How might AI-generated videos be tailored to meet the diverse learning needs of students?
2) In what ways might anthropomorphised AI-generated content impact perceptions relating to the authenticity of learning materials?
3) How can AI-generated videos combine with other technologies (e.g., AI chatbots) to enhance formative assessment and feedback practices?

16

CREATING AN ACADEMIC SAFETY NET FOR NEWLY INDUCTED UNDERGRADUATE MEDICAL STUDENTS USING FORMATIVE ASSESSMENTS AND FEEDBACK

SYEDA SADIA FATIMA, ROMANA IDRESS, SATWAT HASHMI, SANIYA SABZWARI, SADAF KHAN, KAUSER JABEEN, AND KULSOOM GHIAS

Discipline and/or Subject/Field: *(Undergraduate) Medical education*

CONTEXT

The Aga Khan University (AKU) in Karachi, Pakistan, has a five-year undergraduate medical education (UGME) program that was established in 1983. The internationally benchmarked program has been recognized globally for excellence in curriculum, assessment, and student engagement, as evidenced by the AMEE ASPIRE-to-Excellence awards received in 2013 and 2022.

The program follows an integrated, spiral curriculum based on common clinical presentations. It is designed to enable learners to acquire and apply biological and social science concepts, technical skills, and professional attributes to health promotion, disease prevention, and clinical care across hospital and community-based settings. The curriculum has multimodal pedagogical approaches and assessment activities. There is an initial emphasis on problem-based-learning and early acquisition of clinical skills with a

DOI: 10.4324/9781003360254-16

transition to problem solving and patient care in the subsequent three clinical years. In the first two years, basic and community health sciences are taught in or alongside systems-based modules through active learning strategies, predominantly in clinical contexts relevant to the country. Individual objectives of the systems-based modules address the knowledge, skills, and attitudes required to understand the basic science concepts, pathophysiology, investigation, and management for each of these presentations. This model permeates the curriculum – all basic science concepts are presented in the context of clinical presentations, and all clinical disciplines revisit the contextual basic science content, thus completing the integrated spiral.

As part of continuous and iterative self-improvement cycles, faculty, external examiners, and students highlighted concerns about retention of basic science concepts in clinical years, a universal concern in medical education (Custers, 2010), especially in anatomy, physiology, and pharmacology. Additionally, it was identified that the modular system did not adequately cover important and emerging concepts related to molecular biology and public health. To address these concerns and ensure a deeper learning of core concepts, a novel 15-week "foundation module" was introduced in Year 1 of the program. The module includes courses on human body systems and disease, molecular biology, pharmacology, and public health with robust formative and summative assessments and opportunities for global and targeted feedback, both in person and online. As the courses were foundational in nature, satisfactory performance in the end-of-course assessment was deemed essential for student progression. This meant that any student who failed the summative assessment could be required to repeat the year and retake these courses when offered for the next academic year. Therefore, frequent formative assessments in the form of gamified content and online quizzes, laboratory sign-off, group activities, and a written examination coupled with both targeted and general feedback were embedded throughout the module to create an academic safety net given the importance of understanding foundational concepts and the high assessment stakes.

STRATEGY

Curricular planning for the Foundation module began in 2019; it was designed with the intent to be delivered face to face. With the continued waves of the COVID-19 pandemic, the module had to be converted to an entirely online experience for its first iteration in 2021 and had a hybrid format in 2022 with both online and onsite interactions. The case study presented here focuses on experiences across both these years and iterations of the module. As an introductory interaction with students, it was always important to ensure student engagement and understanding. This became even more critical in the online and hybrid versions and was compounded by an additional challenge of limited internet access and experience with online modalities for some in the student body.

A cognitive learning theory approach was adopted (Dong et al., 2021), and assessment-for-learning (Schuwirth & Van der Vleuten, 2011) was strategically planned and implemented for enhanced student engagement and learning and to ensure that students were prepared to progress to subsequent modules. As a principle, all students were provided with an opportunity to receive regular feedback on performance irrespective of performance. For those students who needed additional support, feedback was documented, and adequate remediation opportunities were built in.

Based on tables of specification developed for each course with the support of medical educators, multiple formative assessments were included in the module in the form of quizzes and activities in individual sessions. Strategically, this created opportunities for clarification of concepts in real time and identification of individuals that may need additional support.

A mid-module written formative examination was also included, designed to introduce students to the pattern of examinations and question types and allow time and space to practise. Attempting the written formative examination continues to be mandatory, and individual feedback graphs help identify specific objectives that require further clarification and attention.

PechaKucha – Japanese for "chit chat" – was used as a tool for formative assessment and feedback, allowing students focus on the essential information and present it in a clear and concise manner. This was driven by the recognition that effective communication is a key skill for medical professionals. The use of PechaKucha as a formative assessment tool is supported by theoretical approaches such as Dale's Cone of active learning (Masters, 2013) that emphasizes the importance of active learning and feedback in promoting student learning. By providing students with the opportunity to create and deliver presentations and receive feedback from their peers and instructors, this approach helped students develop their communication skills while also deepening their understanding of course content.

Through this multi-modal assessment-for-learning approach, it was possible to create timely feedback to improve students' performance. Linked to this, regular academic counselling sessions were organized every fortnight, with designated teaching associates assigned to each group of nine to ten students. This allowed students a platform to discuss concerns and identify solutions. It also helped identify students struggling academically and/or socially early in their medical school journey.

PRACTICE

In individual sessions taught during the module, various interactive tools were incorporated to engage and assess students effectively. These were limited to the virtual learning environment during the online iteration of the module in 2021 and expanded to sign-off laboratory sessions and debates once physical classes became possible in 2022. Popular platforms such as Kahoot (https://kahoot.com/), Mentimeter (www.mentimeter.com), Padlet (https://padlet.com), and HTML5 (H5P) (https://h5p.org) were leveraged within the existing virtual learning environment (Moodle). These tools served as valuable resources to conduct individual session quizzes and enhance student participation. Kahoot and Mentimeter provided an engaging and conducive learning environment. Students accessed quizzes through their devices and competed against each other in real time. This gamified approach not only motivated students to actively participate but also made the learning experience enjoyable and memorable. The instant feedback provided by Kahoot allowed students to assess their knowledge and identify areas that required further attention. These interactive platforms fostered a collaborative learning environment, allowing students to engage in discussions and share their perspectives. Padlet served as a digital collaboration board for students to share and discuss their ideas. Interactive boards were created where students could post their thoughts, questions, or even multimedia content related to the topics covered in the module. This collaborative approach encouraged peer learning and knowledge exchange. Students had an opportunity to engage in meaningful discussions, gain insights from the contributions of their peers, and expand their understanding of the subject matter. Original content was also created to best fit the outcomes of the module utilizing H5P for interactive presentations, quizzes, and interactive videos to deliver engaging and interactive lessons. These interactive elements helped students grasp complex concepts more effectively, as they could actively interact with the content instead of passively consuming it.

The PechaKucha approach was operationalized by providing students with topics and guidelines on how to create effective PechaKucha presentations. Instructors also provided support and feedback to help students refine their presentation skills. The process was managed through regular check-ins with students to ensure that they were making progress and receiving the support they needed. On the day of presentation, peer feedback utilized three stars and a wish strategy (Mullane, 2013). This is a structured format for providing feedback where peers share three points from the presentation that enhanced their learning and one area that hindered learning with a tangible solution for future use. Overall, the use of PechaKucha as a formative assessment tool was an effective way to manage the needs of students by providing them with opportunities for active learning and feedback (Fatima et al., 2023).

The mid-module written formative examination composed of 60 best-choice questions (multiple choice, extended matching) and 4 short-answer questions (one from each course) per the course-wise tables of specification. Questions were equally split between those that required recall of knowledge and higher order application of knowledge. In the online version administered in 2021, it also oriented students to the discipline and requirements of online test-taking (Fatima et al., 2021). A feedback session was arranged with course leads to share overall class performance and clarify concepts that may have been incorrectly attempted by most students, as determined by a statistical post-hoc analysis of the difficulty and discrimination indices of questions. Students were also provided with descriptive guidance on how to attempt short-answer questions with an emphasis on key concepts. Individual objective performance graphs were generated and disseminated to each student. Those students who were unable to achieve a pass percentage of 55% in one or more courses were flagged for one-on-one counselling sessions with the course, module, and year leads. Individualized feedback, guidance, and counselling were provided and additional support arranged through teaching associates, course leads, and faculty. These encounters were carefully documented and stringently monitored to ensure a tight academic safety net that ensured steady learner's progress. In 2021, 38 students were flagged and supported through this mechanism; in 2022, when the module was delivered in a hybrid format of online and onsite sessions, this number reduced to 4 students.

Several students who were unable to attempt formative assessment activities online because of internet connectivity issues were also accommodated per availability to ensure learning. Additionally, faculty and course leads provided guidance, clarifications, and support via email and phone. Scheduled review and counselling sessions for academic and social issues ensured that students received the necessary assistance. Teaching associates maintained regular communication with course leads and faculty members to report any concerns that required immediate attention.

IMPACT

The Foundation module is placed at the start of the five-year program. The entering class is diverse in terms of familiarity with adult learning pedagogies that have student engagement as a core principle. Introduction of learner-oriented sessions such as PechaKucha, hands-on laboratory sessions, and other active small group learning strategies during this intensively supported module provide an opportunity for students to become comfortable with these strategies with a safety net.

In 2021, evaluation of the module was completed by 85/100 students, with 78% of students agreeing that it was an enriching and enjoyable learning experience. Students appreciated course organization, content, pedagogy, formative assessment, targeted review and feedback sessions, and faculty commitment and accessibility. Specifically, with respect to formative assessments and feedback sessions, students were asked whether formative sessions helped monitor learning and if feedback/review sessions were helpful; the responses as percentages are provided in Table 16.1. Across all four courses – Human Body Systems and Disease, Molecular Biology, Introductory Pharmacology, and Introduction to Public Health – the majority of students in both the 2021 and 2022 cohorts strongly agreed/agreed that formative assessments helped monitor learning and that feedback/review sessions were helpful. For the Human Body Systems and Disease and Introduction to Public Health courses, more students in

Table 16.1 Student evaluation of formative assessments and feedback in foundation courses across cohorts

| | The formative assessment(s) helped monitor learning |||||| Feedback/review session(s) were helpful ||||||
| | 2021 ||| 2022 ||| 2021 ||| 2022 |||
	SA/A	N	D/SD	SA/A	N	D/SD	SA/A	N	D/SD	SA/A	N	D/SD
Human Body System and Disease	75.3	16.5	8.2	77.7	17.6	4.7	69.4	22.4	8.2	77.6	15.3	7.1
Molecular Biology	84.9	10.5	4.6	79.5	15.7	4.8	83.7	11.6	4.7	77.1	15.7	7.2
Introductory Pharmacology	84.7	11.8	3.5	83.1	13.3	3.6	79.8	15.5	4.7	78.0	15.9	6.1
Introduction to Public Health	70.6	12.9	16.5	72.3	24.1	3.6	51.8	30.1	18.1	69.9	25.3	4.8

The percentage of students who strongly agreed/agreed (SA/A), were neutral (N), disagreed/strongly disagreed (D/SD) with the given statements regarding formative assessments and feedback in the foundation courses – Human Body Systems and Disease, Molecular Biology, Introductory Pharmacology, Introduction to Public Health – in 2021 when courses were delivered online (85/100 students completed the evaluation) as compared to 2022 when courses were delivered both online and onsite (83/100 students completed the evaluation). Responses represent the percentage of those students who completed the evaluation.

the 2022 cohort indicated that the feedback/review sessions were helpful. In 2021, 69.4% of respondents strongly agreed/agreed with this statement for the Human Body System and Disease course and 51.8% for the Introduction to Public Health course as compared to 77.6% and 69.9%, respectively, in 2022.

While the percentage of students who concurred with the statements regarding formative assessments and feedback decreased somewhat in 2022 as compared to 2021 for the Molecular Biology course, narrative comments provided by students emphasized the importance of multimodal formative activities and faculty support in learning in all courses, including Molecular Biology, across both cohorts:

> The different activities helped us to understand the matter in a fun way. – Human Body Systems and Disease, 2021

> All the instructors for the course were extremely good and were always willing to answer questions (especially outside the lecture where they were very responsive on email). – Human Body Systems and Disease, 2021

> The instructors were very cooperative. – Molecular Biology, 2022

> [R]evision sessions really helped. – Molecular Biology, 2022

> The Kahoot quizzes and review sessions were very helpful to get an idea where you stand as well as PechaKucha. – Human Body Systems and Disease, 2022

Narrative feedback also highlighted the need for additional types and more formative assessments across all courses:

> [A]dd a couple more formative essays akin to the essay on blood pressure regulation. – Human Body Systems and Disease, 2021

> Better question formats, case studies in the exam with SAQs would better help with application of the ideas and concepts learnt . . . rather than MCQs. – Introduction to Public Health, 2021

> Perhaps incorporating more Kahoot sessions, because I feel Kahoot quizzes would further solidify what we learned [sic]. – Introductory Pharmacology, 2022

> [H]ave some sessions to practice how to tackle these [MCQ] questions. – Introduction Public Health, 2021

The rigorous planning and execution of formative assessments, feedback, and support led to improved student performance in the summative assessment at the end of the module, with 4 out of 100 students who were unable to pass the summative examination in both 2021 and 2022. Students identified early through the Foundation module academic safety net also benefited from additional support in subsequent modules.

KEY LEARNING

Driven by student feedback and module evaluation, continuous improvement in the planning and implementation of the Foundation module and formative opportunities has led to improved opportunities and student outcomes with every iteration. In 2022, as the COVID-19 wave relented, the module was delivered using a hybrid approach with both traditional in-person contact and digital learning and assessment. Continuous academic support provided by faculty and teaching associates allowed for effective assessment and monitoring of student performance and provision of relevant feedback and support as needed.

The experience with frequent formative assessments in the Foundation module gained during COVID-19 provided confidence to implement formative assessments in subsequent modules across Years 1 and 2. The process of formative assessment and targeted feedback to students overall strengthened the assessment at our institution and is an experience that can be considered by other institutions with similar context. The following box details key lessons about the formative assessment and feedback approaches and is supported by the literature in the field (Konopasek et al., 2016; Watling & Ginsburg, 2019).

> **PRACTICE POINTS FOR AN ACADEMIC SAFETY NET**
> - Design an integrated and comprehensive formative assessment program that complements the summative assessment system
> - Identify purpose of formative assessments and map optimal strategies accordingly
> - Provide students data and feedback in different forms, from a variety of sources and timepoints
> - Provide learner-centric, targeted feedback focused on continuous improvement
> - Build a relationship between learners and facilitators of learning for effective feedback and academic counselling
> - Monitor progress and document feedback to close the loop
> - Evaluate formative assessment and feedback mechanisms for continuous programmatic improvement

REFLECTION POINT

1) For courses that have high-stakes assessment, using multiple formative assessments and feedback opportunities allows students and faculty to gauge academic standing expediently and improve outcomes. This learner-centred strategy increases engagement and student-faculty interaction. How can purposeful formative assessments be designed to empower students, particularly in online/hybrid contexts?
2) Incorporating multiple formative assessments requires thoughtful planning and gives students the opportunity to self-assess and obtain timely feedback. How can an academic safety net be created using formative assessments?
3) The quality of an academic program improves with student partnership. As recipients, students are in the best position to provide critique and feedback on teaching/learning sessions. Their input allows faculty to optimize learning/outcomes. How can students be positioned as equal stakeholders in learning and assessment through formative activities?

17

USING E-PORTFOLIOS AND VIDEO REFLECTIONS TO SUPPORT POSTGRADUATE STUDENTS' PERSONAL AND PROFESSIONAL DEVELOPMENT

CHARLOTTE CHANDLER

Discipline and/or Subject/Field: Sport and Exercise Science/Exercise and Physical Activity Psychology

CONTEXT

This case study presents the formative assessment strategy for an exercise and physical activity psychology module delivered on an applied sport and exercise science (SES) MSc course. Formative assessment and feedback form a central part of the course and module design, not least because SES as a human science is predicated on multidisciplinary work and interpersonal interaction and therefore requires collaborative discussion and sharing of ideas. The case study will articulate how formative assessment is progressively embedded within the module to support students' personal and professional development, contextualised to the subject area but with examples that transcend delivery in SES alone. The course emphasises the importance of practitioner development by advancing students' theoretical knowledge across the SES discipline and promoting self-awareness and critical astuteness as key attributes. Anecdotally, those within the profession have acknowledged that graduates are often not prepared for the realities and challenges of applied work; a shift in emphasis from 'what you know' to 'who you are' is therefore required so that those who enter applied practice are prepared for situations whereby a textbook solution does not exist (Watson et al., 2023). The course, and therefore module, are thus framed within the wider context of industry requirements and designed to provide students with relevant learning experiences that support their preparedness. Formative assessment was therefore used to not only support students' summative work but as a platform from which to develop the skills associated with applied practice. As such, the formative strategy was devised to promote a collaborative and reflective approach to learning, foster independence, authenticity, and creativity and develop both theoretical and self-knowledge.

STRATEGY

The formative assessment approach incorporated both overt and structured opportunities for feedback (i.e., through draft submissions) and ongoing, less-structured support via consistently engaging students in discussion and reflection. This support allowed the module leader to formatively assess students' learning and development throughout the module by identifying topics that needed revisiting and highlighting where discussions could inform their summative work. It was important that students felt a sense of ownership over their assessment and therefore learning and that the focus of their work was personally meaningful. Interactive teaching styles have been shown to be more enjoyable for students, may lead to improved retention and performance (Costa et al., 2007), and can help personalise learning as students bring their 'self' to the classroom. Formative and digital assessment also play a critical role in developing a sense of ownership by enhancing students' self-regulation and autonomy over their learning (Oldfield et al., 2012; Thibodeaux et al., 2019). This notion aligns with the need to develop accountable and self-aware SES practitioners who are comfortable making decisions and working authentically and thus effectively (Chandler & Donovan, 2023). It was important that students not only had the opportunity to engage in collaborative discussion related to their assessment ideas but that they also had accessible and fit-for-purpose tools through which to capture and present their thoughts.

Formative approach

The summative assessments were an intervention mapping (IM; Eldredge et al., 2016) e-portfolio submitted via PebblePad (Pebble Learning, 2023) and reflective presentation recorded via Panopto (Panopto, 2023). Formative assessment was embedded both within taught module sessions and through directed independent study tasks using three main strategies: 1) clearly defined draft submission deadlines, 2) in-class discussion activities, and 3) support for student reflection.

Assessment 1

Students completed their e-portfolios on PebblePad, a 'Learning Journey Platform', which offered a flexible structure that could be adapted to specific assessment requirements. The platform therefore acted as a parallel to the students' ongoing development by offering a space for them to creatively demonstrate their knowledge. Students were encouraged to select a personally meaningful participant group for their IM process, a six-stage approach to a behaviour change intervention. IM is a valuable tool for practitioners, as it offers a clear and comprehensive structure against which to develop impactful initiatives and uses both behavioural and environmental lenses through which to view behaviour change (Eldredge et al., 2016). Students could develop their ideas and e-portfolio in the knowledge that they would be able to engage in in-class discussions and reflections to inform their work (strategy 2) and submit two draft submissions to gain formative feedback (strategy 1).

Assessment 2

Reflective practice (RP) is an important tool for applied practitioners; they will work closely with clients to develop relationships and therefore need to understand who they are and how they impact others (Huntley et al., 2023). RP therefore plays a key part in the development of self-awareness but is often assessed through written work and based on practical experience. A summative digital assessment that could capture students' development throughout the module, as informed by formative feedback and discussion (strategy 2) and targeted reflective questioning (strategy 3), was considered a novel and challenging approach to encourage reflection through a more creative medium.

PRACTICE

The two summative assessments were 'launched' at the start of the module, with the PebblePad portfolio submitted in teaching week 10 and the Panopto reflection submitted one week after the completion of teaching. This approach supported the progressive development of students' ideas alongside specific taught content related to the IM process and broader theoretical and conceptual content to encourage student discussion and reflection. Given the flexible approach to assessment, providing opportunities for structured, formative support was essential, as it encouraged students to feel confident in their ability to manage and make decisions about their learning. It also supported a focus on the process rather than the outcome, as students could evidence their learning at multiple points in time, and the frequency helped monitor progress, support learning momentum, and aid retention (Prashanti & Ramnarayan, 2019). Finally, the formative approach was underpinned by consistent messaging regarding expectations for student engagement; from the outset of the module, students were aware of the teaching style adopted. This was based on Prashanti and Ramnarayan's assertion that "creating a healthy, safe, and supportive environment enables learning to happen in more enduring ways. Formative assessment should involve mutually interactive participation between teachers and students, leading to a joint productive activity" (2019, p. 101). The approaches to formative assessment are outlined in further detail in the following.

1. Clearly defined draft submission deadlines

For the e-portfolio, students were set two pre-determined formative submission points during the module which were presented within their handbook and communicated at assessment launch. IM steps 1 and 2 were submitted for the first formative deadline, followed by steps 3 and 4 for the second; steps 5 and 6 carried less weighting so were not formatively assessed with regard to feedback; however, the module leader was able to offer feedforward based on the draft work. Feedforward is important in shaping future responses and clarifying assessment expectations (Nicol & Macfarlane-Dick, 2006); this was essential given the progressive nature of the IM process. PebblePad is a useful platform for formative assessment, as the module leader could pause 'live' assessments at a given point in time; the paused view is maintained whilst the students continue working on their portfolio. Feedback focused on the strengths of the work and anything that needed clarifying or that could be added, whilst feedforward was provided with regard to how the student could build on their work to complete future steps.

2. In-class discussion activities

Formative assessment was embedded within taught sessions using discussion-based teaching (DBT), which included the lecturer asking open-ended questions to encourage depth of answers from students, offering varied responses depending on student input, and facilitation of student-student interaction (Henning, 2008). This approach created a sense of community and therefore support within the cohort, which is important for the wider student experience (Coneyworth et al., 2019) and provided the foundation for sharing of ideas and constructive debate related to both assessments. DBT as formative assessment was both structured and unstructured, in that students were set specific group discussion tasks and independent study questions (structured) and were also engaged in ad-hoc discussion week-to-week (unstructured). For example, in week one students were set questions related to exercise identity to help explore their biases and personal relationship with exercise, which were then discussed in week two when we started to explore their practitioner philosophy. Through discussions around their own exercise engagement and biases, and their potential impact on their work with a client, students were engaging in formative assessment by considering aspects that could 1) inform their approach to IM and 2) be included in their recorded reflection.

3. Support for student reflection

Although an important tool for applied practitioners, it can be challenging to teach and support students in developing RP skills and self-awareness. The formative approach was therefore designed to engage students consistently yet subtly in active reflection. The author incorporated reflective 'touch points' within the module whereby certain topics were explored in a way that helped build a reflective 'bank' of insights that the student could draw from. These touch points were framed as both structured opportunities for reflection but also used on an ad-hoc basis as the module leader felt was required. The exercise identity-related questions are one example of this, as the DBT approach encouraged students to share their thoughts and thus reflect on both their answers and those of others. Expressing and explaining one's views, thinking, and reasoning to others is key to student learning, particularly with regard to how it relates to the 'real world' (Weurlander et al., 2012). Another formative tool used to support students' RP was the use of personality testing; students completed an online test to understand their personality type, shared and reflected on the insight gained, and collectively discussed how both practitioners' and clients' personalities could impact the therapeutic relationship. Finally, students were taught motivational interviewing (MI) as a behaviour change intervention, with a follow-up session whereby they could practice their MI skills with client actors. Students received feedback on their MI technique and skills and were encouraged to reflect on this experience to include in their summative assessment.

IMPACT

The formative assessment approach described was underpinned by a learning process that progressively developed students' self-awareness and reflective capabilities alongside subject-specific knowledge and skills. This encouraged students to engage with the *process* rather than the *outcome* and allowed students to portray their learning journey in a meaningful and long-lasting way. As the module progressed, it became clear that explicit, structured formative assessment needed to be combined with regular, facilitative discussions; these elements complemented each other and enabled the module leader to maintain a consistent message related to both assessment requirements and student development.

Learning

Timmis et al. (2016) argue that assessment policies are "out of date" as compared to the needs of 21st-century society and therefore need to better represent educational priorities related to creativity, problem solving, and resilience. Digital assessment methods enhanced the student learning experience by being accessible and fostering creativity and long-term learning after submission of the summative work. For example, students fed back that they had used the knowledge gained by completing their e-portfolio within their placement and in job interviews. The approach embraced formative assessment as a collaborative and interactive, rather than passive, activity, which worked because it was embedded in a DBT approach within a supportive and engaged postgraduate community. This approach better represents the reality of applied practice, whereby practitioners will share ideas with and learn from colleagues and creatively identify solutions to applied challenges. External examiner feedback highlighted this as a specific strength of the module's assessment strategy, in particular the autonomy afforded to students in using PebblePad to present creative, research-informed work. The observed impact on both short- and long-term student learning emphasises the need for a holistic approach to formative assessment as part of the postgraduate student experience (Coneyworth et al., 2019), which should include the development of communities of practice to help students find their voice and cope with challenges (Wenger, 1998).

Ownership and confidence

Providing students with choice promotes ownership over their learning giving them a voice to rationalise their choices and cultivates skills fundamental to human development (Thibodeaux et al., 2019). In the context of developing SES practitioners as human scientists, this is essential. Students' comfort with both open discussion and the creativity required for their assessment was varied initially, but it was evident that their willingness to engage with these elements evolved as the module progressed. Research has emphasised the value students can gain from dialogue and discussion (Sambell, 2010), and this was apparent in both formal and anecdotal student feedback for the module. Students praised the use of DBT as valuable for their self-development and self-awareness and in creating a challenging yet safe space to explore their ideas. Their willingness to engage in discussion, and be creative in their assessment, was underpinned by assurance that engagement with these approaches would enhance both their learning and achievement. For example, by the time they submitted their summative work, students were confidently reflecting on their relationship with exercise by embedding short videos delivered to camera. Developing ownership in students through their learning experience represents accountability, an essential attribute for the applied practitioner, and it is therefore recommended that formative assessment approaches be housed in the wider context of long-term, discipline-specific learning.

KEY LEARNING

Formative assessment helps create authentic and collaborative learning experiences and promotes the shift away from outcome-focused learning about 'what you know' to process-focused learning about 'who you are' (Prashanti & Ramnarayan, 2019; Watson et al., 2023). As educators, we must offer creative and flexible approaches to assessment which incorporate collaborative formative opportunities and support the personal and professional development of students. It is also important to have a formative 'blueprint' that we can adapt for each cohort, as the developmental needs of individual students will be different each year. The challenge comes in embedding such a creative, flexible, and personal approach whilst ensuring formal learning outcomes can still be met. Thibodeaux et al. (2019) highlight that "choice, ownership, and voice cannot exist within a program that is not consistently interconnected" (p. 58). Formative assessment should therefore be structured to ensure learning according to intended outcomes but flexible to support the individual needs and strengths of students and cohorts. It was clear that academic involvement in students' formative process is key to creating a safe space within which they can feel comfortable being uncomfortable; they expect to be challenged, understand the value in their contribution, and feel safe sharing their thoughts. It is essential that such a formative approach be communicated clearly from the outset and rationalised so that students understand its purpose and value. The formative assessment strategy described is therefore a cog in a more complex machine of student support and engagement but essential to its effectiveness.

REFLECTION POINT

1) Digital assessment can be framed in a way that develops discipline-specific skills and provides optionality so that assessment is personally meaningful for the student. What is the purpose of digital formative assessment, specific to your discipline area and learning outcomes?
2) The balance between student ownership and academic guidance is key to overall development, so how can you use available digital tools to provide flexible assessment and student choice alongside structured formative assessment?
3) Reflect on whether the formative and digital assessment methods promote self-awareness and development in the student and the potential for it to promote critical reflection and ownership. What can these formative assessment and learning opportunities offer, beyond the development of theoretical knowledge and understanding?

18

USING DIGITAL MULTISOURCE FEEDBACK TO PROVIDE MEDICAL STUDENTS WITH FORMATIVE FEEDBACK ON THEIR WORKPLACE BEHAVIOUR AND PROFESSIONAL PROGRESS

SARAH ALLSOP, JOANNA HOWARTH, AND JANE WILLIAMS

Discipline and/or Subject/Field: Medical Education

CONTEXT

Every year 250–300 students graduate from Bristol Medical School and enter the UK NHS workforce as trainee (Foundation Year 1) doctors. Our course aims to make students part of the healthcare workforce from the outset, helping them develop the professional behaviours, skills and knowledge laid out by the General Medical Council (GMC) Outcomes for Graduates (GMC, 2018). Students meet and observe patients in clinical settings within the first few weeks of starting their course and throughout their studies learn to be part of a multi-professional team.

All students are assigned a professional mentor (personal tutor) from a team of around 300 clinicians and academics to provide oversight of their personal and professional development (PPD). Mentors meet their students regularly throughout their 5-year journey to review their progress. Students also have a professional undergraduate ePortfolio in which they track their PPD across multiple aspects of their training including, carrying out reflective practice, recording conversations with their mentor, documenting workplace-based assessments and clinical skills. They can also share their achievements within and extra to their curriculum.

Receiving and giving feedback are an integral part of PPD both during and after undergraduate medical training. Detailed as a 'professional values and behaviours' outcome by the GMC, maintaining a professional development portfolio, including evidence of refection, achievements, learning needs and feedback from patients and colleagues, is becoming commonplace in undergraduate curricular (GMC, 2018). However, assessing the development of a student's performance and professional behaviours is complex (Lockyer & Sargeant, 2022), particularly when they are studying in a wide range of contexts across many different environments distributed across multiple dispersed locations.

Multisource (or 360-degree) feedback attempts to assess professional behaviour by collating feedback from a range of staff and peers with whom students work closely. Importantly, this feedback activity is a formative process, building to a must-complete summative assessment by the final year of study to reflect the requirement of completing this process successfully within the workplace.

STRATEGY

Multisource feedback is a formative performance assessment tool popularised in the corporate business world in the 1950s and 1960s to offer feedback to employees on their performance. The theory behind this technique is to combine feedback on direct observation of practice with a discussion and opportunity for self-reflection to provide individuals with an action plan that can lead to improved performance and behaviour change. The technique was adapted and adopted in medicine in the 1990s and has become an established and validated assessment and feedback tool in a variety of settings in both postgraduate training and undergraduate medical education (Berk, 2009).

For doctors training in the NHS in the UK, typically multisource feedback uses a version of this technique known as Team Assessment of Behaviour (TAB) (UK Foundation Programme, 2023). The practice of TAB involves requesting and gathering feedback responses from a range of assessors in four domains: attitude and/or behaviour, verbal communication skills, team working and accessibility. For each domain assessors are invited to say if they have no concern, some concern or a major concern and add written feedback. The process of requesting and summarising feedback is carried out digitally in a professional ePortfolio. Responses are reviewed and summarised by the supervisor before being discussed and, during a meeting with the trainee, a reflective action plan is created to promote continued cycles of improved performance and professional development (Donnon et al., 2014).

During our medical programme curriculum review (2017–2022), the implementation of TAB was embedded throughout the undergraduate curriculum to mirror the continuing professional development (CPD) that doctors undertake.

PRACTICE

TAB is an annual programme-wide assessment undertaken in the student's ePortfolio. Students from all years must complete their TAB satisfactorily (i.e., receiving the correct number of responses, from an appropriate mix of assessors, by a given deadline) alongside other formative and summative assessments before they can progress to the next year of the course. TAB supports students to become increasingly familiar with sending requests for and receiving feedback from their peers and staff and to practice giving feedback to others. The overarching aim is that by the end of their final year (year 5), students can proficiently complete a version of TAB that mirrors that used by doctors in clinical practice (Donnon et al., 2014).

Students are encouraged to be autonomous in the process as part of developing their assessment literacy but are supported where needed by their mentor and the portfolio administrative team. Students are required to complete a self-assessment, a judgment of their behaviours, before they can invite assessors (staff in different roles and student peers) to complete a feedback assessment of their behaviour by emailing a link that directs assessors to an online form. Students can view whom they have requested feedback from and who has submitted feedback and send reminders after an appropriate length of time to non-responders but cannot initially view the content of the submitted feedback.

A key aspect of TAB is learning to actively manage the process and select appropriate assessors to provide meaningful feedback. To this end students are encouraged to send more requests than required, ensuring they reach the required mix and number of responses appropriate for their year of study (see Figure 18.1). For each year of study, no more than two pieces of student feedback can be counted towards the overall total, but additional feedback from all assessors is welcomed for their personal development. Once responses have been received, students arrange a meeting with their mentor.

The meeting between the student and mentor is a critical part of the practice. Ahead of this meeting an anonymous and randomised summary view is autogenerated within the ePortfolio system, which is reviewed by the mentor. At the meeting, together they review the student's self-assessment with that of their assessors. This process is usually positive, affirming their progress in learning to become a doctor and providing space for discussion about professional development and growth.

The complexity of the TAB process increases for students as they move through the programme as an iterative process which develops a greater understanding (assessment literacy) and proficiency of completing the process over

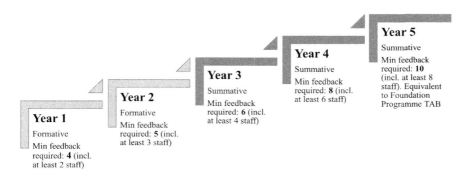

Figure 18.1 Team Assessment of Behaviour requirements over time. The specified minimum number of pieces of feedback increases each year, and the process becomes summative from year 3 onwards. Students send out requests to both students and staff and must achieve the specified ratio of staff to student feedback to count towards the TAB at each stage.

time. If TAB is not completed by the deadline, students are given an extended period within which to finish the process, and those who fail to complete TAB are supported with any difficulties and issues. From year 3, students must complete TAB to progress. Those failing to engage with the process are required to do an additional reflection on the role of TAB as a medical student and a doctor to help them understand the importance of the assessment within the workplace setting. Once reaching their final year (year 5), students with an incomplete first TAB cycle must repeat TAB for a second time before progression to show full and timely engagement as is expected in the workplace after graduation. It is noted that students who do not complete TAB to a satisfactory level are often struggling with aspects of their course. In this instance, the missed TAB can provide an important flag to identify students and offer support.

IMPACT

Gaining personalised feedback whilst on placement in a large cohort is difficult; everyone is busy, and students interact with many people from multiple distributed settings. TAB offers a key opportunity to get a broad perspective of their progress. It empowers students to ask how they are progressing and provides choice in whom they wish to invite to give feedback, along with discussing their feedback with a trusted staff member to consider directions of potential growth. It also supports students to expand and strengthen their repertoire of professional skills and capabilities, including skills relating to time management and following detailed instructions, both important aspects of patient safety.

Importantly, TAB also makes provision for assessors (staff or student peers) to highlight areas of concern around a student's professional behaviour which can be followed up appropriately. Students are encouraged and empowered to provide honest and constructive feedback, including if they feel others are not contributing to their full. Voicing concern is an important attribute when working within a team, particularly in clinical settings, so cultivating this culture is a positive impact of TAB.

Most concerns when reviewed are considered minor and can be explored at a local level with the student's mentor, encouraging the student to reflect and resolve issues through creating a support plan. In this way, through dialogue, students who may be struggling with aspects of the course and expectations of them being student doctors can be supported. More serious concerns are referred to the fitness to practice team, thus ensuring any potential patient safety or professionalism issues are not missed.

Student evaluation responses recognise TAB as an important way of gaining timely, meaningful feedback on their development and performance throughout medical school and learning to manage a digital feedback process in preparation for their future career. The authors of this case study are professional mentors to many students. Together with other mentors, we witness the delight of students when they receive a truly positive set of TAB feedback reflecting their achievements. In this way, the digital process and post-digital conversation together provide affirmation that students are progressing and developing.

Feedback received from our graduates highlights the value of practicing TAB (and other work-placed based assessments) in preparing them for the challenging transition to becoming a doctor.

> From the very first day, I was able to get stuck in and start doing the job. Don't get me wrong, I was terrified, but skills-wise I felt very prepared. I knew what my role was and what were the habits of a good [Foundation] doctor.
>
> Bristol graduate, 2022

KEY LEARNING

The practice of running TAB in medical education is not static, and over the seven years of implementing TAB, our practice has developed as attitudes and language around collecting and reviewing feedback have changed. This includes regularly reviewing and adapting our digital platform and post-digital practice to ensure authenticity and relevance to workplace practices.

Digital planning and support

Successful integration of this authentic and tailored formative feedback process across all years of a large programme (>1300 students) requires collaboration and training for students, academic leads and mentors, administrators, technologists and digital design specialists. The use of technology is critical, requiring comprehensive digital planning to ensure smooth running and timely delivery of the process for students and staff who are geographically dispersed at placement sites across the southwest of England.

Consistently available support from a team of assessment and technical administrators is important, tackling any problems staff or students encounter with logistics or the technology they are asked to use. Continuous review and refinement of the software system used for TAB is needed to ensure any digital barriers for staff and student users are identified as early as possible. The system must also be able to integrate responses into a meaningful anonymised version for each student to enable a constructive post-digital conversation and reflection. When working well, this online system removes unwanted and burdensome administrative barriers and enables a sense of autonomy, increasing reflection, self-awareness and insight (Whitehouse et al., 2007).

The importance of the human interaction within the feedback process

Whilst TAB is initiated and driven through the student's ePortfolio, dialogue between the professional mentor and student is fundamental to provide meaning to the practice. Without this, TAB becomes a process or tick-box exercise, and students may fail to gain full insight from feedback provided; the digital element of TAB enables efficient collection and administration of feedback, and the conversation and supported reflection of feedback received ensure the value.

Importantly, staff and students are reminded not to leave feedback about performance or behaviour issues until the TAB process starts. Concerns or developmental advice should usually be provided concurrently to the behaviour witnessed so that students can learn, reflect and grow in a supportive environment. Likewise, it is important that TAB feedback reflect a student's overall performance rather than singular instances of a particular behaviour (this is clearly stated as part of the feedback entry form).

Training

Training and support for all users about the delivery and systems used for TAB is essential. For students, dedicated sessions are provided about the practice and timeline for TAB and on how to write constructive feedback, as well as online resources on the virtual learning environment (Blackboard).

For mentors, annual training and updates are offered as well as a dedicated online resource providing key information, such as deadlines and assessment dates to highlight when students might need additional support. Specific support is offered to mentors less familiar with multisource feedback approaches and those who are not from a clinical background. When running this process with large cohorts, there is inevitable variability in the student-mentor relationship and availability of mentors to meet students at a pre-designated time. In the rare occasions where a professional mentor is unavailable, trained 'interim' mentors are asked to meet students and ensure the feedback and reflective process can be completed.

Evolution of the process

Over time, the design of TAB has changed through understanding more about the learning curve of the students and developments in the ePortfolio technology. For example, TAB was originally performed twice in year 1, designed as a 'practice' TAB and then a 'real' one. In reality, instead of being helpful, the doubling of the task created confusion and anxiety and so was changed to a single formative TAB in year 1 and year 2 to introduce the process to students across a longer period. The number of assessor feedback responses needed for the earlier years of the programme was also reduced, as students found it challenging to get to know enough people well to meet the original targets.

The language used in TAB has also been reviewed, with the criteria for assessors carefully re-tailored for each year of the programme and the language updated to reflect the increasing diversity within our student population and workforce.

Ongoing challenges

TAB is one of several formative assessments undertaken by students within their ePortfolio. Now fully embedded in the programme, a shift is needed to help students focus on the benefits for their professional development of the feedback received during TAB rather than simply focusing on completion of the task. We know students get out what they put in, but many still complete their self-assessment selecting 'no concern' for each domain without qualifying this with a written reflection. This should be an important part of the process that helps drive the post-assessment dialogue around how they perceive their performance against the feedback received from assessors. More work is needed to maximise staff and student understanding of the value of this part of their practice, further enhancing their assessment literacy. Future evaluation will therefore focus on how meaningful students find the process, the importance and value they give to it and how it is embedded and presented to them in the ePortfolio along with other formative assessments.

REFLECTION POINT

1) How are you currently supporting students within your programme to develop skills of professional behaviour?
2) How are your students supported to develop reflective practice and to engage constructively in feedback processes?
3) Do your students get timely feedback from a range of different assessors to give them a rounded view of their progress and development over time?
4) How could engaging in a 360 multisource feedback process help your students to develop their skills around professional behaviours?
5) Do your students engage in a digital portfolio of practice? Would they benefit from a guided portfolio to track their progress?

19

FORMATIVELY ASSESSING COMPETENCY IN PRACTICAL SKILLS IN THE BIOLOGICAL SCIENCES THROUGH DIRECT OBSERVATIONS AND ORAL FEEDBACK

ANNA NOUSEK-MCGREGOR, LAURA MCCAUGHEY, AND LESLEY HAMILTON

Discipline and/or Subject/Field: Biological Sciences

CONTEXT

Development of practical skills is an essential component of learning within most STEM-based degree programmes, allowing students applied experience with the key techniques related to their disciplines. A crucial example of active learning, these sessions are embedded widely throughout science curricula and typically consist of demonstration of a particular methodology followed by the opportunity for students to complete the procedure themselves. Summative assessment of this learning is typically delivered through a written laboratory report that follows the structure of a peer-reviewed journal article, outlining the context and significance of the research question, the procedure performed and the results and implications of this study. Although preparing students well for research dissemination in academic careers, this method of assessment rarely directly evaluates competency in the skills themselves (Reiss et al., 2012).

Moreover, since undergraduate students frequently conduct practical work in pairs or small groups, some students may never perform the skills themselves.

Professional degrees such as medicine and veterinary science place considerable focus on demonstrated competencies with applied skills, as high levels of proficiency with these skills are required before entering the workplace. As a result, these degree programmes include individually assessed formative and summative assessments based around completion of specific skills in front of a trained observer, known as Objective Structured Clinical Examinations (OSCEs). Although these exams have clear benefits for learning, such as increasing student confidence and improving the learning experience, this practice is extremely time consuming for staff and can be stressful for students, limiting its use for large cohorts (Norcini & McKinley, 2007). Improving student motivation and confidence are key benefits of skills tracking, with the formative approach to its delivery essential in providing repeated opportunities for development, provided there are time-effective tools for use with large cohorts of students (Chen et al., 2013). This case study demonstrates an effective, time-efficient approach to documenting skills development with large cohorts of students, incorporating formative assessments into a digital record accessible to students from the beginning of their course.

STRATEGY

The importance of direct assessment of practical skills for biological science students was highlighted by the Royal Society of Biology (RSB) during the process of gaining accreditation for the 16 undergraduate life science degrees[1] at the University of Glasgow in April 2022. A requirement for obtaining and maintaining degree accreditation was deciding on which practical skills were essential for students within each degree and ensuring that individual students could demonstrate competency in these skills on completion of their degree, and therefore achievement of the programme Intended Learning Outcomes. These requirements also aligned extremely well with the University of Glasgow's new Learning and Teaching Strategy that focuses on improving the student experience both through work-related learning and improved signposting of professional skills development.

The aim of this requirement was to increase student awareness of confidence in, and competency in the key practical skills related to their degree while also providing students with a record of their progress and achievement. Given the challenges of delivering this framework, it also needed to be feasibly delivered with large cohorts of students (600+) and embedded into existing practical sessions, rather than creating stand-alone alternatives such as practical skills courses.

Life science degree structure

At the University of Glasgow, BSc honours students complete four-year degrees that consist of two years of more general biological content followed by two years of discipline-specific content. In their second year, all students across 16 BSc honours degrees, see endnote 1, must complete one compulsory 30-credit course in their first semester (BIOL2039 Fundamental Topics in Biology 2X; approximately 650 students), and all students are required to take one of four 30-credit courses,[2] whichever is most closely associated with their degree area (Figure 18.1). Most students choose to take a second life science–related course from the list to satisfy their credit requirements (120 credits per year) and keep a second life sciences degree possibility open. In third year, all students take a mandatory 120-credit degree-specific course, and in the final year, all students take one core discipline-specific course and three optional courses.

The framework developed to meet the RSB's accreditation requirements involved staff observations providing formative feedback to students during in-class sessions, combined with a set of course checklists embedded into students' learning management system (Moodle). This framework provides a flexible record of students' competencies in their learning of technical skills and a starting point for self-reflection to align with post-university career trajectories. It is more associated with the cognitivist end of the spectrum, as outlined by Evans' (2013) review, where students are more passive in the process, working towards corrective improvements. However, some of the additional functionality allowed by the digital side of this project (see 'Key Learning Points') could be adjusted to involve students with more co-creation of learning.

PRACTICE

This framework was embedded into the practical sessions of five compulsory level 2 life science courses at the University of Glasgow during the academic year 2022–2023 for staff to formatively assess and provide real-time feedback on skills development during practical sessions, recording attainment of these skills within the course LMS for use beyond university. Although not used in our implementation, it also could incorporate student reflections for each skill and provide asynchronous feedback on content uploaded by students. The digital content within this tool consisted of a series of Checklist activities contained in Moodle (v3.11) uploaded by staff and then verified when each skill was observed during a practical session. Given Moodle has both staff- and student-facing interfaces, these digital lists were accessed using tablets or mobile phones during practical sessions to ensure all individual students were observed and received oral formative feedback on their level of competency for each skill listed. Over the duration of a course, completion of all skills is shown with progress trackers based on the elements completed within each Moodle Checklist (Figure 19.1), allowing students to have a record of skills performed and staff to ensure all students were formatively assessed on them. Students also are able review these skills holistically at the start of the course, which may reduce any anxiety or uncertainty about what to expect.

Level 2 course	Fundamental Topics 2X	Animal Biology 2A	Molecular Biosciences 2B	Human Biology 2C	Microbiology & Immunology 2D
List of essential skills	Pipetting Agarose gel loading Changing pH of solution Data analysis in R Creating a LinkedIn profile	Scientific drawing Species identification Field-based data collection Data plotting using ggplot	Loading SDS page gels Streaking out yeast plates	Plotting of data Use of a dissecting scope Physiological measurements on a human volunteer Apply reproducible methodology to increase accuracy & precision & avoid error	Sterile pipetting Streaking out bacterial samples Microscope set-up on 100x oil objective

Figure 19.1 List of essential skills as decided by course coordinator and project team. Each skill was covered in at least one practical session in the course listed at the top. All courses happened in the second year of a four-year degree programme. The left-most course (Fundamental Topics 2X) was compulsory for all students and ran in Semester 1, whereas the other four courses ran in Semester 2 and were mandatory for students only within a specific discipline.

Full guidance and implementation steps are available online at https://edshare.gla.ac.uk/id/eprint/1550 (Figure 19.2).

Design and development of this framework included three stages: 1) creation and scaffolding of skills lists, 2) implementation of checklists during practical sessions and 3) future directions for student reflection and employability.

Creation and scaffolding

To create the skills lists, the project team met with course coordinators and reviewed course materials such as laboratory manuals and course information documents to list the skills currently delivered in practical sessions in each of the five courses and determine which were essential and which were desirable (Figure 19.1). Depending on the degree, these skills included laboratory work, field-based work or data analysis skills such as R programming, each selected by course coordinators according to the priorities of the course. Each list was then imported from a template Excel file to the course learning management system (Moodle v3.11) using the Checklist Import function. Informational materials were also added to student-facing course information documents and included in the introductory Microsoft PowerPoint presentations that are delivered during the first practical session of each course. Course coordinators also briefed postgraduate teaching assistants (GTAs) in advance about which skills to observe, setting out a list of the intermediate steps to verify competency of each particular skill (Figure 19.3).

FORMATIVELY ASSESSING COMPETENCY IN PRACTICAL SKILLS   153

Figure 19.2 QR code to access Course Coordinators Guide (.doc format) for implementing this Practical Skills Tracking framework.

Figure 19.3 Summary of delivery for three essential skills assessed for one second-year course (BIOL2044 Microbiology and Immunology) in which the Practical Skills Framework was embedded. The upper two arrows show when skills were used in lab sessions, either first introduced (orange) or given feedback from staff for formative assessment (light blue). The lower three arrows (dark blue, green and purple) show each of the specific skills assessed, the colours of which correspond to the dots in the upper arrows, and the individual feedback points that staff used to support students' demonstration of competency in each skill.

Implementation

Two or three practical sessions within each course included the direct observations of one skill. During these sessions, staff (which included both lecturers and GTAs, typically at a ratio of 12 students to 1 staff member) observed each individual student perform each of the designated skills and gave immediate formative oral feedback to them on it. In some courses, one staff member per session was designated to observe and give feedback, and in others all staff would participate in this capacity. After the introduction to the session, including the aims and a demonstration of the tasks involved, students were given time to practice the skills. After that period, staff would circulate around the students and ask for individuals who were ready to be observed. Staff would access the skills section in their Moodle account, which would give them a list of skills and students. Once a student demonstrated the ability to perform the skill correctly, the staff could select that box from the checklist, confirming competency. If the student did not demonstrate attainment, they would be given more time to practice and be observed again later or in a subsequent lab session, for as many times as necessary. Feedback was only given orally; however, the Checklist activity does allow written feedback to be included, presenting the potential for future functionality.

Future directions

Although this framework was built around practical skills, its relevance across skills and curricula became clear immediately. Creating similar lists based around other degree programme aspects would greatly enhance the student experience through many of the same advantages explored here. In particular, transferable skills such as presentation, time management, teamwork and problem-solving were frequently mentioned during discussions of essential skills to be included. Although outside the scope of the current project, additional skill lists could be easily and rapidly incorporated into this framework.

IMPACT

At the end of their course, students were asked to complete an online questionnaire that included a combination of Likert-scale and open-ended questions, with a total of 50 students completing it. An optional follow-up focus group was also held and attended by eight volunteers that had completed the practical skills tracking in at least one of their second-year courses. Percentages of positive responses were compared to negative ones for the Likert-scale questions, while a thematic analysis was applied to the open-ended responses looking for themes related to Nelson and Schunn's (2009) three main purposes of feedback, either motivational, reinforcement or informational, with our initial aims most connected with the last of these.

The student response to this framework was overwhelmingly positive, with 77% of students agreeing with improved competency in the skills assessed, 69% agreeing or strongly agreeing that the practical skills tracking had an impact in their engagement with the theory of practical skills and 73% agreeing or strongly agreeing that this framework had influenced their understanding of the theory of the practical skills assessed. Only a small portion of students (25%) felt anxious about being observed, with 42% having no concerns. Of those who concerned about being watched, some further expanded that the benefits of feedback outweighed any discomfort.

From the open-ended questions, students frequently mentioned the connection between repeated skills training and improved learning, increased confidence and understanding the context and motivation behind learning practical skills. Although both large and small amounts of feedback result in a strong improvement of students' practical skills competency, the more feedback that is given, the more efficiently this improvement happens (Bosse et al., 2015). Confidence is another key area where direct feedback can drastically support student skills development; working with surgical interns, Acosta et al. (2018) found that a practical skills learning curriculum improved interns' feelings of confidence in their technical skills. The formative assessment provided by this framework promoted feelings of autonomy and competence (Leenknecht et al., 2021) and therefore more independent motivation than previous unsupervised laboratory teaching. Supporting such independent motivation aligns with self-determination theory, suggesting that learning is further improved as it meets more of the three basic psychological needs: autonomy, competence and relatedness (Deci & Ryan, 1985). Practical Skills Tracking motivates students by giving them the opportunity to demonstrate their competency in skills that are related to the subject-specific knowledge taught in lectures but also related to their potential future career aspirations.

KEY LEARNING POINTS

Overall, this practice was highly successful and well received by both staff and students. Students found it very engaging, feeling increased confidence in their practical abilities. External validation was also important; students valued knowing they were doing skills correctly from someone with experience. Many staff also felt that the opportunity to interact with every individual student was highly beneficial and rewarding. Given this feedback, use of a similar framework with either only self-reflection or peer formative assessment may not be as effective. To reach a more socio-constructivist approach, additional steps would be needed, such as asking students to write reflections on the alignment of skills acquired with available careers (which are possible within the framework used but would require more recognition or summative assessment to promote engagement).

After initial implementation, focus group evaluation helped identify areas of improvement. Consistency of feedback from different staff members was one aspect mentioned, and students would queue to get their skill lists completed, which devalued the experience of getting individual formative advice on their competency level. One student commented:

> you couldn't sit and practise for ages because you knew you had to get into the queue, because if you didn't get into the queue you weren't going to be seen. So sometimes you found yourself waiting a really long time. Which I do understand all this isn't the fault of the GTAs or anything, it's just really big labs. . . . But I do think it was worth it.

From our experience, most staff found this practice straightforward to embed in their courses, and using Moodle was helpful to manage the system with large numbers of students. Similarly, creating skills lists in Moodle allowed students to access the comprehensive list at the start of the course, providing the students with the target skills to achieve and creating a learning goal for practical activities (Lizzio & Wilson, 2008). However, consistency in feedback was extremely important to ensure fairness in implementation, and implementation required genuine observation of students to verify competency. Staff training (particularly for GTAs) was essential in ensuring that quality feedback was delivered in a positive, constructive way consistently across students. The biggest challenges that this approach faced were determining an appropriate number of skills to include and supporting those students who had missed those laboratory sessions in which the practice was implemented. To resolve these issues, we designed the skills lists on content that was delivered in repeated sessions across semesters and years or considered some skills desirable, as there was only one delivery of that material. Finally, adding a summary checklist that mapped skills onto sessions and signposted students' assessment and reassessment possibilities should also mitigate those concerns.

Overall, both staff and students recognised the considerable benefits of this framework, and most students engaged in the framework without formal requirements for completion such as inclusion as a credit-bearing course or as a summative assessment. Similarly, staff found it straightforward to provide formative assessment of individual students, even supporting a large cohort of 650 students. Representing a highly transferable system that could be used across institutions, this framework balances the needs for a unique learning experience, with advantages that were quickly recognised by the students.

REFLECTION POINT

1) Do your programme and course Intended Learning Outcomes align with the skills embedded in your coursework? Do the skills embedded in your coursework accurately reflect those that are required for future employment in your discipline?
2) This method of providing a record of skills competency is excellent for student awareness of learning during a degree, but the next step is connecting that with post-university careers. How could you embed activities in your programme that take this next step in supporting students transitioning from a student identity into a graduate one?

3) Many professional degrees use observations of practical skills in summative assessment or as the basis for reflective portfolios. This skills assessment contains options that could integrate reflective statements and/or self-assessment of skills development. Would you see those options as having advantages or disadvantages to the staff-observed method we have used here?
4) This tool focused on practical skills but could be incorporated into a larger framework to evaluate the whole university experience for students. What other types of skills could you integrate for your discipline or programme? Would co-generating these skills lists with students further strengthen its advantages?
5) Feedback was given orally to students during practical sessions, allowing for synchronous improvement and reassessment; however, this tool has the capacity to include written feedback. Immediacy of feedback is beneficial to students, but does more detailed asynchronous feedback work better for your discipline or teaching?

[1] *Degrees consist of: BSc (hons) anatomy, BSc (hons) biochemistry, BSc (hons) genetics, BSc (hons) human biology, BSc (hons) human biology and nutrition, BSc (hons) immunology, BSc (hons) marine and freshwater biology, BSc (hons) microbiology, BSc (hons) molecular and cellular biology, BSc (hons) molecular and cellular biology with biotechnology, BSc (hons) molecular and cellular biology with plant technology, BSc (hons) neuroscience, BSc (hons) pharmacology, BSc (hons) physiology and sports science, BSc (hons) physiology, sports science and nutrition, BSc (hons) zoology.*

[2] *BIOL2041 (Animal Biology, Ecology and Evolution), BIOL2042 (Genes, Molecules and Cells), BIOL2043 (Human Biology) and BIOL2044 (Microbiology and Immunology).*

20

EMBEDDING FORMATIVE ASSESSMENT IN THE FLIPPED STATISTICS CLASSROOM

YEH-CHING LOW

Discipline and/or Subject/Field: *Computing/Statistics*

CONTEXT

Final-year students in an undergraduate computing-related degree in our university in Malaysia are required to take a subject on probability and statistics. Due to students' varying level of familiarity with statistical concepts, there is a need to narrow the existing gap before students are introduced to new concepts. The flipped classroom approach (Farmus et al., 2020) in which students engage with pre-class asynchronous learning activities requiring lower levels of cognitive learning taxonomy before coming together for in-class sessions is introduced in the subject. This approach serves two objectives: to (a) allow students some flexibility to learn at their own pace in the asynchronous component and (b) focus on higher cognitive learning taxonomy levels which will benefit from discussions and active learning strategies during synchronous in-class sessions.

However, a crucial requirement and major challenge in flipped classroom implementation is student engagement in pre-class content. Neither of the objectives is achievable if students are not engaged or prepared through the pre-class materials. This lack of engagement or preparation is attributed to various factors such as lack of self-regulatory skills (Jensen et al., 2018), amongst others. Therefore, remedial measures need to be in place to ensure that students who do not do the necessary pre-class preparation are not totally "lost" during the in-class session. In order to balance between being sufficient for students who are not prepared and useful for those who have done their preparation, these remedial measures are implemented in the form of formative assessments embedded within the flipped classroom session's design.

STRATEGY

The flipped classroom approach has gained significant interest in recent years. As an active learning technique, the principal idea behind flipped classroom is to stimulate learners' cognitive activities by creating an intentional learning design which moves low level learning activities to pre-class time. In-class time is then directed towards learning activities of a higher level which would benefit more from the presence of instructors, peer collaboration or physical learning enablers such as learning resources and facilities. Therefore, for an effective flipped classroom approach it is crucial to structure and identify levels of Bloom's taxonomy (Krathwohl, 2002) for the content to be covered and learning outcomes so that students' learning process is well supported. Although active learning is often more emphasized or evident in the in-class sessions, pre-class learning activities which include watching pre-recorded lecture videos, reading tasks or listening to podcasts can also incorporate active learning strategies.

Previous research has shown both positive and negative reactions towards flipped learning (O'Flaherty & Phillips, 2015; Akcayr & Akcayr, 2018). The positive aspects of flipped learning are increases in academic satisfaction, learning experience and achievement. On the other hand, due to the increased responsibility from the students, especially in managing their time and behaviours for pre-class preparation, some studies indicate that students may experience frustration. In particular, students with lower self-regulation skills and a tendency towards task avoidance do not adapt well to the flipped classroom approach (Lai & Hwang, 2016; Hyppönen et al., 2019) and thus may fall behind in their studies (Chen et al., 2014). The incorporation of low-stakes formative assessments thus serves as an external prompt for students to manage their time and learning behaviours.

Talbert highlighted that assessment and regular feedback throughout the flipped course are necessary to support students' self-directed efforts as compared to a traditionally taught course. Formative feedback has been proposed by McLaughlin and Yan (2017) and Yeung and O'Malley (2014) for developing students' higher order cognitive skills. Moreover, individual feedback (Tusa et al., 2018), structured guidance and in-time support from teachers are factors that lead to better student motivation and overall learning experience. In-video quizzes have been shown to be effective for student engagement in pre-class content delivery in various courses such as programming (Cummins et al., 2016), pharmacy (Jones et al., 2021), biochemistry (Shelby & Fralish, 2021) and chemistry (Kinsella et al., 2017).

Technology is an important enabler in the delivery of the flipped approach, especially in the pre-class materials. The digital native generation of students has been shown to be more responsive to digital technology use in learning (Margaryan et al., 2011). In addition to supporting the actual learning process, information and communication technology (ICT) facilitates the flexibility of the content delivery. It is important to emphasize that ICT needs to be considered from the pedagogical perspective to support cognition, not just for the sake of technology use to present information (Abeysekera & Dawson, 2015; Bishop & Verleger, 2013; Tamim et al., 2011). Davies et al. (2013) found that a technology-enhanced flipped classroom was more motivating. Students also preferred using technology to assist their learning over other aspects in the flipped classroom environment (McNally et al., 2017). Using technology-enabled tools such as digital polls and self-assessment quizzes, interactive lectures provide a bi-directional feedback mechanism which promotes reflective learning and empowers the lecturer to be proactive to accommodate classes' understanding as required (Thai et al., 2017).

PRACTICE

The subject was delivered over a semester which consists of fourteen weeks between April and July. In most weeks throughout the semester, through the learning management system, students are assigned to complete a "pre-lecture preparation kit" which consists of curated learning activities such as watching pre-recorded lecture videos and YouTube videos, reading journal articles or going through external websites related to the content. This is then followed by online lecture classes and face-to-face tutorial classes. During the synchronous sessions, there are also formative assessment opportunities through collaborative tutorial work using a digital notebook.

In order to incorporate active learning components in pre-class activities, a combination of approaches which utilizes technology tools is embedded in the pre-lecture preparation consisting of (a) ungraded quizzes, (b) branching scenarios and (c) a discussion board via Padlet wall. Ungraded quiz questions are embedded strategically in pre-recorded video lectures to highlight key or threshold concepts. These questions also serve the purpose of encouraging and monitoring students' engagement with pre-class learning activities (Jones et al., 2021). Through these questions, students can obtain instant feedback to check their own factual recall and understanding before proceeding to the next part of the lesson. The assessments also serve as a low-stakes goal for students to attain.

In the topics related to hypothesis testing, the expected learning outcome is that students can select the best hypothesis test for a given scenario. To incorporate active learning into the content delivery, a branching scenario is designed whereby the students have to select the correct hypothesis test in order to be able to view the associated pre-recorded lecture video. This interactive element seeks to engage student directly with the concept and required decision-making process.

For concepts requiring application, analysis or evaluation of learning constructs which would benefit from in-class learning opportunities, students are directed to post their answers to prompt questions on Padlet wall. These points are picked up and discussed during in-class sessions. These levels of cognitive complexity are based on Bloom's revised taxonomy (Krathwohl, 2002).

For selected topics, formative assessments are blended into instruction during face-to-face sessions. This approach is driven by two motivations: (a) just-in-time feedback on students' understanding about the instruction and (b) inclusivity due to some students' circumstances or special needs, which lead to them shying away from collaborative learning activities. These circumstances or special needs range from lack of preparedness on pre-class content to medical reasons. In these classes, lesson content is interspersed with ungraded quiz questions using Quizizz, which is a web-based tool for assessment and instruction. The functionalities in Quizizz allow seamless integration and delivery of content slides and quiz questions. In this setting, the question types focus on application and analysis. These low-stakes formative assessments are intended to highlight key concepts and provide opportunity for instantaneous, just-in-time feedback to students. It should be noted here that the lesson is a complement and not a repetition of pre-class content. The design of this approach is similar to the Self-Assessment Quizzes (SAQs) framework proposed by Gibson and Morison (2021), which has been shown to increase student engagement and improve student academic performance.

IMPACT

The effectiveness of the approaches is determined using several data sources: (a) students' engagement via learning management system's analytics, (b) students' feedback via questionnaire survey and (c) instructor's observations.

From the learning analytics statistics of the pre-recorded lecture videos, it is observed that the videos are viewed in the days leading to the in-class session, with the highest number of views during the hours before the in-class session is scheduled to take place. All students who watch the videos are required to attempt the embedded quizzes, and overall students' response rate is positive for these quizzes.

A questionnaire survey was administered in the middle of the course, in which around 20 students participated. Participation is voluntary with consent, and no compensation is given to participants. The items in the survey are intended to measure four student engagement factors, which are emotional engagement, physical engagement, cognitive engagement in class and cognitive engagement out of class (Burch et al., 2015). Each item is measured on a scale of 1 (strongly disagree) to 5 (strongly agree). The survey results show that the mean score for all items is skewed towards 4 (i.e., agree) and 5 (i.e., strongly agree). Items on emotional engagement scored lower than the other factors, which is within expectation, as most students are not positively inclined towards the subject because a direct application cannot be established between the subject and the field/discipline. Positive student engagement is evident for both cognitive-related factors since the items score relatively high.

Based on the instructor's' observation whilst conducting in-class sessions with formative assessments blended with instructional content using an online quizzing platform, students are evidently more engaged throughout the session. This is also captured through the open-ended comments given during the questionnaire survey. Students commented that the approach is a good method to evaluate, reinforce and understand students' knowledge and understanding. The approach is also found to be interactive and improves the students' participation and focus.

For this study, impact on academic performance is not evaluated at this point in time due to the inevitable changes made in assessment modes due to the COVID-19 pandemic.

KEY LEARNING

A key observation has been that some of the students would view the videos immediately after or over the next few days after the in-class session. Although this is not the optimal behaviour for a flipped classroom approach, it highlights the flexibility afforded by such access to pre-recorded content. In general, digital tools have increased the accessibility of learning content, which can now be made available anywhere and anytime.

Students are favourable towards multimodal learning tools. This is observed through the introduction of digital quizzing platform during physical classes, which attract a positive response in terms of participation and overall student sentiment towards the learning experience. Formative assessments have been previously administered through the learning management system, but student engagement was low. Nevertheless, it is observed that there are some students who shy away from collaborative learning activities, although use of digital tools enables anonymity to a certain degree. This could be due to cultural differences, lack of preparation or certain learning needs. Blending activities which cater to different learning processes would be more inclusive, ensuring that no one is left out.

Despite positive responses towards cognitive engagement factors, the adopted approach has less impact towards the emotional engagement factor. This reveals an interesting insight that emotional and cognitive aspects of student engagement correlates to a certain degree. Since emotions towards subject learning are managed more effectively in face-to-face sessions, careful design of the activities during these sessions will potentially help to alleviate issues related to students' emotions towards the subject.

REFLECTION POINT

1) How can formative assessments be used effectively in a flipped classroom for improving student engagement?
2) What is a good design behind the scaffolding of formative assessment questions?
3) How can digital tools be incorporated in physical sessions for improving students' emotional and physical engagement?

21

EMBEDDING FORMATIVE FEEDBACK THROUGH DIFFERENTIATED INSTRUCTION USING MICROSOFT ONENOTE CLASS NOTEBOOKS

SAMANTHA GOONERATNE

Discipline and/or Subject/Field: Chemical Engineering/Process Simulation, Reaction Engineering

CONTEXT

Teesside University (TU) is a post-92 public university based in the northeast of England. Approximately 16% of TU students are enrolled in engineering-related courses (HESA, 2023), of which chemical engineers form a small portion.

This case study presents three scenarios in which differentiated instruction is used to provide formative feedback to students in undergraduate (UG) and taught postgraduate (PG) chemical engineering courses at TU. The scenarios cover synchronous and asynchronous feedback practices related to a range of pedagogic activities.

Scenario 1 details the provision of synchronous feedback on an in-class activity relating to chemical process simulation. In this scenario, students traditionally sketched the process on paper and received verbal feedback. Whilst this worked well to foster a collegial atmosphere, the feedback was not retained beyond the session, and errors were repeated throughout subsequent submissions.

Scenario 2 explores the provision of asynchronous feedback to support preparation for examinations in reaction engineering, a major branch of chemical engineering with a heavy mathematical bias. Traditionally, out-of-class work on this topic was presented on loose papers (which were subsequently discarded) or via email; this made it extremely difficult to provide scaffolded revision support.

The final scenario explores the provision of synchronous and asynchronous feedback on project activity. Most taught degrees culminate in a significant piece of project work, and whilst tutor guidance is provided, self-directed project management is a key learning objective, typically evidenced via a logbook. Historically, students maintained physical logbooks. This was initially convenient for tutors, as no setup was required; however, various operational limitations resulted in a negative pedagogic impact.

When these challenges are coupled with an overwhelming increase in administrative burden for academics, the notion of a single digital platform via which all formative feedback can be disseminated becomes increasingly attractive.

STRATEGY

The value of formative feedback in student attainment is well established. Nicol and Macfarlane-Dick (2006) highlighted the role of formative feedback in facilitating learner self-regulation and identified principles of good feedback practice. Handley and Williams (2011) also investigated student engagement with formative feedback and posited that the public nature of cohort-wide opportunities may limit student engagement due to an aversion to appearing ignorant. The desire to encourage self-regulation whilst addressing this concern was a key driving force for exploring the use of technology-enabled differentiated instruction presented here.

This exploration coincided with the launch of TU's future facing learning (FFL) initiative in 2018, designed to empower students to succeed within a connected global workplace (Teesside University, n.d.). A key element of the FFL strategy was to issue an Apple iPad to all new full-time UG students. This iPad was pre-loaded with educational software tools linked to students' university accounts. One of these was Microsoft OneNote, the note-taking tool within the Office 365 suite.

To fully appreciate the nature of tutor-student interactions in this case study, familiarity with the OneNote platform is beneficial, at least within the context of its ability to facilitate formative feedback practices. In recent years, Microsoft has devoted considerable resources to improving its educational offerings, and OneNote has been a focal point, albeit with emphasis on its use in primary and secondary education. It is nonetheless popular in higher education, even more so due to necessities brought on by the COVID-19 pandemic (Marvin, 2020).

Table 21.1 Summary of content areas in ONCN, with member permissions

Area	Member permissions
Content Library (CL)	All sections view-only
Collaboration Space (CS)	All sections normally viewable and editable; owners can set availability of each section (to view-only or hidden) for individual members; owners can lock CS to prevent further edits
Teacher Only (TO)	All sections hidden
Personal Workspace (PW)	Content area has one named section per member; can only be edited/viewed by named member (and owners)

OneNote is fundamentally formed of unconstrained 'pages' organised in tabbed 'sections' within distinct 'notebooks'. The pages allow various input methods, including typed text, weblinks, file uploads and digital ink, and all entries are timestamped and attributed to the author. The platform is accessible via desktop, mobile and browser-based apps, and synchronisation occurs automatically when online.

OneNote Class Notebooks (ONCNs) are notebooks with enhanced collaboration capabilities. The sections and pages sit within distinct areas, as detailed in Table 21.1. Whilst notebook owners (i.e., tutors) can edit and view all sections and pages, the permissions vary for members (i.e., students).

The flexibility for all users in the choice of data input method combined with the tiered structure of the ONCN presented an opportunity to ease the administrative burden of providing feedback without diminishing the student experience. What began as a pilot with final-year UG students has developed over time (accelerated by the pandemic) into the three scenarios presented here.

PRACTICE

Scenario 1 – synchronous formative feedback on in-class activity

In this activity, Year 2 students are required to demonstrate that they can interpret the description of a chemical process and present it in a simple format recognised by all chemical engineers (Step 1) and then simulate this process using industry-standard software (Step 2). The in-class tasks are designed to mimic the summative assessment.

When Step 1 was completed on paper with verbal feedback, the reflective cycle was limited to the current session, with no real opportunity for improvement across sessions. The hypothesis was that if students were able to review feedback provided for attempts in previous sessions, the reflective cycle would be more impactful. TU's FFL strategy presented an opportunity to use ONCN to retain feedback from in-class activities, thereby facilitating reflection across sessions.

The overall session plan was not modified; instead, students are now instructed to present their Step 1 attempts via their PW, and feedback is provided on the same page. Students can sketch their attempts directly onto the ONCN page using digital ink or upload a photograph of attempts completed with pen and paper. Those who wish to use the sessions as an opportunity to develop their proficiency in engineering drawing software can upload the completed MS Visio file. Regardless of the method of student data input, tutor feedback is generated by typing onto the page accessed via a browser.

Scenario 2 – asynchronous formative feedback on assessment preparation

This scenario focuses on revision support on 2nd- and 3rd-year modules in reaction engineering. In both modules, concepts are introduced during lectures and understanding is tested via example questions issued during seminars and self-test questions issued for independent study. Whilst worked solutions are provided for example questions, they are not provided for self-test questions; instead, individualised feedback is given for all attempts presented to the tutor. The high mathematical content makes reaction engineering difficult to master, and students have reported struggling with the concepts in both tutor-led and independent study (Azizan et al., 2018); therefore, this tiered support structure is designed to progressively reduce student reliance on worked solutions and improve confidence ahead of the examination.

Traditionally, students would make use of tutor office hours or arrange an appointment to request feedback on batches of work. These requests were typically made close to the examination date, limiting the opportunity for skills development. Furthermore, attempts were frequently made on loose sheets of paper, making it difficult to encourage reflection during revision. It was hoped that a structured formative feedback schedule incorporating the use of ONCNs would encourage scaffolded independent study and enable students to reflect on feedback and update their approach, echoing the observations of Favero and Hendricks (2016).

As part of this initiative, a weekly formative feedback schedule is communicated to students at the start of each module. The tutor reviews the ONCN at the agreed-upon times and provides feedback on presented work; this could be a new attempt or an improvement made using prior feedback. As with Scenario 1, students use their preferred data input method; due to the mathematical nature of the work being reviewed, tutor feedback is typically generated using digital ink.

Scenario 3 – synchronous and asynchronous formative feedback on project activity

This scenario explores the use of ONCNs in project logbooks for UG and PG students. McAlpine et al. (2006) analysed a variety of engineering logbooks and categorised their content as follows:

- Management – meeting notes, personal notes
- Design – personal notes, calculations, technical drawings
- Research – personal notes, calculations, external documents

Whilst a physical logbook was historically fit for purpose, various issues were observed:

- Students would forget to bring logbooks to meetings and/or leave them in public spaces;
- University policy required logbooks to be retained for a fixed duration, resulting in a significant storage demand;
- Students wouldn't maintain logbooks regularly during the project, instead choosing to collate evidence shortly before the deadline;
- Design work was increasingly being completed electronically (e.g. via MS Excel, AutoCAD), rendering physical logbooks no longer fit for purpose.

OneNote's cloud-based operation meant that space- and information governance-related concerns could be easily addressed. Timestamps on all entries would address concerns relating to the timing of logbook generation and enable students to organise their work thematically. Finally, as OneNote can display weblinks, the weblink for any cloud-based file (such as a dissertation draft or calculation file) could be shared to give both tutor and student live access as required.

The use of OneNote for project logbooks was initiated within the Year 3 project module. This module comprises both group work and individual work, and in 2019, MS Teams was introduced as a collaborative platform for module activity to facilitate HyFlex engagement (Gooneratne & Russell, 2021). An ONCN was set up via this team, enabling students to record both group and individual work from within the same platform. Each group had their own supervisor who could review group members' individual logbooks at any time via OneNote.

An ONCN was also used to manage logbooks for PG students completing their dissertations. As these projects are entirely individual, an MS Team wasn't considered necessary. Instead, a single ONCN was created by the tutor, and students were given access for the duration of their project. This module required students to upload evidence of project management as an assessment; students who maintained their logbooks in the ONCN exported the timestamped notebook pages to PDF and no further collation was required.

IMPACT

Due to the small cohort size, evaluation has been primarily anecdotal. Students took longer than expected to familiarise themselves with the expectations, but once the operational aspects had been clarified, they appeared comfortable with the platform and feedback practices. One student shared their recognition of the variety of data input methods:

> Using the OneNote class notebook was extremely easy, and massively helped me for the preparation for my assessment. There were many different ways to submit work and receive feedback.

The use of digital ink by the tutor in Scenario 2 was also appreciated, with significant focus on its impact in differentiated instruction:

> The feedback helped as this was personally tailored to your work. The use of comment boxes and the function for Dr Gooneratne to draw/write over my work with feedback was really helpful.

A benefit of this technology-enabled differentiated instruction is that physical proximity to campus is not a prerequisite for engagement. This is routinely useful for part-time students who attend campus one day per week, but it was a necessity for all students during the pandemic-related lockdowns, as social distancing made face-to-face instruction more difficult:

> The use of the class notebook was a major help to me during Covid . . . as this would allow me to present work whenever suitable rather than on a once a week basis. The notebook and feedback helped me in all areas of my preparation, to clarify questions, check any working I had done and give confidence with the exam style questions.

In Scenario 3, students were apprehensive about the logbook aspect of the assessment. They were therefore pleasantly surprised to find that the informal notes they'd created in the ONCN would satisfy the requirements of a project logbook.

The impact of these interventions on the tutor cannot be disregarded. The use of ONCN for formative feedback has resulted in a drastic reduction in emails from students requesting in-module support. Seeing all student work in one space has promoted consistency in addressing common areas of poor understanding, which has then informed discussion points in subsequent taught sessions. It has also made it easier to spot potential academic misconduct in advance, enabling the tutor to advise students accordingly.

KEY LEARNING

Beware the 'digital native' fallacy

Kirschner and De Bruyckere (2017) opined that the idea of a 'digital native' is a myth, and their study suggested that whilst students do make frequent use of digital technologies, this use is limited in scope and functionality. Their view was mirrored within this case study. ONCN video guides were created for students and tutors; whilst tutors adopted the practice with relative ease, students appeared not to engage with the videos to the same extent (even when listed as required viewing). A live demonstration was the only form of support that had lasting impact, as students could test the features of both OneNote and ONCN in real time. Students should therefore be proactively trained to engage with the platform.

Dialogue is key to differentiated instruction

The privacy afforded by the PW area makes ONCN an ideal platform for 'embarrassment-free' formative feedback. However, this only works if the student is assured of the tutor's support, and Orsmond et al. (2005) found that student engagement with feedback was impacted by perceptions of individual tutor approachability.

Anecdotal evidence of this phenomenon has shaped the way tutor feedback is provided across the interventions discussed here. The use of digital ink to generate feedback for Scenario 2 was in part due to the personal feel of handwritten ink, and casual language was used when providing encouragement, which required a change in tutor mindset with regard to the notion of professional communication.

As a result, students saw the PW as a safe space in which to "reduce gaps between current and desired states of learning" (Narciss, 2013). This was evidenced through their own use of language and demonstration of appreciation in the PW.

The fear of missing out is a powerful driver for engagement

Students who engage with the practice presented here recognise its merits, as evidenced by the comments presented previously. Despite this, overall engagement has been underwhelming when viewed at scale. Winstone et al. (2017b) observed the same trait in UG psychology students and concluded that complete removal of barriers to engagement would require a shared responsibility between tutor and student.

Whilst this aspect is still in development, building a rapport with students has helped to convey the value of formative assessment and feedback. Early adopters of the practice within a class have also been observed promoting it to their peers, which will hopefully encourage more students to participate.

REFLECTION POINT

1) Am I using the correct tools, and am I getting the most out of them? ONCN was used in this study, as all TU members have Microsoft accounts and therefore the platform would integrate seamlessly with their existing technology usage. However, there are several note-taking applications available, and the tutor should choose an application with

which they feel comfortable. They should also familiarise themselves with the behaviour of the application across different platforms.
2) How do I encourage engagement?
It isn't sufficient to assume that students will automatically appreciate the value of formative exercises, nor that they will be comfortable with digital technologies. The tutor should provide appropriate support to remove motivational and operational barriers. The nature of this support will depend on the relationship between the tutor and students.
3) How do I maintain engagement?
Once the initial barriers to engagement have been overcome, it is important to create an environment that promotes continued engagement, as this is where self-regulated learning can be explored. A feedback schedule can help students plan their self-directed learning, and it can help tutors consolidate the time spent supporting a specific module.

22

SCALING UP AND AUTOMATING FORMATIVE ASSESSMENT IN COMPUTER SCIENCE

NEIL GORDON

Discipline and/or Subject/Field: Computer Sciences

CONTEXT

The rise in student numbers in computer science creates a challenge to ensure resources match students. Computer science has some of the worst attainment and retention profiles across subjects (Woodfield, 2014; Gordon, 2016). As a discipline based on development of digital solutions, it is a subject where digital technologies have long been integrated into teaching and assessment and so can be considered to have passed through the digital age earlier than others. Within computing, there is sometimes a tension between the use of technology in teaching computer science, and the teaching of computer science technology. This latter may be taught with or without learning technologies per se. Flexibility in teaching – considered a key part of the post-digital world – can be a challenge with large cohorts and limited resources. Moreover, the practical nature with labs and support means that there can be further tensions between allowing students to take ownership of their learning and in providing suitable support through, for example, live workshops.

The examples in this case study are based on the author's experiences, teaching across a range of year groups, from foundation year up to

DOI: 10.4324/9781003360254-22

postgraduate masters. The author has experience of teaching a wide range of classes. with different class sizes and resource pressures, from small postgraduate cohorts of less than 10 up to large undergraduate cohorts of 300 and more, with very different backgrounds and preparation. This experience is further tempered by the experiences of teaching during COVID, where the nature and use of digital-based education shifted and adapted due to the unprecedented situation.

The growth in computing in general has seen a routine increase in class sizes (IT Pro, 2022). Whilst this is not consistent, and at some points individual institutions see their student cohort go down as well as up, it has created an environment where planning of teaching and assessment is challenging. Given the macro environment, with changes in student caps being removed, with the changing of the fee structure in the English higher education (HE) environment, plus the demand for the specific subject, the expected size of a class in the first-year or at postgraduate level is highly erratic, though generally increasing. For example, looking back at over two decades of teaching practice on a core first-year subject, the class size there rose from around 25 to 50, then 80, then 120. This peaked in 2016, declined briefly for a couple of years, and is growing again, thus making for challenging planning.

As a practitioner in higher education, there are several factors that impact what and how we teach and assess. These include the following:

- The syllabus and subject needs – which now need to reflect the digital environment of education and the world our graduates are going to enter;
- Practical constraints, such as staffing resources, and where digital technologies can help;
- The subject expectations, which typically identify digital skills (e.g., subject benchmarks (QAA, 2022b));
- Professional requirements and external needs such as accreditation bodies, as for computing (BCS, 2022).

STRATEGY

This case study describes an approach to use computer-based assessment that enables students to explore their understanding and competence with activities and assessment to guide and encourage them. The strategy exploits digital assessment, with a hybrid formative and summative assessment to give feedback and engage students in their learning, within a broad range of assessment activities and practices to allow students to demonstrate their competencies as computer scientists. A driving factor is the need for formative assessment to help students develop their understanding, whilst acknowledging the challenge of getting students to do formative work.

The strategy developed partly due to necessity, as a way to address the challenge of variable and hard-to-predict class sizes. It utilises digital technologies to enable flexible teaching and learning, with flexible assessment within the constraints identified in the context previously.

A benefit of the post-digital era is that students generally have the necessary skills and background to be able to adopt and use a variety of digital platforms. They are generally familiar with the idea of user-generated content and of the practicalities of interaction via social media and online platforms. This makes it easier to put together suitable collections of technologies to teach and assess without losing too much time in training and support for the platforms. Of course, not all students are in that situation, so there will be some students needing that support, but for the majority, this is not a barrier and so does not become a resource constraint. The majority still benefit from explanations of etiquette and practice and the need for professional behaviour in online environments, as well as in the physical classroom.

PRACTICE

The approach aligns assessment activity with the teaching activity to encourage regular and routine interactions with learning materials. It provides students with a flexible approach to allow students to have some autonomy on when to attempt assessment (Gordon, 2014). The assessment is a hybrid one, functional essentially as a benchmark assessment (Gordon, 2010) for students to monitor their performance. The assessment is integrated with the teaching materials and activities to encourage them to access these as they attempt the assessment. This utilises gamification in assessments, utilising game mechanics to aid engagement (Gressick & Langston, 2017). The practice is based on identifying the key aspects of a course that need to be evidenced in terms of the module outcomes (intended learning outcomes or competencies) and selecting mechanisms to encourage students to develop the necessary skills, knowledge, and practice. Given the constraints identified in the context section, this has developed over time into the following approach:

1) Provide core and essential learning via lectures (live lectures or recorded ones);
2) Splitting up as far as possible the module outcomes to focus on
    a) knowledge and application activities,
    b) the more reflective and analytical requirements;
3) Identifying suitable assessments for (a) and (b) that are viable given resources and timing, with formative and summative activities utilising digital technologies.

The details of this vary across modules, but in the following short case studies we describe some of the solutions based on the strategy and overall practice previously.

First-year professional skills and development

This first example is based on material developed over two decades. The available technologies and the detailed content of this have changed and evolved into the following approach which provides some flexibility to students, utilises several digital platforms and techniques, and encourages students to engage with formative assessment as a path to their summative outcomes. For the sort of large module with highly variable student numbers, this is operationalised in the following way:

1) Students are provided with the key module content and knowledge via lectures. These are provided live to encourage attendance/engagement whilst also signposting the resources that students should be accessing. Resources are a mix of lecture notes, guided activities, and the module reading list (including websites, interactive digital documents, and more traditional eBooks and other media);
2) The teaching material is partitioned into blocks (essentially into weeks, say, into a 2- or 3-week block), to aid students in managing their time and resources. Students are given explicit guidance on expected time to be spent studying and on assessment.
3) For a given block of material, there is a computer-based (i.e., digital) assignment
    a) requiring students to attend or watch the taught material to engage with the supporting resources to answer the questions;
    b) this activity is typically a formative one in the first instance. Given the digital computer assessment nature, this can be done multiple times.

Questions can be a mix of knowledge based, so essentially book work, and application based, where students must apply techniques and approaches to find an answer. Moreover, given the ability to utilise question banks or computer-generated questions, students can get feedback on their attempts, then retry, so this is acting in a truly formative way. However, it aggregates with the other activities to become a final course mark and so is also a summative part of the module when considered at the end.

As part of its formative role, this block-based approach also enables student engagement to be monitored, prompted, and developed (another aspect of the formative influence), with students being approached and prompted if they weren't attempting the formative activities to remind them of the benefits of doing them in a timely way.

To aid and encourage students to develop some of their other skills, including developing an appreciation of how assessment is carried out, another complementary activity is to get students to write about a topic or issue from the discipline that is in the news. They are given illustrations of different forms of writing within computing, from technical writing, through to writing for the general population, as well as the specialised nature of academic writing.

The students are briefed on the way this would be assessed if this was a summative piece of writing and are shown and have a rubric explained. They then produce their own written piece, and that is shared using the peer marking option within the VLE. The students utilise the rubric to assess other students, and this process gives some formative feedback. Within the course, there may be scope for individual feedback from staff or, where resource does not allow that, to have some more generic feedback on the writing based on sampling of student submissions and highlighting common issues.

The third element of this example is to use group-based projects to encourage student interaction and team building to develop their teamworking skills and to provide more formative feedback from their teammates and from the module staff. One way that this is typically delivered is through setting teams specific problems to solve to generate some form of digital artefact. The focus of the teamwork is the process to achieve the outcome, not the artefact itself. Students can score one another in terms of their relative contribution to the team activity. This includes several stages of feedback so that the module staff can see how people are apparently contributing and can use that to give feedback to teams and individuals to aid their development. The formative elements are those during the process – this leads on to the final summative mark, established by marking the team deliverable, then assigning an individual mark based on the final peer score of relative contribution. The learning material and skills in this example are explored further in Gordon (2015).

Mathematics and computational thinking

This second example has a similar context, with the same sort of changing student cohort. The students have varied backgrounds in mathematics, from GCSE grade C (4 under the current grading), up to advanced mathematics and further mathematics. This created similar resourcing challenges and the additional problem of motivation – since some students often found this sort of material difficult and were antagonistic to start with, not seeing why mathematics was deemed critical to computer science. Whilst early approaches to engagement and formative work included example sheets and in-class tests, as the student numbers moved into three figures, the alternative was to focus on recognising the impact of digital tools for learning and on how to utilise digital platforms for formative assessment. For this module, the approach to operationalise it was to introduce:

1) Interactive digital worksheets to illustrate the concepts identified in the lectures/recorded sessions.
2) Weekly example sheets illustrating the material covered in the lectures, with activities for students to attempt. The example sheets included purely formative assignments as well as assignments that were developmental but also counted towards the module overall summative mark.

These hybrid questions allowed for multiple attempts – formula-based questions and question banks enabled multiple attempts.

This example is an evolution of the approach considered in Gordon (2010), where the author explored the way that splitting assessment into formative or summative does not reflect practice, and it can be better to consider the hybrid role of assessment as both formative and summative.

IMPACT

The approach has been used by the author on several modules for two decades and has been adopted by others within and beyond computing. Student feedback has been positive; they find the opportunity to attempt work and get rapid feedback helpful. Monitoring this has shown how students will repeatedly engage with the activities and have multiple attempts. The gamified approach (Gordon et al., 2013) of allowing students to have multiple attempts (lives) at low-risk (formative) assessments is generally appreciated by students. This approach has been adopted and adapted for other modules and material, including programming and computer architectures and systems.

Providing a wide range of resources, and by routine recording of lectures and live workshops, students have flexibility in how, where, and when they study. The use of low-risk multiple assessments utilises game mechanics to engage students and lets them try and risk failure, knowing they can learn from then process and try again up to the final deadline (typically at the end of the teaching trimester). This is shown by the way that students have taken this opportunity and is also reflected in positive comments in student feedback. The approach can also be seen to be positive through the attendance and engagement figures, which show some of the highest values when compared to other modules within the author's school.

This approach is scalable and can cope with large and variable student cohorts – and is also easier to maintain in the medium term, as the overall structure and assessment can be updated and refined for the subsequent academic session.

One aspect of student feedback worth considering in more detail is where learners identified the use of multiple-choice assessments, with multiple attempts as potentially enabling them to get marks without necessarily studying. However, this approach is commonly used in continuing professional development (CPD)-style activities – academic staff may well do such forms of assessment to fulfil annual training requirements on things such as equality and data protection. This is used where the aim is to ensure that students have engaged with certain core topics and is more focused on the threshold aspect. Indeed, in attempting the assessment and having to reattempt it, they are reading through and considering the issues, even if they are not necessarily going through the longer recommended resources. Thus, this seems suitable for competency-style assessment, where we are most concerned about achieving the pass threshold. The use of assessment as both formative and summative and to ensure a threshold pass/competency and to grade does create some tensions and compromises.

KEY LEARNING

Today's students now expect digital tools to support them in their learning; they expect immediate access to resources and expect some form of rapid feedback. The growth in student numbers, with the change in the demographic and their preparedness, means that adapting assessment to guide and support students is a key instrument for educators. The two case studies illustrate this with examples of rapid feedback and utilising digital tools. Furthermore, the digital tools allow the use of game mechanics, flexible teaching, and assessment, focusing on student engagement and experience.

This is not always easy to achieve – institutional policies on extensions and mitigation for non-attempts tend to get bogged down with multiple assessments and check points. Students may request extensions on formative activities or not engage in a timely way, which makes team activities problematic. Another challenge in developing flexible and different assessment is that it is harder to check – creating assessment becomes akin to writing software, and it is only when it is used (run) that some bugs can be discovered and fixed. This can require a change of mindset – from having "perfect" assessment to allowing for more flexibility in process.

Open assignments can lead to potential collusion or the use of tools in inappropriate ways. If the work is deemed too onerous, students may avoid it or try to circumvent it. This is especially coming to the fore in this period, with the rise of foundational AI systems and the apparent easy access to convincing and novel work. There needs to be a balance of quality and academic rigour, as well as the student experience itself.

REFLECTION POINT

Readers may want to consider:

1) How to use digital technology to give students flexibility in attempting (and reattempting) assignments to ensure that they are fulfilling their formative intentions;
2) How far is your assessment focusing on the necessary skills, knowledge, and application to meet the programme/course outcomes? How do you assess sufficiently but not over-assess;
3) How to identify the most appropriate parts of a course to focus on, with the appropriate pedagogic approach.

23

A DATA-DRIVEN APPROACH TO STUDENT SUPPORT USING FORMATIVE FEEDBACK AND TARGETED INTERVENTIONS

SIMON COUPLAND, CONOR FAHY, GRAEME STUART, AND ZOË ALLMAN

Discipline and/or Subject/Field: Computer Games Programming

CONTEXT

De Montfort University (DMU) has approximately 30,000 registered students, primarily at its Leicester campus in the United Kingdom (UK) but also at campuses internationally, as well as UK-based and transnational education partners. Based in Leicester, DMU's community was particularly hit by the impact of COVID-19, with Leicester being the first city to be placed in local lockdown, extending the period of lockdown beyond the broader national experience. The approaches described in this case study were motivated by the need to capture information about student progress in the lockdown-necessitated online environment but have been equally impactful in in-person classroom teaching.

In the subject area of computer games programming (CGP) at levels 5 and 6, students are required to use theoretical underpinning to develop solutions to practical problems, often demonstrating mastery of learning through completing a single, large piece of coursework over a medium-long timeframe,

DOI: 10.4324/9781003360254-23

usually three–five months. Through the learning and assessment journey, students plan, meet, and reprioritise a series of dynamic sub-objectives. This all takes place during weekly timetabled workshops where most of the valuable learning occurs. These are student and assessment-centred learning environments where learners, facilitated by tutors, incrementally develop their coursework projects. These workshops are natural opportunities to monitor engagement and to provide instant, formative feedback personalised to the learner and directly related to assessment.

CGP as a discipline attracts students with a wide range of learning preferences and differences; the classical approach of 1–1 in-person tutoring may not be the best approach for these students (Amoako et al., 2013). Additionally, the temporary move to online teaching necessitated by the COVID-19 pandemic meant this established approach was not possible. Continual support and feedback are critical in an online setting and facilitated through sustained interaction between tutor and learner (Gikandi et al., 2011). Maintaining this interactivity is important, and it has been observed that continual documentation and sharing of learner-created artefacts is a key feature of meaningful interactivity (Gikandi & Morrow, 2016). In response the CGP team have developed a suite of innovative tools and processes to facilitate the real-time monitoring of student progress through using digital artefacts and the metadata associated with these digital artefacts. This approach provides students with timely formative feedback at key milestones in their progress and facilitates interventions for students requiring additional support to fully engage for best attainment. This approach is grounded in constructivist theories of learning. The individual learner is at the centre of the process, and the feedback process is an iterative, continuous part of learning (Carless et al., 2011; Molloy, 2014).

STRATEGY

Learning analytics (LA) approaches are widely used across higher education (Ifenthaler & Yau, 2020). LA can broadly be defined as the collection, measurement, and analysis of data generated from learners and their engagement with learning materials. Among recent studies there is strong evidence that data-driven monitoring and subsequent meaningful interventions can change learner behaviour (Wong, 2020; Tsai et al., 2020). For example, an early alert application which facilitates instructor-learner interactions showed better academic performance, retention, and graduation rates (Star, 2010). Furthermore, there are indications that LA supports the provision of meaningful and timely feedback to learners (Lim et al., 2020; Zheng et al., 2022). In these studies, feedback is framed as a learning process with both tutor and learner actively involved. Without LA support it is for the tutor in the classroom to determine where individuals are in their learning journey and provide appropriate support and feedback. This case study describes a LA approach which gives metrics on student progress. These metrics allow tutors to give formative feedback to students as they reach a milestone. These discussions can strengthen the students' understanding of their knowledge achievements through reflection after the action. Tutors can also help students consider how to build on their work, smoothing progress to the next milestone.

The approach presented in this case study requires student work and assessment submission to make use of cloud-based storage. It has become commonplace for people to use cloud-based computing platforms to work collaboratively on all manner of digital artefacts and documents. In CGP cloud-based computing platforms are used to collaborate, often remotely, on large-scale coding projects. As professional academics we are required to use cloud-based systems to work together on live documents, presentations, and spreadsheets. Indeed, this very manuscript has been collaboratively worked on by four authors asynchronously at different times and locations; this activity is how the modern world works. What may be less obvious is that the cloud-based platforms that enable this collaboration have to perform a significant amount of bookkeeping underneath. Every edit made to a shared document leaves a digital footprint. The footprint may vary with the system and type of digital artefact, but a record will always be made of when, what, and who made the change. These records are kept so that it is always possible to go back to a previous version, explaining why such systems are often termed 'version control systems'. This digital footprint is stored as metadata, data about the changes to the digital artefact. To some extent the production of such a digital artefact can be retraced and recreated through this metadata. It is this journey of the construction of a digital artefact which is key to understanding where a student is on their learning journey.

The ability to obtain digital artefact metadata varies with each system; however, many systems, including OneDrive and GitHub, provide access via a RESTful interface, a code application programming interface (API) which allows those with permission to extract the metadata through a series of queries. You can think of a rest API as a website used by other computers to access data. As such, rest APIs are not for use by the average end user but rather are intended to be used by computer programmers. This approach allows bespoke, user-friendly interfaces to be built which provide the analytics data to see where a student is on their learning journey and even to suggest when it may be a good time to give some formative feedback to the student to help them progress to the next stage. In the next section we describe how such an infrastructure has been developed and deployed by the authors and how it is used in the on-site and virtual classroom.

PRACTICE

In this case study the digital artefact is a code repository created with the Git version control system (Chacon & Straub, 2014). Git is a distributed version control system that allows users to create, manage, and share repositories. A repository in Git terms is essentially a filesystem folder in which all files and subfolders are treated as data. Every file in a Git repository is tracked for changes. When changes are made the user can view exactly which lines of code were modified and the user can decide to 'commit' these changes to create a new snapshot to which they can return at any time. Each commit made by the user is accompanied by a text-based message, which should describe the changes made in that commit. Thus, a Git repository is more than just code; it is an annotated history of the entire development process.

Student repositories can be managed via the web interface provided by GitHub. However, GitHub also offers a RESTful interface which provides an interface through which custom applications can be programmed to access metadata for each of the various components of the system. These include, but are not limited to, 'organisations', 'repositories', 'commits', and 'branches'. Using these tools, it was possible to create a simple system for interrogating student progress automatically and creating summary metadata (Stuart, 2023). Each student's coursework is a digital artifact in the form of a code repository. As students work on their coursework, metadata about their progress is automatically generated. It is this metadata which provides a rich source of information on each student's progress. This metadata was analysed using a spreadsheet package giving a set of metrics chosen to support formative feedback for each student.

In this case study we examine how this data is analysed and used and what impact that has had on a final-year advanced programming module. For this module we have metrics for engagement. Each student's data is used to place them in one of four categories:

- Have not started the work, zero engagement.
- Have very low engagement.
- Have previously been engaging but not engaged in the preceding two teaching weeks.
- No engagement issues.

This information was acted upon on a weekly basis via a simple protocol. Students with zero engagement were contacted directly. If it was the second week in a row, then the personal tutor was also contacted and requested to follow up with the student. If it was the third week in a row, then the lack of engagement was escalated to the faculty pastoral team. If the student had disclosed a disability, then the university disability team would also be contacted as appropriate depending on the nature of the disability and the data privacy position of the disclosure. For students with low engagement, tutors were contacted and asked to spend time with each of these students to speak to them about their work and ask them what would help them progress. Students whose engagement had declined were contacted directly by the module leader, and lab tutors were asked to speak to these students to make sure they had the help they needed to overcome whatever obstacle(s) had slowed their progress. The module leader and lab tutor could, of course, help the student with subject specific technical issues. In addition, it is mandatory for all staff to be trained in personal tutoring and therefore know and understand when to signpost student to appropriate services within the university and beyond.

Experience has shown that identifying students in these categories based on the LA gathered has had positive impact on attainment and progression. However, it is also possible to take the data extracted from the repositories and produce a broader set of analytics for a range of uses. One such example is the distribution of engagement over time, which is used when assessing a student's professional practice. This data informs the student's mark and has been used in evidence in cases of suspected academic offences. The data clearly shows when code has been created and edited over time, and copied and pasted code shows up clearly in the metadata. In the next section we present the impact this practice has had on attainment and progression for a final-year advanced programming module.

IMPACT

Module attainment data has been collected over four academic years spanning 2018/2019 to 2021/2022. For the first two years metadata about student activity was collected and formed part of the grading process but was not looked at prior to feedback. In the following two years this data was used to give formative feedback to students, as described in the previous section. Figure 23.1 depicts the distribution of grades grouped by grade boundaries. Each coloured band gives the percentage of that year's students whose final mark sat within that respective grade boundary. This data shows a change in student attainment, summarised as follows:

- The percentage of students failing the module has broadly halved.
- The percentage of students obtaining a lower second- and first-class mark is broadly stable.
- The percentage of students obtaining an upper second-class mark has increased by broadly the same amount as the percentage obtaining third-class marks have decreased.

The data does not show a uniform shift in marks of the sort associated with grade inflation. Rather the data shows students in the lower grade areas improved attainment, whilst the attainment of the high-achieving students was unaffected. This suggests that this approach has had little impact on the highest-achieving students. This is not surprising, given the metrics used focused on engagement and higher-achieving students tend to have high levels of engagement. Furthermore, such students often reach milestones before their peers, leading tutors to spend time giving them formative feedback, as they are the only students in the cohort ready to usefully engage with feedback. The remainder of the cohort have benefited from being

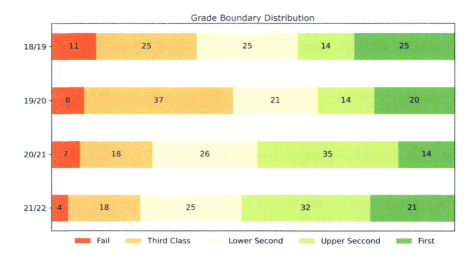

Figure 23.1 Distribution of student attainment by grade boundary over academic years 2018/2019 to 2021/2022.

reminded of the need to keep progressing or perhaps from contact from wider student services brought about by this process. For these students the knowledge of their progress obtained from metadata on their work has improved their attainment.

KEY LEARNING

Ongoing feedback and support are required in all learning environments. An authentic facilitation method for this in CGP is the observation and formative review of learner-created artefacts; with the need to engage with learning online during the pandemic, this also provided an appropriate method for student engagement and support. Students create digital artefacts and associated metadata automatically as part of their assessment. This rich source of valuable information is useful for monitoring student progress and providing feedback and should not be ignored. When using metadata from digital artefacts, having a simple but thorough protocol for acting upon analytics can help identify students who need support and who, with timely personal feedback and support, can improve their attainment. It can be common for students who have not been engaging with learning materials throughout the module to seek help or additional support as the assessment deadline gets closer; it is often difficult to provide adequate support in these situations, and so continual real-time monitoring helps to mitigate this.

REFLECTION POINTS

1) Consider the technologies you invite students to use for their assessments. Could the work be completed on a cloud-based platform underpinned by version control, allowing tutors to review engagement data about the progress of individual students?
2) Where students may be reluctant to ask for help, what mechanisms do tutors have at their disposal to review a student's progress to date and provide individualised support?
3) How can tutors embrace a data-driven approach to ensure fair and equitable support for all students within the cohort?

24

BEYOND THE UNIT

A COURSE-WIDE, ITERATIVE FORMATIVE ASSESSMENT AND FEEDBACK FRAMEWORK FOR ENHANCING LEARNING AND EMPLOYABILITY SKILLS IN COMPUTER SCIENCE EDUCATION

IOANNIS BENARDIS, ALAN HAYES, AND JAMES H. DAVENPORT

Discipline and/or Subject/Field: Computer Science/Software Engineering

CONTEXT

Formative assessment and feedback are increasingly recognised in higher education (HE) (Morris et al., 2021) for their positive impact, including enhanced outcomes, engagement, self-regulation, and student-educator communication. In computer science (CS) education, formative assessment and feedback play a crucial role in fostering knowledge, skills, and problem-solving abilities akin to real-world professional settings. A key aspect of these in CS is achieved through peer review and collaboration in group work assignments. These activities encourage students to evaluate and provide constructive feedback on each other's work (e.g., code, design choices), enhancing criticality, communication skills, and collaboration, which are essential graduate attributes.

However, certain limitations have been observed regarding formative assessment and feedback in the educational setting of the Department of Computer Science at the University of Bath, UK. Indeed, when considering the scope of individual units, it is challenging to assess various topics and skills comprehensively. Moreover, students have limited opportunities to reflect on and utilise feedback before progressing. This is particularly detrimental for transferable and other employability-related skills that need to be practised through iteration to be internalised (Hager, 2006). Finally, the biggest observed limitation is that feedback effectiveness depends on meaningful engagement and receptiveness by the students. Far too often, feedback is used as a tick-box exercise to increase the final grade during the learning process and is forgotten when a unit is passed.

To address these challenges a *course-wide approach* has been adopted offering greater flexibility in planning formative educational interventions across diverse themes. To ensure active student engagement, this approach emphasises *grade improvement*, *professional relevance*, and *employability*, extending formative assessment and feedback beyond subject knowledge to encompass transferable and employability skills. This *programme portfolio* approach allows students to consolidate and showcase their assets to interested stakeholders, providing actual and perceived value. An additional benefit of looking at formative assessment and feedback at a programme level is that it provides the opportunity to receive different *types* of formative feedback from various channels (including peers), which is a key characteristic of any professional computing practice.

STRATEGY

A course-wide formative assessment and feedback approach is a key driver for the current practice at Bath. This approach leverages formative assessment and feedback to consolidate subject knowledge and considers transferable skills and desired graduate attributes. However, several historical and practical factors have contributed to shaping this approach.

Despite the myth of the lone software genius, most software products are the products of teams. Hence professional bodies (in the case of the University of Bath, this is the British Computer Society) require group work to be included in programmes of study for their accreditation. Beyond the requirements of the accrediting body, collaborative working experience and related transferable skills are key attributes for professional placements and employability in general. Therefore, an additional important driver for the practice at Bath is to incorporate group work opportunities.

Moreover, as mentioned before, employability skills must be iteratively practised to be assimilated. This skills accumulation "by doing" and the *scaffolding* of these throughout a unit or across a programme is embedded in active blended learning (ABL) frameworks that are becoming the norm in the post-digital era (Armellini & Rodriguez, 2021). ABL follows a constructivist pedagogical philosophy where students are empowered to actively participate in building their knowledge and skills to achieve the desired learning objectives (ibid.). Active learning approaches are also effective in encouraging students to reflect on this process (Bonwell & Eison, 1991), which is highly congruent with formative assessment and feedback.

ABL is particularly suited for CS education due to its problem-based nature, which fosters higher-order thinking processes such as analysis, evaluation, and creation. ABL is also typically implemented in collaborative and cooperative environments, ideal for developing interpersonal skills (Prince, 2004; Armellini & Rodriguez, 2021). Thus, another key driver for the practice at Bath is harnessing the benefits of active blended learning as the theoretical foundation of an evidence-based approach.

In summary, the evidence-based course-wide formative assessment and feedback approach at Bath aims to:

- Foster group work and peer formative feedback
- Scaffold subject knowledge and skills through ongoing formative opportunities beyond individual units
- Iteratively develop transferable skills and desired graduate attributes, including problem-solving, critical thinking, leadership, resilience, adaptability, creativity, teamwork, presentation/demonstration, and project management skills
- Leverage the potential of active blended learning to enhance student engagement and educational outcomes.

PRACTICE

As established, in Bath programmes of study, integrating and assessing group work is vital for accreditation and employability. Placing it solely in Year 1 does not align with assessment goals (as this year typically does not count towards the degree classification in the UK). Conversely, placing it in the final year, with its substantial weighting (68% of the overall degree programme), is an unpopular and high-risk programme choice. As a result, Bath computer science traditionally included a group project in the second year.

However, this approach has drawbacks. The second-year weighs 32% towards the overall degree, which means students undertake a significant group project (that counts toward their degree) with minimal prior experience. Also, students applying for professional placement at the end of Year 1 or the start of Year 2 lack relevant group working experience to discuss in interviews.

In 2000, the director of studies proposed introducing a group exercise in Year 1, an idea that, while unpopular at the time, was endorsed by the Department Learning and Teaching Quality Committee. The current practice builds upon this idea and is driven by the strategic aims mentioned previously. It is designed to scaffold knowledge and skills across two units in the first two years of study (to optimally prepare students for placement happening typically between Years 2 and 3).

At the core of this practice are formative assessment methods and feedback that allow students to reflect at suitable stages of their education journey. This model aims to empower students towards metacognitive skills (e.g., self-reflection, self-regulation), foster cumulative learning via appropriate sense-making activities, and encourage the use of appropriate digital and physical tools.

Year 1: the first exposure

Competency for developing computer-based systems in a team setting is a key programme learning outcome for Year 1. The rationale is to expose the students early on to challenges such as project management, group dynamics, communication, and conflict resolution. This is achieved through the Software Process and Modelling (SPAM) unit, which shifts student focus away from intensive programming and towards process, modelling, and management aspects of the discipline. In SPAM, students form groups, typically consisting of six to eight students, and are tasked with developing a prototype system requiring the use of technical skills in specification, design, and implementation. At this stage, the coursework specification is rather prescriptive to "railroad" students to the required competence through appropriate assessment tasks.

To support their progress, students attend lectures introducing them to agile principles and development using sprints. Weekly laboratory sessions provide opportunities for formative feedback from lab tutors who also serve as sprint masters, guiding students to reflect on and monitor their progress and development. Students also receive summative feedback comments and a grade on their work. As previously mentioned, degree classifications at Bath are based upon a student's academic performance from Year 2 onwards. In this context, the entire first year serves as a low-risk formative experience. It allows students to develop their skills as they transition into the discipline without the pressure of affecting their degree classification.

Year 2: Scaffolding for internalisation

Year 2 aims to build upon the skills acquired in Year 1 while expanding and iterating on the practice of transferable and employability skills. The formative feedback provided to students in Year 1 (e.g., on their process, use of tools, prototype) becomes crucial in this subsequent stage of their studies. This is explicitly communicated in Year 1 to ensure full engagement with the learning process and the feedback received.

In the second year, the unit that ensures the aims of the practice are achieved is the year-long experimental systems project (ESP). Similar to SPAM, the ESP is not development focused but rather aims to guide students in adopting an incremental software process, using appropriate tools, and managing risks in the context of group-based system production. In ESP, students are asked to self-assign to groups of seven to nine students.

A significant distinction between this unit and SPAM is the level of creativity and autonomy students are expected to demonstrate. While methods, tools, and requirements were previously prescribed, ESP encourages students to use their experiences from the first year to adopt a more exploratory and research-oriented approach. This shift aligns with the desire to help students progress from lower levels of educational objectives, such as understanding and applying methods and concepts in Year 1, to higher-level educational goals, such as evaluating/justifying design decisions and creating novel systems in Year 2.

ESP's assessment requires groups to propose, specify, design, test, implement, and evaluate a novel system solution based on a real-world problem. They are encouraged to develop their system iteratively and incrementally, leveraging user-centred design principles and benefiting from formative feedback from multiple sources, including lecturers, tutors, peers, end users, domain experts, and other project stakeholders. The assessment includes four deliverables distributed throughout the academic year, each building upon the previous one. Students receive formative feedback and a summative mark based on the criteria of each deliverable. Additionally, students reflect on their project's process, project management, and risks in their reports to foster iterative engagement. The third deliverable is assessed through an oral presentation and a demo video to evaluate relevant transferable skills.

The feedback in ESP primarily aims to guide groups on improving their performance in subsequent stages of the project and their studies overall rather than focusing solely on establishing grades. To supplement this feedback, students attend weekly tutorials where unit tutors provide formative feedback on the stage of the project the student groups are in. Students are encouraged to seek peer feedback in these sessions, fostering discussion and comparing approaches, methodologies, and tools used.

ESP's diverse learning settings (e.g., lecture theatre, computer lab, in the wild) and modes of study (e.g., asynchronous, flipped classroom, workshop-style), along with the multitude of tools and technologies employed, demand careful planning. The approach used to achieve this is constructive alignment (CA), where educational activities and assessment tasks are designed to directly align with the intended learning outcomes for a unit or overall program (Kandlbinder, 2014). The role of feedback in helping students achieve their goals is carefully planned within this framework, too (Figure 24.1).

To enrich the learning experience, students attend lectures on various topics throughout the project. These lectures adapt their format depending on the educational goal, leveraging active blended learning opportunities. Some are traditional lectures where students receive formative feedback on subject knowledge through polling software. Others are offered as curated resources and recorded lectures in a virtual learning environment (VLE), allowing students to receive feedback by posting in dedicated forums. Additionally, some lectures are conducted as workshop-style sessions where students use physical artefacts to learn practically (e.g., employing design thinking), receiving feedback on their applied tasks from relevant stakeholders. Flipped-classroom lectures are also employed, where students engage

BEYOND THE UNIT 191

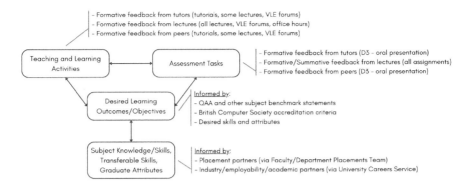

Figure 24.1 Constructive alignment for ESP showing the opportunities for formative and summative feedback in the learning process.

with the material in advance and then apply their knowledge collaboratively in class, with formative assessment and feedback taking the form of peer and cohort discussions (Figure 24.2).

In summary, implementing this comprehensive practice requires meticulous planning and coordination among various stakeholders across the two units involved. Selecting realistic case studies or real-world problems in both units enhances the practice's value and student engagement. Clear guidelines and expectations are established to ensure effective teamwork, task distribution, and accountability within groups. Digital tools and technologies play a prominent role throughout the process, ensuring the operationalisation of the practice. Online collaboration and team communication platforms, project management systems, and code repositories, among other tools, facilitate efficient communication and collaboration among students and educators.

IMPACT

Colleagues in employability teams report in their testimonials enhanced collaborative working skills, technical skills, and adaptability in students who participated in the practice, making them better prepared for professional roles.

> The feedback I have received from undergraduate students on placement this year has been overwhelmingly positive regarding their degree preparation for the placement. The majority have reflected on how well-advanced programming knowledge, understanding of agile scrum framework and the groupwork have helped their transition to the workplace. . . . Students also commented on how the programme provided introductions to industry terms and tools, so that these were familiar when they started their placement.
> (LO, Placements and Industrial Engagement Manager, Faculty of Science)

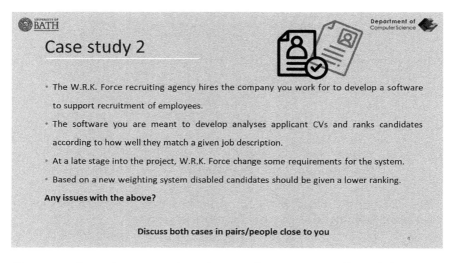

Figure 24.2 Example case study and group discussion on a flipped-classroom lecture on the importance of legal, ethical, and professional practice.

In addition, feedback from industry partners indicates a preference for graduates with experience in formative improvement opportunities in group work settings. Such graduates are better at teamwork, communication, and handling real-world challenges due to frequent iterative evaluation and scaffolding of their applied practice.

> This year our students have continued to impress our placement providers. . . . They are able to work effectively as part of experienced professional teams, contributing to daily stand-up meetings and retrospectives. Students will highlight what they have completed and what they are focussing on next, requesting feedback from the wider team. Students are able to successfully transition into using new programming languages, tech stacks, and technology fields that they won't have had any prior exposure to. Students are able to contribute to technical discussions, sharing valuable ideas and solutions.
> (LO, Placements and Industrial Engagement Manager, Faculty of Science)

KEY LEARNING

Perhaps the key takeaway from this case study is that formative assessment and feedback sometimes need to be viewed from different perspectives (e.g., course-wide v. within-units) and via diverse lenses (e.g., group work setting, different educational approaches) to achieve distinct goals (e.g., academic learning outcomes v. applied employability skills). These considerations inevitably affect the *scope* (timing, frequency, and duration) and *types* of interventions used (educational activities, assessment tasks, feedback channels/forms). It is important that, irrespective of any manipulation to adapt to the learning goals, the key principles of gap identification for improvement, increased motivation, and engagement, as well as self-regulation, remain at the core of the practice. An implicit benefit of this multi-dimensional approach is that students, through the varied opportunities, develop enhanced skills in receiving, interpreting, and utilising feedback effectively, achieving a different level of *feedback literacy* that is transferable to professional settings.

An additional valuable insight yielded by the practice outlined here is that careful *planning* (e.g., through constructive alignment) as well as following a successful, contextually relevant *evidence-based educational approach* are essential. At Bath, the adoption of active blended learning as the theoretical foundation of the practice has highlighted the importance of social interaction and collaboration in knowledge construction concerning formative educational opportunities. Aligning the practice with ABL also promotes the effective use of educational tools, technologies, and physical educational artefacts that elicit meaningful engagement among students as they are seen as tailored around the different tasks. This becomes especially relevant when integrating *authentic assessments* which expose students to real-world problems, bridging the gap between theory and practice.

However, a novel take on formative assessment and feedback does not come without risks. Extending the scope and diversity of types of formative opportunities, particularly across years of study with complex educational and vocational goals, presents challenges. Indeed, risks were identified around the programme-wide nature and the group-working setting of the practice. These were addressed with planning, application, and refinement based on lessons learnt. Examples of risks include the way scaffolding between different units and years is handled coherently (e.g. with tutor mentorship and resources to bridge gaps in skill development); the way groups are formed (e.g. self-appointment vs. based on skills efficacy); equality, diversity, and inclusion considerations within groups (e.g. non-male student pairing or disability "buddies"); and roles students undertake in different project teams across units and years (e.g. rotating to ensure diversity of skills). All of these were tested and calibrated over several years based on student evaluations, internal/external reviews, QA regulations, and feedback from teams/services in the university.

To mitigate potential risks in similar practices, it is advisable to adopt an iterative and incremental approach with frequent evaluation points. This involves systematically collecting feedback from students, assessing actual performance, evaluating employability potential, and monitoring various process-related metrics. Such an approach ensures the ongoing success and effectiveness of innovative formative assessment and feedback strategies.

In conclusion, the Bath case study sheds light on the complex yet rewarding nature of formative assessment and feedback. By considering various perspectives, adhering to evidence-based approaches, and embracing iterative refinement, educators can create impactful learning experiences that equip students with essential skills for both academic and professional success.

REFLECTION POINT

1) What changes in scope and type of formative assessments and feedback need to be made for your desired learning (or other) goals?
2) What is the method or mechanism by which student motivation and engagement with formative opportunities will be achieved?
3) What are the key challenges and benefits of utilising a variety of types of formative assessments and different channels for formative feedback? Is there a theoretical educational framework that could help determine these?

25

FORMATIVE DIAGNOSTICS FOR STUDENT TRANSITIONS AND SUCCESS THROUGH PERSONALISED GUIDANCE

JACK HOGAN AND LUKE MILLARD

Discipline and/or Subject/Field: *The Abertay Discovery Tool applies to all subjects and disciplines as it is embedded within a first year, credit bearing multi-disciplinary micro-credential. This micro-credential is focused on building the academic and social foundations for students' success and is completed by all first-year students upon entry to the university.*

CONTEXT

This case study will explore an institutional approach to using self-assessment diagnostics (known as the Abertay Discovery Tool) as a formative assessment tool that seeks to help students build the foundations for academic and social student success (Lizzio, 2006; Wainwright et al., 2020). The diagnostic tool is embedded within a core first year undergraduate, credit-bearing, transition-supporting microcredential (Millard et al., 2023) that is mandatory for all entering first-year students (Thomas, 2012; QAA, 2022a).

The COVID-19 pandemic created many issues for transitioning first-year students. Foremost within this was the traditional ability to prepare for university based upon a personal confidence in one's academic ability and an understanding of the expectations of the university gained through visits and study days (Wong & Chiu, 2021). This reassurance had been removed by the pandemic, and Abertay University sought to address this change through the creation of a suite of transition supporting microcredentials that can help students build confidence by reflecting on their strengths and challenges and gain direct access to institutional advice and guidance to enable them to set effective goals.

This disruption to the normal process of transition saw Abertay University embark upon a radical curriculum journey to personalise first-year student learning. Abertay decided to build a personalised academic and social curriculum through microcredentials with the aim of fostering a sense of purpose and belonging within the curriculum (Felten & Lambert, 2020; Lizzio, 2006; Thomas, 2012). At the heart of this, transitioning first-year students complete the Abertay Discovery Tool (Hogan & Millard, 2022). Through this embedded curriculum construction, activities within a core module (ABE101 Being Successful at Abertay) were designed for students to create a personalised action plan driven from results received in the formative assessment and wider reflective activities within the module.

A key facet of this new approach was to normalise access and engagement with student development services such as wellbeing, careers, study skills, and the student's association. The aim was to move away from a deficit-based approach to accessing services (something is wrong) to one where it was expected that students should access these development opportunities.

STRATEGY

In July 2020, recommendations from a university working group were approved, confirming that it should initiate developments that would see a microcredential framework implemented for students in September 2021. The development would replace the existing, poorly regarded electives with a new suite of microcredentials (Millard et al., 2023).

A university development group sought to turn this ambition into reality and define the framework. It placed an emphasis on students utilising the framework to personalise their own development journey as they prepared themselves for their university career. The group drew upon expertise from across the academic, student, and professional service spheres.

Strategically, the development aligned with the university's learning enhancement strategy with a specific focus on student transition and retention efforts. In addition, the strategic direction was met through the stated ambition:

> We will extend the range of support available to students and capitalise on advances in technology such as learning analytics and artificial intelligence (AI), where appropriate, in order to increase flexibility, improve efficiency and also enhance personalised student support from the point at which a student accepts an Abertay offer.

These microcredentials aimed to build the foundations for academic and social success for transitioning first-year students. This was structured by introducing a 5-credit module called ABE101 Being Successful at Abertay. ABE101 sought to help students identify successful student behaviours. ABE101 also detailed the expectations of university study (Wong & Chiu, 2021) and allowed students to set effective goals through evaluating their strengths and areas for growth by completing the formative assessment.

Upon completion of the formative discovery tool and reflection on strengths and areas for growth, students had the opportunity to choose three choices options (Figure 25.1). The options mapped against the topics within the Abertay Discovery Tool (Studying at University, Academic Skills, Digital Skills, Careers and Employability, and Wellbeing). Each of the options was delivered by the most appropriate academic or professional service team. For example, ABE108 Your Student Life, which focuses on student representation, getting involved, and living independently, had been designed and delivered by the Abertay Students Association.

From a sectoral perspective, there was also a great deal of interest in this approach, and a funding bid was made to the Quality Assurance Agency Scotland Enhancement Themes on creating resilient learning communities (QAA, 2023). Four universities supported the bid for the project entitled Personalised Approaches to Resilience and Community (PARC). The project has been in operation for three years and has now involved ten universities, all looking at how they can best deploy formative diagnostics to better support the student experience. Project partners explored the use of diagnostics for wellbeing, academic skills, English language, and professional development at both undergraduate and postgraduate levels. Institutional case studies can be found at the website identified in the PARC footnote together with challenge

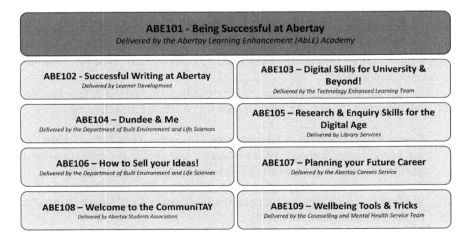

Figure 25.1 Microcredential options.

papers that offer institutions questions at the macro, meso, and micro levels, for those universities considering such a move.

PRACTICE

The Abertay Discovery Tool (the formative assessment activity) is completed by students during the ABE101 Being Successful at Abertay transition microcredential (Millard et al., 2023). All first-year students complete this early in the module, and it is worth 5 academic credits. The purpose is to provide students with early indicators of their strengths and areas for development to enable them to reflect and action plan accordingly. The module learning content is built around the Abertay Discovery Tool and includes topics on navigating institutional systems, a student's sense of purpose for higher education study (Lizzio, 2006), expectations of university (Wong & Chiu, 2021), and successful student behaviours. Broadly the ambition through ABE101 is to set student expectations for study at their new university and to enable them to reflect on the challenges they may face.

The Abertay Discovery Tool is delivered using quiz functionality in the university's virtual learning environment. To ensure the philosophy of the tool as a supportive student development activity, settings within the quiz were carefully chosen. Points allocated to questions were hidden, scores on completion were removed, and the structure of the tool emphasised the self-reflective element. It is important that this tool be seen as a self-assessment reflective activity rather than an assessed quiz to ensure that students understand the positive purpose in helping them to gain insights into their strengths and areas for growth to enable them to be successful at university.

Each student receives instant feedback on completing and submitting the Abertay Discovery Tool. This is achieved through automated marking and individualised feedback which is generated through pre-prepared responses based on student answers. Ensuring students received instant feedback on the formative assessment was seen as important to enable them to proceed with the wider module content using the results as a reference point for their own student development.

The Abertay Discovery Tool includes five sections which cover different aspects of student success. In total 45 questions are asked around the following areas:

- Studying at University – 10 questions exploring study habits, preparing for assessments, purpose of assessment and feedback, expectations of university, and understanding of independent learning.
- Academic Skills – 20 questions identifying students' understanding of academic writing styles, academic reading conventions, purpose of reference, and basic numeracy skills.
- Digital Skills – 5 questions exploring digital competencies, including the ability to work collaboratively in a team environment and the ability to use core software applications such as Microsoft packages.

- Careers and Employability – 5 questions which link to career registration to measure students outlook on career prospects. These questions also considered students' previous and current experiences.
- Wellbeing – 5 questions reflecting the five ways to wellbeing (Aked et al., 2008) to understand the individual student's lifestyle and connections.

On completion of the self-reflective questions, students receive personal feedback with recommended actions to implement within their student journey. The actions relate to advice, guidance and activities aimed at normalising access to student development opportunities. Actions are suggested as short, medium, and long term. The module content introduces students to reflective frameworks (Gibbs, 1988) and encourages them to complete a series of activities utilising the feedback. These activities required students to complete a strengths, weaknesses, opportunities, and threats (SWOT) analysis and ask them to set short-, medium- and longer-term goals. These learning activities encourage students to engage with the feedback from the Abertay Discovery Tool and take ownership of their learning journey. Part of the reflective process encourages students to make an informed choice on which three optional microcredentials from a suite of eight options they choose to complete to fulfil the remaining 15-credit space in the curriculum. The options align with the themes of the Abertay Discovery Tool, with options outlined in Figure 25.1.

To capitalise on the data generated by students, programme-level insight reports are also created. These reports analyse student cohort data and provide insights into perceived student strengths and areas for development for the given undergraduate programme. Included within this are recommendations to programme leaders and module leaders. These recommendations include actions which they could embed within curriculum activities to address the perceived need. The reports are circulated by week 4 of semester 1 to ensure that actions can be implemented quickly and efficiently to address cohort need in the formative stages of their university journey. To support this, resources are provided or referrals made to student development services such as the wellbeing and learner development teams.

IMPACT

The 2021/22 academic year saw the introduction of the Abertay Discovery Tool. Since its inception, a process of evaluation and analysis has taken place. The evaluation considered qualitative and quantitative data, including student engagement and success alongside focus groups and surveys.

During 2021/22 the Abertay Discovery tool was attempted 758 times, and 652 students (96.4%) of the students enrolled on the module engaged with the tool. Only 24 students (3.6%) did not engage with any element of this formative activity. The data shows that some students engaged with the tool on multiple attempts. Focus groups revealed that some of these students wished to track their development and progress through a second attempt.

Reports to students provided suggestions of further microcredentials to engage with (based on identified areas of development), and there is evidence that this signposting led to increased take-up in some areas. For example, the responses from across the cohort for the Careers and Employability section were less positive and confident than other sections. This could be explained by the lack of work experience opportunities students were able to access during the pandemic. Perhaps, as a result, this saw a significant student uptake of the careers microcredential as 67% of first-year students chose to undertake this option.

The aim of the Abertay Discovery Tool was to create a formative assessment which enabled students to become self-aware of the skills required and the expectations of university. This was confirmed by student feedback. Students reflected upon how the Abertay Discovery Tool had increased their self-awareness.

> It helped me identify my strongest skills and qualities and also where I can improve in order to become the best version of myself in my university life.
>
> BA (Hons) Criminology Student

> This has been informative and well structured. It allowed me to identify areas that I struggle with such as procrastination – and provided me with possible solutions to manage this. It also allowed me to identify areas of support from other sources for when it is required.
>
> BSc (Hons) Psychology and Counselling Student

Students provided feedback on how the discovery tool increased their self-awareness. This was particularly important in creating action plans, making informed choices, and normalising access to student development services.

> I found the self-reflection tasks to be very beneficial because they helped me put into perspective what I would like to achieve during my time at university.
>
> BA (Hons) Accounting and Finance Student

> I went through a lot of epiphanies and realisations about living on my own, studying, and problems I discovered. I do thank myself for choosing these modules. . . . I truly needed them.
>
> BSc (Hons) Ethical Hacking Student

Overall, the Abertay Discovery Tool aimed to increase student self-awareness, give students control of their learning journey, and create an action plan based on evidence and reflections. Through this approach, students were able to choose what they considered to be the appropriate micro-credentials options for their development.

KEY LEARNING

The Discovery Tool is under annual review as the team seeks to better understand the implications of its deployment. Through the Quality Assurance Agency Scotland collaborative group called Personalised Approaches to Resilience and Community, external perspectives are sought through regular discussions. These perspectives include feedback on questions, advice, and guidance to ensure the tool is operating effectively.

At present, Abertay is content with the model developed and is now considering the learning from the second year of deployment. Student success rates across the microcredentials is at around 96%, and academic staff are starting to see the possibilities for better relating them to their disciplines. This remains a work in progress and is an inevitable growth point for any institutional change. The number of students taking each microcredential has slightly altered, but ABE107 Planning Your Future Career remains the most popular choice.

The university is exploring the technology that is utilised to see how best this can evolve as there is a belief that a more visual feedback tool would benefit student understanding. In relation to this, the possibility of generative AI engagement is also being considered to support student feedback processes.

REFLECTION POINT

1) How can diagnostic formative assessments contribute to enhancing students' sense of belonging, identity, and connectedness to the university?
2) How can expectations for university be set through diagnostic questioning and feedback?
3) What specific challenges do transitioning first-year students face, and how can the personalised academic and social curriculum address these challenges?
4) In what ways does individualised feedback and recommended actions provided to students through the diagnostic support their engagement with university central support systems and early integration into the university community?
5) How does the analysis of insights and the production of programme-level reports contribute to informing and implementing strategies for further enabling student success?

26

USING AN ONGOING FORMATIVE FEEDBACK APPROACH TO SUPPORT EARLY CAREER ACADEMICS MAKE PROGRESS TOWARDS THEIR END POINT ASSESSMENT

BIANCA FOX AND ADAM TATE

Discipline and/or Subject/Field: *Higher Education Apprenticeship provision/Early Career Academics Education*

CONTEXT

Despite the widely acknowledged positive impact of feedback on student learning, development, and professional identity beyond graduation (Eraut, 2006; Ferguson, 2011), several studies reveal a discrepancy between the effort made by academics to provide feedback and the level of student engagement with it (Winstone et al., 2017b). In the current landscape of Higher Education (HE), there is a growing emphasis on finding innovative solutions to enhance student engagement with feedback and develop student feedback literacy, a term that encompasses students' 'understanding of what feedback is and how it can be managed effectively; capacities and dispositions to make productive use of feedback; and appreciation of the roles of teachers and themselves in these processes' (Carless & Boud, 2018, p. 1316).

In this context, this study aims to contribute to addressing the issue of student engagement with formative feedback and puts forward solutions to increase student uptake of formative feedback by presenting the findings of a case study of how NTU's Academic Professional Apprenticeship/Postgraduate Certificate in Learning and Teaching in Higher Education (APA/PGCLTHE) course participants utilise formative feedback. Through an examination of the experiences and practices of APA/PGCLTHE course participants (who have dual identity, staff and students), as well as the analysis of relevant course data, this case study delves into various processes associated with student uptake of feedback. In doing so, it seeks to address the following research questions:

1) To what extent do students (who are also members of staff at NTU) review and utilise their formative feedback to enhance subsequent coursework?
2) How effective is the formative feedback provided, and to what degree does it translate into improved overall grades?

This case study aims to offer insights into the effectiveness and impact of formative feedback practices within the context of the APA/PGCLTHE course. Given the specialised nature of this level 7 course, the findings of this case study will provide a significant contribution to the existing body of knowledge regarding feedback uptake among postgraduate students. By exploring the feedback practices of this particular group (early career academics), the case study offers unique insights that can enrich our understanding of postgraduate students' feedback uptake as well as inform interventions aimed at supporting the development of Early Career Academics. Moreover, the intention is to provide practical recommendations and guidance to practitioners in the design and implementation of effective formative feedback practices that can be seamlessly integrated into higher education curricula.

The APA/PGCLTHE is a postgraduate course specifically designed for early career academics who are new to teaching in higher education in the UK. In March 2021, NTU's APA/PGCLTHE course underwent a redesign and relaunch. The challenge was to develop content for two long, very thin, modules of 64 and 40 weeks. Considering the length of these modules, knowledge previously organised in modules had to be planned and delivered in teaching blocks (between 3 and 10 weeks per block) designed though a process of triangulation between the learning outcomes of each module, the Academic Professional Apprenticeship (APA) standard (Institute for Apprenticeships, 2022) and the Professional Standards Framework (Advance HE, 2023) dimensions of practice for Fellowship (D2) of Advance HE, two frameworks that reflect a widely recognised set of professional standards for those involved in teaching in higher education in the UK. Each teaching block was designed to focus on introducing essential concepts and theories related to learning and teaching in HE. These concepts and theories were carefully selected using the threshold concepts theory proposed by Meyer and Land (2003). Additionally, the teaching blocks incorporate various scaffolding elements to support the learning process. These elements include problem-solving scenarios, activities tailored to the specific disciplines, work-related tasks, opportunities for career development learning, and networking events.

To shift our approach to curriculum design and delivery, a conscious decision was made to move away from the traditional knowledge transmission model that solely focused on meeting learning outcomes. Instead, a more flexible approach was adopted that prioritises skill development through work-integrated learning. Our curriculum planning and delivery now revolve around fostering skills and competencies through workplace activities. Our vision for developing the curriculum focused on internalising learning outcomes and creating independent thinkers, self-governing academics who understand the value and impact of their teaching and will continue to reflect on their practice and engage in CPD beyond the duration of the course.

The course provides opportunities for both patchwork and synoptic assessment to enable knowledge transfer and support students to make connections between modules and teaching blocks, culminating with the End Point Assessment (EPA). Assessment opportunities allowing for ongoing formative feedback were created, and formative feedback was provided at appropriate time intervals to allow students to have an optimal interval period of being able to recall the origination of work and use the feedback in a meaningful manner to improve future work. Formative assessment was designed to integrate the skills learnt in the most recent teaching blocks and provide synoptic links across the course to help course participants use a range of skills and apply knowledge that will provide insights that will be useful for and draw on their own practice. Through providing this timely actionable feedback, our aim is to encourage students to actively engage with feedback, further develop their work, and better meet the requirements of the APA/PGCLTHE End Point Assessment.

STRATEGY

Assessment across the APA/PGCLTHE course was designed to enable learners to critically evaluate and demonstrate their own development in the context of their discipline, building on their prior professional knowledge, behaviours, and skills. In line with an experiential professional practice-based mode of study, the assessment strategy for the APA/PGCLTHE is varied, which enables course participants to both experience and personalise a range of tasks and feedback opportunities relevant to their practice, including peer and self-assessment, presentation, and teaching observations.

As our teaching blocks transcend the boundaries of a module and to avoid 'silo' thinking (Gibbs, 2006) and the feeling of working to a tight modularised course, the APA/PGCLTHE course offers opportunities for both patchwork and synoptic assessment. According to the Quality Assurance Agency, synoptic assessment is 'Assessment through a task that requires students to draw on different elements of their learning and show their accumulated knowledge and breadth and depth of understanding, as well as the ability to integrate and apply their learning' (QAA, 2016). To support learners in demonstrating their accumulated knowledge, patchwork assessment was designed for each module that feeds into the overarching synoptic End Point Assessment. In designing the assessment strategy, we adopted Winter's (2003, p. 112) view that 'the essence of a patchwork is that it consists of a variety of small sections, each of which is complete in itself, and that the overall unity of these component section, although planned in advance, is finalised retrospectively, when they are "stitched together".'

In addition, we aimed to create assessment opportunities that allow for continuous formative feedback to further develop skills and knowledge, which is one of the key principles of patchwork assessment. For students to engage with feedback, a number of conditions must be met, the most important of which being the need to ensure that the feedback provided gives students a clear indication of where they are in relation to achieving learning outcomes or standards, where they need to progress to and what they need to do to reach the expected level (Sadler, 2010). Our strategy therefore aimed to provide opportunities for formative feedback in relation to the progress made on formative assessments designed to prepare participants for the End Point Assessment. This means that throughout the course, lecturers role model different methods of providing constructive, developmental feedback in line with Haines' (2004) feedback sandwich approach. Haines (2004) suggests two types of frameworks for providing feedback, as follows: the feedback sandwich and the interactive dialogue approach. The feedback sandwich approach includes three stages: 'First, strengths are identified (praise). Next, weaknesses (development needs) are identified. Then, options for improvement are explored – ending on a positive note' (Irons & Elkington, 2021, p. 37). On the APA/PGCLTHE course we used a modified version of the feedback sandwich approach: First, we write an overall evaluation of the work summarising key feedback points. Next, we identify strengths. Then, we outline opportunities for further development, starting from identified weaknesses of the work with clear suggestions on how to address them. Key here is to ensure that feedback extent is manageable and proportionate to the assessment that has been undertaken and enables students to have a clear indication of whether they met the learning outcomes. As a result, we usually identify three to four strengths and three to four areas for development and align our feedback comments to the learning outcomes and the APA standard.

PRACTICE

Progression points through formative assessment and academic and workplace mentor progress review meetings are built into the course, with opportunities for feedback, review, and personal evaluation at each stage. Formative assessment opportunities were included in the assessment strategy to support learners to meet the APA standard and build evidence for the End Point Assessment. Table 26.1 shows the succession of formative assessments designed as patchwork elements to the End Point summative assessment.

In this way, we moved away from what the literature refers to as the traditional 'old paradigm' (Carless, 2015) of approaching feedback in an intermittent way restricted to a series of end-of-module summative assessments and towards the 'new paradigm' (Carless, 2015; Winstone & Carless, 2019) that conceptualises feedback as a 'process' and a continuous 'dialogue' between students and tutors embedded at module and/or course level with the intent to allow students to receive ongoing feedback and use it in a developmental way to enhance their learning (Boud & Molloy, 2013; Carless, 2015; Winstone & Carless, 2019) and academic practice. This approach includes the submission of draft work at various points of the course followed by individual feedback meant to support students to continue to develop their work and recognise how they could use it in the End Point Assessment. This 'process view' feedback framework promotes learning and enables students to build evidence for the EPA throughout the course. Not only does this feedback aim to provide support for the summative assessment but also enable students (early career academics) to develop knowledge, skills, and behaviours that will be useful beyond the course in their own teaching and careers.

The rationale behind this range of assessment and feedback experience was threefold: to support early career academics who are learners on this

Table 26.1 APA/PGCLTHE assessment strategy

APA/PGCLTHE assessment strategy	
Module 1	*Module 2*
Eight hundred-word written reflective piece on your teaching philosophy	
Teaching observations	Review of two research papers
Inclusive practice – a narrated PowerPoint presentation responding to a given scenario	Research poster
Three-minute video tour of the NOW learning room showcasing your approach to blended learning	Written portfolio (3000-word reflective journal with relevant supporting evidence)
Video submission of a selection of classroom-based sessions accompanied by a session plan and short reflective video about your choice of recorded content	Practice professional conversation
End Point Assessment (Summative), consisting of:	
Academic Professional Practice Assessment (APPA)	Written Portfolio of Practice (WS) Professional Conversation (PC)

course to accumulate knowledge and evidence for the End Point Assessment; to assess their work against the learning outcomes and the knowledge, skills, values, and behaviours included in the APA Standard (Institute of Apprenticeships, 2022); and to allow them to undertake experiential learning through formative work-based learning assessment techniques which form the basis of an authentic assessment experience.

IMPACT

The new assessment and feedback strategy implemented in 2021 led to 100% completion rate. This meant that all course participants were able to submit their End Point Assessment on time, either directly to Advance HE (for those on the APA route) or via the NOW learning room (for those on the PGCLTHE route). Building opportunities for formative feedback throughout the course increased course participants' confidence and enabled them to better understand what evidence to collate for their End Point Assessment. This approach also supported course participants to improve their feedback literacy and self-assessment skills. We purposefully decided that at least one formative assignment was going to be shared in peer support groups so course participants could engage in peer feedback. Engagement with formative feedback therefore increased gradually after the submission of the first formative assignment (please see Table 26.2).

APA/PGCLTHE participants said that they had benefitted from being exposed to a range of different formative feedback media, as this has given them a framework from which to trial that with their own students. For example, recorded verbal feedback as a method being structured around the overall summary, three to four strengths, three to four areas for development, and no more than 4 minutes. However, no difference was noted in student outcomes based on the type of feedback received (written vs. audio).

In only one academic year, since implementing this formative assessment approach, the achievement rate has increased from 23.1% to 72.2%, with a predictive 83.3% for the 2022–23 academic year. The pass rate based on first-time submissions is 71% (with only two fails) and 100% since the launch of the new course in 2021. The success rate for the PGCLTHE also remains at 100%.

Engagement with formative feedback has increased since the implementation of the new assessment and feedback strategy. The best engagement with formative feedback was recorded for the elements of the End Point Assessment (e.g., APPA or WS – see Table 26.2).

Data presented in Table 26.2 only includes submission of assessments through the dedicated learning room, which means that exceptional submissions via email were not included in this analysis. However, what data shows is that there were two learners (the same two for both the APPA and WS) who didn't read their formative feedback on the APPA and WS from the May21 cohort and only one APA learner from the January 22 cohort. We noticed that

Table 26.2 APA/PGCLTHE student engagement with formative feedback overview

Assessment Type	May 21 cohort			September 21 cohort			January 22 cohort		
	Total no. of submissions	No. of participants who read their feedback	No. of participants who didn't read their feedback	Total no. of submissions	No. of participants who read their feedback	No. of participants who didn't read their feedback	Total no. of submissions	No. of participants who read their feedback	No. of participants who didn't read their feedback
Formative 1 (Academic identity)	36	35	1	33	32	1	21	19	2
Formative 2 (Teaching observations)	30	29	1	25	25	0	9	9	0
Formative 3 (Module enhancements)	32	30	2	Submitted in peer support groups for peer feedback			21	20	1
Formative 4 (Inclusive practice, began Jan 22)							20	20	0
Formative 5 (Research poster)	18	16	2	25	25	0	12	11	1
Formative 6 (EPA–APPA)	40	38	2	29	28	1	21	20	1
Formative 7 (EPA–WS)	34	32	2	25	25	0	21	20	1

Table 26.3 APA/PGCLTHE student outcomes

	May 21 cohort			September 21 cohort			January 2022 cohort			
	Overall no. of EPA submissions	*Distinction*	*Pass*	*Overall no. of EPA submissions*	*Distinction*	*Pass*	*Overall no. of EPA submissions*	*Distinction*	*Pass*	*Fail*
APA	13	10	3	14	11	3	15	12	2	1
PGCLTHE	25	N/A	25	15	N/A	15	5	N/A	5	0

more PGCLTHE learners tend to not engage with formative feedback compared to their peers on the APA route. However, PGCLTHE learners who didn't engage with formative feedback managed to secure a marginal pass. While not checking the formative feedback did not lead directly to a fail, not acting on the formative feedback did, as was the case for one APA learner from the January 22 cohort who failed the End Point Assessment (see Table 26.3).

KEY LEARNING

This approach to assessment had its inherent challenges. One of the main challenges was to make sure that each formative exchange feeds into the summative End Point Assessment supporting course participants to gain knowledge and essential skills gradually. This meant that the assessment strategy had to be adjusted three times to make sure that we were not over-assessing course participants.

Making clear connections between each formative assessment and the End Point Assessment has massively increased learners' engagement with formative assessments and feedback compared to previous iterations of the course. This was later reflected in better overall outcomes. The new assessment and feedback strategy has contributed to the programme's success outside of NTU, the APA being recognised as the programmes with the highest number of distinctions compared with the sector (Advance HE, Quarterly Call, 2023).

Providing three to four clear areas for development for most formative assignments meant that the process of further enhancing skills and knowledge was a more achievable task, which led to better student engagement. Similarly, through adopting an approach of inviting students to discuss their feedback either in class or by booking a one-to-one meeting further increased student engagement with feedback and meant that feedback became more of a dialogue.

Modelling of good practice in providing actionable formative feedback to students has also proved effective in supporting course participants to better understand their feedback but also enabling them with skills to enhance the feedback they provide to their own students. The emphasis on actionable feedback that must highlight strengths and what to continue doing more of, as well as areas for development and how to go about addressing that area for development, has further improved our course participants' feedback literacy and has transformed their practice, leading to the adoption of better feedback practices across the institution. Furthermore, showcasing a range of formats for providing feedback, including audio, video, and written, has enabled course participants to experience and experiment with different types of feedback.

Informal peer support groups helped to provide a low-stakes setting for students to discuss their feedback and gain peer feedback on the work that they had done. Students were assigned to peer support groups from the start of the course to create opportunities to network with colleagues from across the institution and become part of a community of students. The peer support groups held potential and proved very efficient for sustaining the conversation about feedback and how learning from that can be applied to future assessments and work.

One of the biggest challenges that deserve further consideration is the additional workload for the APA/PGCLTHE course team caused by the high volume of formative assessment opportunities that learners expect individual feedback on. Here, formative feedback opportunities need to be intentional and designed to enable the best use of time for staff and students. One potential solution identified was to split the number of submissions between all members of the team and allow for sufficient time for these to be reviewed and feedback released. Each member of the course team would oversee submissions from one learning room and make sure that feedback on formative assessments is released on time.

REFLECTION POINT

1) How can you redesign your assessment strategy to include feedback strategies that could help students to continuously develop and shape their work?
2) How do you know your students are engaging with the formative feedback provided?
3) Is your formative feedback proportionate and actionable?
4) How do you encourage your students to engage with formative feedback?
5) What strategies/interventions do you put in place when you notice that your students do not engage with the formative feedback provided?
6) What mechanisms do you use at the module or course level to ensure students have the opportunity to act upon the formative feedback received?

27

REIMAGINING FORMATIVE ASSESSMENT AND FEEDBACK

PROPOSITIONS FOR PRACTICE

SAM ELKINGTON AND ALASTAIR IRONS

INTRODUCTION

Framed by a post-digital view of educational assessment, this volume has sought to ground a meaningful analysis of the wide-ranging practices associated with formative assessment and feedback in a practical consideration of how the fusion of digital technologies and socio-material practices intermingle with the diversity of student learning experiences. On account of this diversity, there are many factors that make the effectiveness of formative assessment and feedback complex and far from an automatic feature of conventional pedagogic designs and approaches. Not having access to a suitable means of recognising and working with such complexity can lead to the application of reductive categories of formative assessment, where digital technology tends to be understood as an additive feature of existing pedagogical practices and learning experiences which can be predicted through structured design and functionality (Bearman et al., 2022; Knox, 2019). Though such categorisations may, at first glance, seem to represent a common-sense approach reflecting an understanding that assessment and technology are connected at some practical level, it does not sufficiently capture the subtleties of learning in action, nor is it able to speak with any authority to the

DOI: 10.4324/9781003360254-27

significance of agency in determining how individuals can effectively navigate and work with different materials, tools, and technologies to create new dynamics and relationships for the purposes of learning.

Even with the technological advancements that afford opportunities to enact new approaches in university assessment, all too often this leads to such technologies being used to replicate or augment traditional practices (Bearman et al., 2022; Selwyn, 2016). But technologies themselves do not produce change; they only offer affordances (Fawns, 2022). To the extent that we see evidence of change in formative assessment and feedback practice, this is fundamentally social, situated in the everyday communicative relationships and actions of students and educators, and is part of a complex socio-material environment that includes diverse assemblages of tools and other materials that continually shape student learning and teaching practice. There is a need to consider the pedagogical implications and opportunities afforded by these changes and particularly how educational technology can be used to provide personalised and contextualised formative feedback for learners.

In the case studies captured in this volume, a range of perspectives have been articulated concerning the scope and purposes of formative assessment and feedback. Taken together, the case study work represents a range of different viewpoints – including student and professional (academic) learning development – and scales of application – including module-level interventions, programmatic approaches, and institutional initiatives. As curators of this collection of work, we have not sought to constrain, limit, or categorise these interpretations since they reflect the variation of disciplinary formative assessment and feedback practices across a global academic community. Each case study offers a practical illustration of how digital learning tools and techniques can be combined and configured to provide assessment-for-learning opportunities that generate real-time, actionable insights into individual and social learning processes and provides a timely look into how useful these tools and technologies are when working with the complexity of today's learning environments. With many students demanding greater flexibility to fit their studies around other aspects of their lives, the boundaries between physical and virtual learning encounters are becoming less clear and more permeable (Saichaie, 2020). Digital learning tools and technologies make a different kind of contribution to formative assessment and feedback practices here, providing not just expanded access to resources 'for' learning but, more importantly, open pedagogical layouts and assemblages of tools and places that afford the reconfiguration and redistribution of learning 'through' practice and meaningful interactions across space and time.

In this final chapter, we do not attempt to summarise each of the approaches captured or suggest where any one approach or method might be fruitful or most effective. What we seek to do is to point to practicable considerations and plausible (near) futures that might be taken up by those wishing to apply these ideas in course development and assessment design. For this reason, our treatment is exploratory, seeking to open up further discussion of how formative assessment and feedback might be effectively considered, structured, and embedded in ever more complex and uncertain learning environments.

RECONCEPTUALISING FORMATIVE ASSESSMENT AND FEEDBACK

All too often in formal education, learning designs and their accompanying assessment strategies are predicated on the acquisition of knowledge structured into recognisable, predictable, and straightforward configurations that prescribe content areas to be learned and approaches to be undertaken in the form of an organised curriculum that is largely determined by the educator. Relatedly, it remains a feature of modern modular course structures that many assignments retain a largely summative (assessment-of-learning) function. Students often look to summative assessment tasks to tell them what it is that they should be learning, especially if there is little in the way of formative assessment to help guide them (Irons & Elkington, 2021). The case studies captured in this volume reflect an ethos of 'participation' in how the various formative assessment processes and practices are deployed, where learning is intentionally situated in social practices and mediated through combinations of digital and material approaches and integrated activities. These participatory assessment designs situate student learning in a system of ongoing practice in ways that are contingent upon a range of complex relations that cannot be wholly determined in advance – rather they are dynamic, provisional, and continuously (re)produced and negotiated between tutor and learner.

In leveraging the availability of digital media, the case study work presented has demonstrated how the tutor need not be positioned as the gatekeeper of assessment and learning, but rather, they can take on the role of orchestrator as they arrange and configure tools, resources, people, spaces, and places that form the substrate from which new understandings and meanings are cultivated. Taking advantage of the affordances of digital learning tools and technologies, educators can devise sequences of activities in which learners are intentionally positioned as active partners in constructing their learning experiences through ongoing evaluation, feedback, and reflection. This coincides with representations of formative assessment practice that illustrate a change in direction of knowledge flows, from more conventional, hierarchical, educator-led knowledge flows to flatter, lateral knowledge flows, and a distributed model of learners shaping and influencing how knowledge is constructed. With the assistance of digital tools and technologies, these changing relationships can be configured to encourage mutual collaboration, dialogue, and active learning between students and educators. What is more, in the process, individual students through their own learnings and associated actions may come to influence and help shape things, which in turn opens new possibilities for learning and creativity. This marks an intentional shift in the balance of agency between tutor and learner, where the learner has considerable scope and responsibility for epistemic action (the construction of knowledge), typically within the frame of sequenced activities that have been carefully scaffolded by educators. Ownership and responsibility for learning by students is a key message to take from the analysis of the case studies in this book.

Generative constraints

Key to this shift is ensuring that there is ample time and opportunity within and across modules for students to benefit from feedback they receive and put their learning into practice in subsequent activities. These formative exchanges might involve multiple sources of feedback information and offer a variety of different ways of locating technology and technological practices within a particular context. For this to be effective, both educators and students need to be able to identify what combinations of technologies and tools in use matter to them and how such combinations are connected to and embedded in the broader learning environment. This, in turn, is contingent upon certain 'generative constraints', introduced in Chapter 2 as the ways in which the tutor orchestrates available digital and material resources to guide the student experience towards effective demonstrations of learning. Crucially, by designing generative constraints to be flexible across time and space, tutors can support student agency through a structured series of learning opportunities that increasingly rely on learners making meaningful decisions with regard to their learning approaches. This structure takes the form of scaffolding that comprises types of generative constraints that emphasise a 'process-focus' and make learning more traceable for students by reconfiguring complex and difficult tasks in ways that make these tasks accessible, practicable, and meaningful, allowing students to integrate them more fully into their individual learning strategies. The shared practice of formative assessment and feedback is revealed to be a relational process that is central to our ability to effectively navigate and trace the complexities of a changing learning environment. It is viewed as occurring in context, as dynamic, iterative, and influenced by previous and present interactions with others and how educators and students position themselves. In this sense, formative assessment and feedback is, we argue, foundational to a reflexive praxis being both an approach and a process that facilitates an understanding of how we can continue to learn about ourselves and the world around us through incremental, everyday practice.

Toward a reflexive praxis

Reconceptualising formative assessment and feedback as a reflexive praxis provides a sufficiently broad lens to help us examine and understand the wide-ranging practices associated with formative assessment and feedback that inevitably involve combinations of digital, material, and social approaches. Indeed, in the absence of such reflexivity, it is easy to see how attempts to optimise formative assessment and feedback through such initiatives as the imposition of standardised protocols and templates or outsourcing to digital tools are likely to meet with limited success. A reflexive outlook is also seen as central to the sustainability of formative assessment and feedback foregrounding a form of shared feedback literacy – emphasising the mutual roles of students and staff in generating and making sense of feedback and developing evaluative judgement capabilities, enabling each of them to track and make better sense of subsequent feedback information and how to use it. The challenge here to established educational practice, however, is the implication that existing curriculum designs may not always be set up to facilitate such reflexive work, and institutional quality assurance processes may not encourage or permit the kinds of participatory approaches shown to be so effective in facilitating meaningful assessment-for-learning opportunities.

So, what exactly needs to happen for such reflexive praxis to be more widely and more effectively adopted? The diversity of methods and approaches showcased in this volume suggests that no single approach is to be fully effective in isolation. The development of effective formative assessment and feedback strategies has been shown to involve more than the introduction of a set of integrated activities to modules and curricula. It involves a repositioning of what it means to be a student within a discipline or profession and a reinterpretation of the notion of student learning development over time and across different spaces and modes of study. On this basis, we propose that such reflexive praxis has the potential to create learning opportunities that will be more engaging for students, more effective, more resource efficient, and more equitable in the face of growing learner diversity and environmental complexity. It prompts a new focus on the role of assessment in learning as it is practised by those involved and how it can contribute not just to the judgement of students by others but to the ongoing reflexive work they engage in when making judgements and decisions about their own learning, shining important light on the micro-dynamics of a learner-centred pedagogy.

A present challenge for educators is to understand how the shifting material, digital, and hybrid assemblages of places, tools, and resources can be effectively configured to promote assessment-for-learning that is manageable and sustainable. With a near-limitless variety of potential entry points to planning and implementing formative assessment, it might be useful to focus on certain features found to underpin such practice as captured in the case studies in this volume. To this end, in the following section, we outline six propositions for practice that, in the process of considering their own contexts, educators might use as both mirrors and lenses to reflect on, evaluate, develop, and embed effective formative assessment processes.

Proposition 1: Formative assessment and feedback need to be intentionally embedded in flexible instructional design to allow us to realise richer, more responsive learning experiences for each student.

As discussed in Chapter 2, a post-digital view of assessment places particular significance on the relations among the formative 'in-process' interactions and socio-material arrangements in particular environments and the forms of knowing generated from these. These assessment arrangements need to be adaptive enough to capture and reflect student learning that takes place in practice as students and staff negotiate and (re)interpret formal assessment processes into situated practices and worthwhile learning. They also need to accommodate students' unique patterns of readiness, interests, and modes of learning. This 'responsiveness' is an important feature running through the case study series in this volume, highlighting how working to embed greater flexibility in assessment holds the potential to prompt significant change in the relational dynamics of learning processes in the form of more participatory assessment designs. Students differ in the ways that they receive, perceive, and comprehend information; the ways that they navigate a learning environment; and the ways in which they are engaged and motivated to learn and express what they know. Factoring such considerations into assessment design decisions helps inform a flexible and adaptive schema of pedagogic praxis wherein assessments are at once anticipatory and responsive to individual learning requirements.

Efforts to embed and activate such flexible assessment designs are often challenging and necessarily utilise a range of available digital tools to diversify how we teach and the methods by which educators can evidence and enhance learning practices. Such adaptive approaches are not just geared towards improving the presence of students in shaping specific learning encounters; they represent a recalibration of the balance of learner and teacher agency to set up a series of reflexive and dialogical relationships with and among learners – the comments on a blog post, the peer and self-review of early artifacts, the conversations with a tutor. Superficial arrangements or one-off formative tasks are problematic here because they narrow possibilities for action and thus the agency of students. Adaptive practices shift priorities from conventional, formulaic approaches of content learning to what Goodyear and Carvalho (2014) have termed 'learntime' and an explicit focus on how learning activities unfold, including ways of generating and engaging with a wide variety of feedback information as a connected and coherent process. This needs to be designed into programmes and modules so that students and educators can use it in supportive and developmental ways.

Proposition 2: With the help of integrated designs, we now have access to so much interim learning and progress data for students; these sources of formative information need to be activated as part of a continuous learning process.

There is compelling evidence throughout the case study series to suggest educators are already working with the sociomaterial affordances of contemporary digital learning environments to devise a wide variety of integrated assessment designs. These are most effectively realised when they comprise practicable and recursive sequences of nested activities intended to engage learners in a process of active knowledge making. Through these processes individuals are encouraged and supported to (co)construct their learning experiences and (re)configure their understandings through ongoing evaluation, feedback, and reflection.

Emerging compositional and communicative technologies and associated sociotechnical practices have great potential for affording recursive feedback systems in response to an increasingly complex educational environment. By combining better access to different forms of 'in-process' assessment information with an understanding of how these configurations can come together to inform rich and engaging assessment-for-learning opportunities, educators are better equipped to adopt learner-focused designs that make use of a broader range of tasks, rapid feedback, and timely student-student and student-staff dialogues aligned to assessment activities. From this perspective, what counts as knowledge is not only a matter of what a student knows and can recall, as such. It is their capacity to navigate the wider epistemic world available to them; it is their ability to discern critically what is salient and what is not in different circumstances and contexts; it is their commitment to acknowledging the social provenance of knowledge by means of making connections and their ability to work with others to create collaborative knowledge; and it is their capacity to synthesise, as well as creatively extend, socially acquired knowledge. This represents a broader view of formative assessment where student self-regulation (autonomy) and the attributes associated with evaluative judgement (self-assessment, peer feedback, engaging with exemplar work) are supported as part of the learning process. The benefit of explicitly identifying to students that such assessment tasks are integrative is that they develop a sense that the primary purpose of the tasks set is to provide feedback on their ability to self-regulate their learning, including their capacity to identify standards and apply their capabilities to present and future learning situations by being able to articulate their strategies and approaches in response to certain tasks and/or situations.

Proposition 3: Because we can assess everything (process and product), there should be no instruction without embedded recursive feedback and no feedback that does not directly and incrementally contribute to student learning development and the improvement of instruction.

When feedback is pervasive in the design of assessment processes, evaluations of learning and associated interventions can be foregrounded throughout the learning process rather than serving as merely monitoring and assessment functions after artefacts of learning are completed (Dawson et al., 2021; Henderson et al., 2019b). Digitally mediated participatory assessment designs provide opportunities for new and varied associations and relationships that conflate more than just modes of communication but can offer a broadened range of timely feedback in the form of meaningful dialogue, reflection, and iterative action. Formative assessment is experienced not as an isolated act on its own; rather it is intentionally positioned as part of a wider context of curricular practices wherein the active roles of tutors, students, and peers are recognised and the developmental role of assessment feedback is made explicit.

Flexible and responsive assessment designs emphasise the recursive and facilitative role of formative assessment designed to actively involve students in assessment processes, bringing feedback to the fore of learning through a focus on developing students' ability to self-monitor, regulate their own learning behaviour, and act upon feedback in timely and meaningful ways. Crucially, in such arrangements, it is not just the tutor who is providing feedback, nor is the feedback coming just at the end – in fact, there are many more potential items of feedback than a tutor alone could realistically offer. Through the social affordances of digital tools such as online discussion forums, blogs, collaborative editing tools, and e-portfolios, there are 'real-time' opportunities for extending decision-making in assessment by sharing assessment challenges and experiences across a wider cohort group. This might come in the form of an automated response in an online MCQ test, a select response question where the answer can be immediately checked, a reply in a discussion board, a response to a blog post, or reviewing an aspect of work in an e-portfolio. It might also come through structured opportunities to engage with generative AI applications (i.e., a designated chatbot tool) as a way of providing learners with personalised formative feedback during the learning process. These tools can handle multiple feedback interactions simultaneously, ensuring comprehensive coverage and responses to students prompts. This data can then be used to provide experiences that are tailored to individual learning needs. Such arrangements are most effective when they are set up to support students to formulate judgements about the quality of their work and calibrate these judgements considering the evidence generated through their active engagement in and reflection at regular points in the assessment process.

At the level of the student, such flexible and responsive assessment designs can encourage them to accept greater responsibility with regard to personal monitoring and engagement in learning, teaching, and assessment activities. Such responsibilities may involve no more than regularly engaging with (a) synchronous class activities, or they may extend to more intentional and participatory practices such as contributing to weekly blog tasks or commenting on peer contributions to a public discussion forum. The central change implied through such arrangements means academics must accept a certain amount of ambiguity. Indeed, an important feature of these assessment arrangements is that tensions, ambiguities, and contradictions are intrinsic to their design. Importantly, from this perspective, assessment for learning is characterised as other than information transfer or reproduction; it is a student-directed process of developing, extending, modifying, and reorganising existing knowledge, with the aim of generating and representing new knowledge forms.

Proposition 4: The focus of assessment designs needs to shift from only measuring individual performance to the process of composition and representation of knowledge artefacts through meaningful approaches that trace and evidence the processes of (co-)construction, feedback, reflection, and revision engaged in by the learner.

Captured throughout the case studies series is evidence that educators are recognising the value of providing structured opportunities for students to create and share multimodal learning artefacts and participate in multimodal disciplinary practices as part of integrated formative assessment and feedback strategies. An important feature of this multimodal work is that the constituent activities and products are themselves emergent, stemming from the choices made by educators and students with regard to the configuration of tasks, tools, and social arrangements for the purposes of assessment. The measurable object of learning shifts to knowledge processes and their documentation in the form of epistemic artefacts or knowledge representations – the recorded object, the worked solution, the modelled practice. Amidst the growing proliferation of multimodal genres of learning, teaching, and assessment in HE, where text, image, sound, and data are now inseparable – the social media feed, the blog post, the mobile app, the infographic, the data visualisation – dealing with and designing for increasing diversity and connectivity in representational forms become central to the pragmatics of learner-centred pedagogy.

University learning management systems still tend to separate mode and media into spaces that have a specialist focus on audio, video, or text. This need not be the case and often is not the case in the ways students navigate and combine different software and tools as they seek to manage and negotiate their learning environments. To value the learning that occurs within and through the multiple, multimodal representations available to learners, educators need to devise ways of actively engaging students with the affordances and constraints of modes, media, and tools for the purposes of learning. Different spaces and arrangements have modal affordances that can help to set up assessment-for-learning opportunities. This can prompt tutors through integrated digital media to provide students with more comprehensive formative feedback that personalises the learning process, strengthens the quality of learning artefacts, and fosters an increased sense of agency. In this sense, multimodal feedback experiences are instructional design opportunities that enable educators to use sound, image, text, and animation to expand and extend their teaching and learning spaces, increasing the potential for dialogic learning exchanges with students as part of feedback-rich environments (Esterhazy & Damşa, 2017). Through such exchanges, students and educators receive, process, and comprehend video, audio, and written comments in different ways, which can lead to broader understanding of feedback quality, relevance, and utility (O'Donnell, 2020; Payne, 2023).

Practically speaking, the digital and/or material productions generated through multimodal assessment embody and reflect a students' shared experiences in a particular social context and requires both participation and reification which are intimately interconnected with the everyday formative in-process work students engage in. These created artefacts reflect the contexts of students' participation that, in turn, foreground relations between materials, knowledge creation, and learning. Emphasis is placed on learners being responsible knowledge producers – that is, when they make an update based upon tutor feedback, when they create work for peer review, and when these works are published and shared. This is most effectively realised when the digital devices and platforms with which learners interact for the purposes of assessment are oriented toward viewing, composing, and revising multiple aspects of multimodal artefacts as they are mediated and produced through iterations of integrated reading, writing, designing, discussion, composition, and reflection.

Proposition 5: Formative processes need to facilitate and enable students to think critically and creatively about their prospects, to begin to generate alternative visions of future possibilities for learning and practice, and to initiate action in pursuit of these.

For learning through assessment to be sustained and relevant long term, focus needs to extend beyond students being able to retain information relative to set assessment tasks and predefined content to what is needed for them to apply and sustain effective learning both in the immediate term and into the future (Boud & Soler, 2016). More specifically, this refers to establishing a sense of how likely it is (based on knowledge of the context and its history) that current learning practices will retain future relevance for disciplinary practice – that is, the ability to make informed judgements as to the level of potential future benefit learning has for individual development and success. Practically, attention shifts to how learners can be supported to engage productively in the kinds of feedback practices they may encounter later in their programmes, as well as after they graduate – what Dawson et al. (2021) have termed 'authentic feedback'. Such prospective practice is contingent upon flexible assessment designs that encourage students to look forward in time as well as paying attention to events as they happen with a view to nurturing the ability to anticipate and plan for future practice relevant to their discipline.

Crucially for educators, working prospectively through formative assessment approaches is suggestive of working speculatively and compositionally, as well as being open to creative and inclusive ways of thinking and working that draw on a range of possible methods. We cannot simply combine a series of distinct methods and call them formative; there are tensions and opportunities that only emerge in the combination and configuration of approaches that need to be worked through, and we need to be equally attentive to their unique affordances and limitations. Understanding the concept of affordances is pivotal here, it being a relational construct where the qualities of a tool or task and the capabilities of a person come together to describe what the tool or task offers the person for their learning (Goodyear et al., 2018; Goodyear, 2020). This means taking up methods and approaches and conceiving new ones (oftentimes in partnership with learners) in ways that are sensitive to the practice realities they produce and the potential for future action they open up. In this way, working prospectively is not only about the future but is rooted in the present, shedding light on current issues of concern and opportunities for improvement.

Proposition 6: Educational technology needs to be proactively embraced and used for its potential to cultivate and harness productive diversity and differentiated assessment-for-learning opportunities.

Given the growing recognition of student diversity in higher education, a prominent challenge is providing appropriate educational opportunities for 'productive diversity' where students' backgrounds, experiences, and abilities are actively valued and harnessed to contribute positively to the learning environment (Cope & Kalantzis, 2017). With today's data dashboards, embedded learning analytics, alternative student pathways, and increasingly adaptive learning management systems, new educational media make the organisational intricacies of productive diversity ever more manageable, opening differentiated learning opportunities for students. Differentiated learning is the ability to take full advantage of technologies as a medium for structured learning opportunities as well as unstructured learning (Haniya & Roberts-Lieb, 2017; Jorre De St Jorre et al., 2021). Put another way, it is about connecting the formal learning settings with informal learning experiences, as well as being sensitive to the micro-steps made by each student in the broader learning process. Here, educators need to provide just enough support through formative processes to enable active knowledge making opportunities, creating meaningful spaces for reflection and dialogue, whilst also being responsive to how students make and enact learning choices within the course of the assessment process. Through the backward and forward movement between tutor and the student along the formative plane related aspects of instruction and learning are considered and reconsidered in practice. It is through this mutually informing process that a reflexive instructional outlook attuned to generative constraints emerges. In this sense, the different features of a learning setting are not in themselves generative; rather what educators determine as the form, structure, and scope of what students do opens certain trajectories of agency and action.

Such a view implies a widening and loosening of the boundaries of assessment as spaces-for-learning (Middleton, 2019) to provide greater potential flexibility in how, where, and when learning through assessment happens. This sprawling characteristic of formative assessment, its proclivity to make connections between instances of learning – both actual and potential – brings both strengths and weaknesses. Strengths lie in its capacity to aid personal growth and even create value. What was previously unattached becomes connected and imbued with meaning so that it becomes valuable in new and different contexts. The weaknesses lie in the inherent fragility of such associations. Connections might not be made; important matters or concerns may be skewed or passed over. Inviting greater flexibility in learning and assessment is also accompanied by dangers of fragmentation, as learners become spread across multiple spaces, devices, and media, interacting with different groups of people at different times. A challenge for educators when working reflexively with formative assessment and feedback is how to utilise material and digital tools and resources to devise pedagogic patterns and assemblages that promotes the kinds of learning that help students (re)connect what they are learning with the world around them.

With a growing emphasis on personalisation through educational technology, a further possible limiting consequence can be to overstate the individualised experience of learning, reducing the learning relationship to a lone enterprise shared between a person and some combination of technology. In learning environments and assessment arrangements designed on reflexive principles, complex structured social interaction may not only be managed but leveraged. As soon as the social aspects of learning come in to view, differences are revealed and can be deployed as a productive resource (Hanesworth et al., 2019). For example, providing opportunities for regular, structured peer dialogue and feedback around assessment work in progress and collaborating on shared learning artifacts exposes learners to different perspectives and ways of thinking and makes visible different points of focus and views on knowledge and progress. Adopting such approaches means learner diversity can be harnessed productively 'for' learning with digital technology and tools allowing for assessment arrangements that accommodate and track the different interests, activities, and trajectories of each learner (Beetham & MacNeill, 2023; Pitt et al., 2019).

Learning does not have to be the same to be equal. It is possible that learners can be doing different things but of comparable cognitive or practical challenge and value. Such flexible and inclusive assessment arrangements have the potential to promote significant learning, allowing a more expansive suite of integrated pedagogic arrangements and practice assemblages that span the digital and physical tools and spaces mediating students' interactions with the wider learning environment. From this perspective, navigating such complexity is not solely a technical or technological issue, as has been noted by Fawns (2022) and Knox (2019), amongst others. To work reflexively means fundamentally rethinking the spaces and places in which assessment occurs, as students and educators are connected and interact through a network of physical and technologically mediated encounters, each playing an active role in constructing knowledge and positioning practices necessary for meaningful learning to take place. Students are already using the affordances of different digital tools and platforms to discover and construct knowledge that is meaningful to their learning needs and, as a result, are increasingly coming to expect wider, sometimes ubiquitous access to educational resources. Set against the backdrop of changing patterns of 'distributed' learning and working brought about through the proliferation of digital learning tools and technologies in HE, the value of formative assessment and feedback practice needs to be considered less in terms of singular moments or tasks and much more in terms of reflexive systems and configurational strategies which consider the ways in which combinations of people and practices interact and interrelate, incorporating networked, inter-connected, physical, and virtual learning experiences in which digital learning tools, resources, and places are integral to holistic pedagogic designs.

(Near) future directions

Considered together, the propositions for practice outlined in this chapter emphasise that the contemporary practice of formative assessment and feedback is multidimensional in its concern for the formal and informal social structures of learning, alongside the combinations of physical and digital tools that mediate students' interactions with their learning environment. The range and variety of technology-supported assessment designs described in the case study series shows that formative assessment and feedback, as it is practised, is a product of a dynamic, shared, relationship between the teacher, the student, the digital tools and technologies deployed, and the environment. Increasingly, students and staff connect and interact through a network of physical and technologically mediated encounters to co-construct knowledge and position learning practices necessary for their work in particular contexts. The practical task in front of formative assessment and feedback is that of devising ways of working with, and learning from, the multiplicity of information flows that our educational environments afford. Although aspects of these environments might be new or unfamiliar to individuals (students and staff) and fraught with uncertainty, complexity, and challenge, having the knowledge, skill, and confidence to work reflexively is crucial to them accessing and engaging meaningfully with relevant and authentic information flows to enable problems to be resolved or opportunities to be taken. In this sense, formative assessment becomes a crucial means of 'practical venturing' (Barnett & Jackson, 2020), that is, how educators manoeuvre and position formative processes to imagine the wider assessment experience to prepare students for a multitude of future possibilities whilst also effectively leveraging such affordances to ensure that a diversity of approaches, points of view, disciplines, and cultures are included that, in turn, offer as rich a palette for learning as possible.

Whilst the integration of information processes and learning technologies has been a precursor to fundamental changes in assessment policy and practice amidst the hybridisation of university learning environments; the effective implementation and management of flexible and adaptive assessment requires a reflexive systems perspective on the broader educational infrastructure, recognising how generic pedagogies change shape in the context of different institutional arrangements, academic departments, and educational agendas. Arising here are a range of aspects of flexibility in teaching and learning that we need to pay attention to, including the flex that educators experience in the shaping of their own assessment approaches, how students navigate across the constituent elements of a programme of study, and the extent to which information systems and digital technologies are effectively harnessed and integrated to enhance the assessment process, improve feedback, and streamline assessment information and administration. Each of these factors needs mapping if the full potential of formative assessment is to be realised.

A reflexive systems perspective offers a useful basis on which to conceptualise the role of generative AI not as a source of knowledge production but as a 'dialogic agent' that fosters critical and personal engagement with learning where students are enabled to work with different forms of knowledge acquisition and application as they receive feedback, are challenged in their thinking, and receive guidance tailored to their individual learning trajectories. Though generative AI applications and tools are increasingly able to reproduce or even surpass human performance in the production of certain artifacts (i.e., the written text), they cannot (yet) replicate the nuances, compromises, and workarounds of the human learning journey. The ability to trace individual learner journeys through the assessment of learning processes ensures the ongoing relevance and integrity of formative assessment in a way that a focus on outcomes and products cannot. GenAI, whilst in part necessitating this shift, also provides tools to facilitate and inform learning processes more efficiently. Through adaptive systems and embedded learning analytics, educators and their institutions have access to an increasingly comprehensive and nuanced understanding of student learning across a variety of educational settings. It is now possible to glimpse every step of a learner's educational journey. But it remains the case that the most important aspects of learning are relational, not transactional, and this very much includes how we assess and the ways we encourage students to engage with different forms of feedback information. While such tools and applications will not be without their challenges, and must be appropriately considered and implemented, it is an essential component of formative assessment practice that warrants deeper exploration.

A reflexive systems perspective also challenges the assumption that an accumulation of assessment in discrete modules will cover the programme outcomes, a view the research evidence shows can result in students and staff failing to perceive a coherence to their programme, diminishing opportunities for formative assessment, and a failure to assess the validated outcomes (Baartman et al., 2022; Jessop et al., 2014; Whitfield & Hartley, 2019). Programme-level outcomes generally require complex learning benefitting from integrated assessment and feedback delivered over time (Baartman et al., 2022). Such outcomes are not well served by multiple narrow assignments and examinations with a summative function (assessment of learning), which can lead to students taking a strategic approach to their studies, potentially limiting their broader learning and independent thinking (Carless, 2015; Sambell et al., 2019). Instead, effort needs to be focused more squarely on leveraging the affordances of adaptive learning management systems and associated assistive tools for the valid and reliable assessment of programme outcomes across tasks and over time rather than poorer-quality one-off measurements of individual module outcomes. There is potential, through embedding such adaptive approaches in programme-wide assessment strategies, to reduce the quantity of summative assessment with its accompanying quality assurance load (second marking, moderation, external examining), thus freeing important resources for use in formative assessment processes. This would provide grounds on which to integrate and simultaneously optimise decision-making about students (assessment of learning) and stimulate student (self-regulated) learning through the longitudinal and frequent use of formative feedback (assessment for and as learning). Such connected, programmatic formative assessment strategies would mean that information about learner development is purposefully and regularly collected, creating longitudinal flows of information about their progress. To contemplate the longer-term considerations for sustaining formative assessment and feedback at a programme level means exploring the relationship between a reflexive systems mode of thinking and the integrated practice of assessment more deeply, alongside critical questions about how best to position university assessment now and in the future.

CHAPTER SUMMARY

If anything has decisively changed amidst the pervasiveness of educational technology in higher education settings, it is that a new economy of effort is rendered plausible, making long-held pedagogic ambitions regarding the access, inclusivity, responsiveness, reach, and impact of assessment arrangements more practicable than ever before. One of the key outcomes of investing in formative assessment and feedback in such environments is that of transformed pedagogic practice and an enhanced student learning experience. Thinking with a post-digital sensibility enables educators to consider what practice elements influence learning, teaching, and assessment. This involves purposefully considering how different social and material elements might limit or enhance possibilities for learning across different modes of study, as well as critically deliberating how and why specific educational practices become stabilised, dominant, and influential in certain circumstances. Such an outlook, we argue, opens possibilities for staff and students to better recognise, understand, and consequentially shape and improve learning and teaching environments. When viewed alongside the propositions for practice outlined in this chapter, what emerges is a future that places participation and the relationships that define it at the heart of the way we assess students. An openness to the generative potential of diversity and accommodating flexible and expansive student journeys requires assessment systems and designs that are sensitive to flows of movement and changing circumstances. We have presented evidence that the opportunities afforded by such flexible assessment arrangements cannot be divorced from the context out of which they arise, as it is part of their conditions of possibility and affect. Relatedly, appropriate digital tools need to be combined with congruent and well-considered pedagogic strategies that account for how physical and digital environments, materials, and social arrangements are not only influenced by educational design but also by institutional policies and internal configurations of technology. In closing, we propose that formative assessment and feedback is integral to figuring out ways of learning, teaching, and assessment – whether these utilise digital resources or not – that work for particular situations and individuals and is fundamental to the development of sustainable learning practices for students, educators, and institutions.

References

Abbasianchavari, A., & Moritz, A. (2020). The impact of role models on entrepreneurial intentions and behavior: A review of the literature. *Management Review Quarterly*, 71(1), 1–40. https://doi.org/10.1007/s11301-019-00179-0

Abeysekera, L., & Dawson, P. (2015). Motivation and cognitive load in the flipped classroom: Definition, rationale and a call for research. *Higher Education Research & Development*, 34(1), 1–14. https://doi.org/10.1080/07294360.2014.934336

Acosta, D., Castillo-Angeles, M., Garces-Descovich, A., Watkins, A. A., Gupta, A., Critchlow, J. F., & Kent, T. S. (2018). Surgical practical skills learning curriculum: Implementation and interns' confidence perceptions. *Journal of Surgical Education*, 75(2), 263–270. https://doi.org/10.1016/j.jsurg.2017.07.013

Adams, D., & Chuah, K. (2022). *Artificial intelligence-based tools in research writing*. CRC Press eBooks. https://doi.org/10.1201/9781003184157-9

Advance HE. (2023). *Professional standards framework for teaching and supporting learning in higher education*. https://advance-he.ac.uk/knowledge-hub/professional-standards-framework-teaching-and-supporting-learning-higher-education-0?_ga=2.152346224.811774939.1713245673–1474597852.1713245673

Akcayr, G., & Akcayr, M. (2018). The flipped classroom: A review of its advantages and challenges. *Computers & Education*, 1(26), 334–345. https://doi.org/10.1016/j.compedu.2018.07.021

Ahmad, K., Qadir, J., Al-Fuqaha, A., Iqbal, W., El-Hassan, A., Benhaddou, D., & Ayyash, M. (2020). *Artificial intelligence in education: A panoramic review*. https://doi.org/10.35542/osf.io/zvu2n

Aked, J., Marks, N., Cordon, & Thompson, S. (2008). *Five ways to well being*. New Economics Foundation. https://neweconomics.org/uploads/files/five-ways-to-wellbeing-1.pdf

Albarqi, G. (2023). Padlet as a formative assessment tool in the online language classroom: Action research. In S. W. Chong & H. Reinders (Eds.), *Innovation in learning-oriented language assessment. New language learning and teaching environments* (pp. 181–199). Palgrave Macmillan. https://doi.org/10.1007/978-3-031-18950-0_11

Alder, G. S. (2007). Examining the relationship between feedback and performance in a monitored environment: A clarification and extension of feedback intervention theory. *The Journal of High Technology Management Research*, 17(2), 157–174. https://doi.org/10.1016/j.hitech.2006.11.004

American Psychological Association. (2020). Journal article reporting standards. In *Publication manual of the American Psychological Association* (7th ed., pp. 71–108). https://doi.org/10.1037/0000165-000

Amoako, P. Y. O., Sarpong, K. A. M., Arthur, J. K., & Adjetey, C. (2013). Performance of students in computer programming: Background, field of study and learning approach paradigm. *International Journal of Computer Applications*, 77(12).

Anderson, L. W., & Bloom, B. S. (2014). *A taxonomy for learning, teaching, and assessing: A revision of Bloom's taxonomy*. Pearson.

Andersson, C., & Palm, T. (2017). Characteristics of improved formative assessment practice. *Education Inquiry*, 8(2), 104–122. https://doi.org/10.1080/20004508.2016.1275185

Arbaugh, J., Cleveland-Innes, M., Diaz, S., Garrison, D., Ice, P., Richardson, J., & Swan, K. (2008). Developing a community of inquiry instrument: Testing a measure of the Community of Inquiry framework using a multi-institutional sample. *The Internet and Higher Education*, 11(3), 133–136.

Armellini, A., & Rodriguez, B. C. P. (2021). Active blended learning: Definition, literature review, and a framework for implementation. In *Cases on active blended learning in higher education* (pp. 1–22). IG Global.

Arts, J. G., Jaspers, M., & Joosten-ten Brinke, D. (2021). Enhancing written feedback: The use of a cover sheet influences feedback quality. *Cogent Education*, 8(1), 1901641. https://doi.org/10.1080/2331186X.2021.1901641

Ashwin, P. (2009). *Analysing teaching-learning interactions in higher education: Accounting for structure and agency*. Bloomsbury Publishing.

Azizan, M. T., Mellon, N., Ramli, R. M., & Yusup, S. (2018). Improving teamwork skills and enhancing deep learning via development of board game using cooperative learning method in Reaction Engineering course. *Education for Chemical Engineers*, 22, 1–13.

Baartman, L., Baukema, H., & Prins, F. (2022). Exploring students' feedback seeking behavior in the context of programmatic assessment. *Assessment & Evaluation in Higher Education*, 48(5), 598–612. https://doi.org/10.1080/02602938.2022.2100875

Banerjee, J., Xun, Y., Chapman, M., & Elliott, H. (2015). Keeping up with the times: Revising and refreshing a rating scale. *Assessing Writing*, 26, 5–19. https://doi.org/10.1016/j.asw.2015.07.001

Barnett, R., & Jackson, N. (2020). *Ecologies for learning and practice*. Routledge. ISBN 9781351020268

Bates, A. W. (2015). *Teaching in a digital age: Guidelines for designing teaching and learning*. Tony Bates Associates Ltd.

Bates, T., Cobo, C., Mariño, O. L. A., & Wheeler, S. (2020). Can artificial intelligence transform higher education? *International Journal of Educational Technology in Higher Education*, 17(1). https://doi.org/10.1186/s41239-020-00218-x

Baynes, K. (2010). John Eggleston memorial lecture models of change: The future of design education. *Design and Technology Education: An International Journal*, 15(3), 10–17.

BCS. (2022). *Academic accreditation guidelines*. www.bcs.org/media/1209/accreditation-guidelines.pdf

Bearman, M., & Ajjawi, R. (2021). Can a rubric do more than be transparent? Invitation as a new metaphor for assessment criteria. *Studies in Higher Education*, 46(2), 359–368. https://doi.org/10.1080/03075079.2019.1637842

Bearman, M., & Ajjawi, R. (2023). Learning to work with the black box: Pedagogy for a world with artificial intelligence. *British Journal of Educational Technology*, 54(5), 1160–1173. https://doi.org/10.1111/bjet.13337

Bearman, M., Nieminen, J. H., & Ajjawi, R. (2022). Designing assessment in a digital world: An organising framework. *Assessment & Evaluation in Higher Education*, 48(3), 291–304. https://doi.org/10.1080/02602938.2022.2069674

Bearman, M., Tai, J., Dawson, P., Boud, D., & Ajjawi, R. (2024). Developing evaluative judgement for a time of generative artificial intelligence. *Assessment & Evaluation in Higher Education*. https://doi.org/10.1080/02602938.2024.2335321

Beetham, H., & MacNeill, S. (2023). *Beyond blended*. A Jisc Report. www.jisc.ac.uk/reports/beyond-blended

Bennett, S., Dawson, P., Bearman, M., Molloy, E., & Boud, D. (2017). How technology shapes assessment design: Findings from a study of university teachers. *British Journal of Educational Technology*, 48(2), 672–682. https://doi.org/10.1111/bjet.12439

Berk, R. A. (2009). Using the 360° multisource feedback model to evaluate teaching and professionalism. *Medical Teacher*, 31(12), 1073–1080. https://doi.org/10.3109/01421590802572775

Biggs, J. B. (1996). Enhancing teaching through constructive alignment. *Higher Education*, 32(3), 347–364.

Biggs, J. B., & Tang, C. (2011). *Teaching for quality learning at university: What the student does* (4th ed.). Open University Press.

Biggs, J. B., Tang, C., & Kennedy, G. (2022). *Teaching for quality learning at university* (5th ed.). McGraw-Hill Education.

Bishop, J. L., & Verleger, M. A. (2013). The flipped classroom: A survey of the research. In *Proceedings of the American society of engineering education annual conference* (pp. 5–7). American Society of Engineering Education.

Bjerknes, A. L., Opdal, L., & Canrinus, E. T. (2024). 'I finally understand my mistakes'–the benefits of screencast feedback. *Technology, Pedagogy and Education*, 33(1), 43–55. https://doi.org/10.1080/1475939X.2023.2258134

Black, P., & Wiliam, D. (1998). Assessment and classroom learning. *Assessment in Education: Principles, Policy and Practice*, 5(1), 7–74.

Black, P., & Wiliam, D. (2018). Classroom assessment and pedagogy. *Assessment in Education: Principles, Policy & Practice*, 25(6), 551–575. https://doi.org/10.1080/0969594X.2018.1441807

Blicker, L. (2005). Evaluating quality in the online classroom. In C. Howard (Ed.), *Encyclopedia of distance learning* (pp. 882–90). IGI Global.

Blondeel, E., Everaert, P., & Opdecam, E. (2022). Stimulating higher education students to use online formative assessments: The case of two mid-term take-home tests, *Assessment & Evaluation in Higher Education*, 47(2), 297–312. https://doi.org/10.1080/02602938.2021.1908516

Bond, N. (2021). So, you want to be a registered psychologist? *InPsych*, 43(4). Retrieved from https://psychology.org.au/for-members/publications/inpsych/2021/november-issue-4/so,-you-want-to-be-a-registered-psychologist

Bonwell, C. C., & Eison, J. A. (1991). Active learning: Creating excitement in the classroom. In *1991 ASHE-ERIC higher education reports*. ERIC Clearinghouse on Higher Education, The George Washington University.

Bosse, H. M., Mohr, J., Buss, B., Krautter, M., Weyrich, P., Herzog, W., & Nikendei, C. (2015). The benefit of repetitive skills training and frequency of expert feedback in the early acquisition of procedural skills. *BMC Medical Education*, 15, 1–10. https://doi.org/10.1186/s12909-015-0286-5

Boud, D. (2010). Assessment for developing practice. In J. Higgs, D. Fish, I. Goulter, J. Reed, & F. Trede (Eds.), *Education for Future Practice* (pp. 251–262). https://doi.org/10.1163/9789460913204_023

Boud, D., Dawson, P., Bearman, M., Bennett, S., Joughin, G., & Molloy, E. (2018). Reframing assessment research: Through a practice perspective. *Studies in Higher Education*, 43(7), 1107–1118. https://doi.org/10.1080/03075079.2016.1202913

Boud, D., & Molloy, E. (2013). Rethinking models of feedback for learning: The challenge of design. *Assessment & Evaluation in Higher Education*, 38(6), 698–712. https://doi.org/10.1080/02602938.2012.691462

Boud, D., & Soler, R. (2016). Sustainable assessment revisited. *Assessment & Evaluation in Higher Education*, 41(3), 400–413. https://doi.org/10.1080/02602938.2015.1018133

Bovill, C., Cook-Sather, A., & Felten, P. (2011). Students as co-creators of teaching approaches, course design, and curricula: Implications for academic developers. *International Journal for Academic Development*, 16(2), 133–145. https://doi.org/10.1080/1360144X.2011.568690

Bozkurt, A., Karadeniz, A., Baneres, D. Guerrero-Roldán, A. E., & Rodríguez, M. E. (2021). Artificial intelligence and reflections from educational landscape: A review of AI studies in half a century. *Sustainability*, 13(2). https://doi.org/10.3390/su13020800

Bracken, S., & Novak, K. (Eds.). (2019). *Transforming higher education through universal design for learning: An international perspective*. Routledge.

Broadbent, J., Panadero, E., & Boud, D. (2018). Implementing summative assessment with a formative flavour: A case study in a large class. *Assessment & Evaluation in Higher Education*, 43(2), 307–322. https://doi.org/10.1080/02602938.2017.1343455

Brookhart, S. M. (2013). *How to create and use rubrics for formative assessment and grading*. ASCD.

Brodie, P., & Irving, K. (2007). Assessment in work-based learning: Investigating a pedagogical approach to enhance student learning. *Assessment & Evaluation in Higher Education*, 32(1), 11–19. https://doi.org/10.1080/02602930600848218

Buber, M. (2003). *Between man and man*. Routledge.

Burch, G. F., Heller, N. A., Burch, J. J., Freed, R., & Steed, S. A. (2015). Student engagement: Developing a conceptual framework and survey instrument. *Journal of Education for Business*, 90, 224–229.

Burton, J. (2009). Reflective writing: Getting to the heart of teaching and learning. In J. Burton, P. Quirk, C. L. Reichmann, & J. K. Peyton (Eds.), *Reflective writing: A way to lifelong teacher learning* (pp. 1–11). TESL-EJ Publications.

Burton, J., Quirke, P., Reichmann, C. L., & Peyton, J. K. (Eds.). (2009). *Reflective writing: A way to lifelong teacher learning*. TESL-EJ Publications. Retrieved from http://tesl-ej.org/books/reflective_writing.pdf

Carless, D. (2007). Learning-oriented assessment: Conceptual bases and practical implications, *Innovations in Education and Teaching International*, 44(1), 57–66. https://doi.org/10.1080/14703290601081332

Carless, D. (2015). *Excellence in university assessment: Learning from award-winning practice*. Routledge.

Carless, D. (2019). Feedback loops and the longer-term: Towards feedback spirals. *Assessment & Evaluation in Higher Education*, 44(5), 705–714. https://doi.org/10.1080/02602938.2018.1531108

Carless, D. (2020). Longitudinal perspectives on students' experiences of feedback: A need for teacher – student partnerships. *Higher Education Research & Development*, 39(3), 425–438. https://doi.org/10.1080/07294360.2019.1684455

Carless, D. (2022). From teacher transmission of information to student feedback literacy: Activating the learner role in feedback processes. *Active Learning in Higher Education*, 23(2), 143–153. https://doi.org/10.1177/1469787420945845

Carless, D., & Boud, D. (2018). The development of student feedback literacy: Enabling uptake of feedback. *Assessment & Evaluation in Higher Education*, 43(8), 1315–1325. https://doi.org/10.1080/02602938.2018.1463354

Carless, D., & Chan, K. K. H. (2017). Managing dialogic use of exemplars. *Assessment & Evaluation in Higher Education*, 42(6), 930–941. https://doi.org/10.1080/02602938.2016.1211246

Carless, D., Joughin, G., & Liu, N. F. (2006). *How assessment supports learning: Learning-oriented assessment in action*. Hong Kong University Press.

Carless, D., Salter, D., Yang, M., & Lam, J. (2011). Developing sustainable feedback practices. *Studies in Higher Education*, 36(4), 395–407.

Carvalho, L., Goodyear, P., & de Laat, M. (Eds.). (2017). *Place-based spaces for networked learning*. Routledge.

Carvalho, L., & Yeoman, P. (2021). Performativity of materials in learning: The learning-whole in Action. *Journal of New Approaches in Educational Research*, 10(1), 28–42. https://doi.org/10.7821/naer.2021.1.627

Cavalcanti, A. P., Barbosa, A., Carvalho, R., Freitas, F., Tsai, Y. S., Gašević, D., & Mello, R. F. (2021). Automatic feedback in online learning environments: A systematic literature review. *Computers and Education: Artificial Intelligence*, 2, 100027. https://doi.org/10.1016/j.caeai.2021.100027

Chacon, S., & Straub, B. (2014). Git internals. In S. Charcon & B. Straub (Eds.), *Pro Git* (pp. 357–388). Apress. https://doi.org/10.1007/978-1-4842-0076-6_10

Chandler, C., & Donovan, T. (2023). Effectiveness in practice: Principles of evaluation. In A. Borrie, C. Chandler, A. Hooton, A. Miles, & P. Watson (Eds.), *The applied sport and exercise practitioner* (pp. 189–196). Routledge.

Chang, Q., Pan, X., Manikandan, N., & Ramesh, S. (2022). Artificial intelligence technologies for teaching and learning in higher education. *International Journal of Reliability, Quality and Safety Engineering*, 29(5). https://doi.org/10.1142/s021853932240006x

Chen, H.-J., She, J.-L., Chou, C.-C., Tsai, Y.-M., & Chiu, M.-H. (2013). Development and application of a scoring rubric for evaluating students' experimental skills in organic chemistry: An instructional guide for teaching assistants. *Journal of Chemical Education*, 90(10), 1296–1302. https://doi.org/10.1021/ed101111g

Chen, L., Chen, P., & Lin, Z. (2020). Artificial intelligence in education: A review. *IEEE Access*, 8, 75264–75278. https://doi.org/10.1109/access.2020.2988510

Chen, Y., Wang, Y., & Chen, N. S. (2014). Is FLIP enough? Or should we use the FLIPPED model instead? *Computers & Education*, 79, 16–27. https://doi.org/10.1016/j.compedu.2014.07.004

Chernikova, O., Heitzmann, N., Stadler, M., Holzberger, D., Seidel, T., & Fischer, F. (2020). Simulation-based learning in higher education: A meta-analysis. *Review of Educational Research*, 90(4), 499–541. https://doi.org/10.3102/0034654320933544

Chiu, T. K. F., Lin, T.-J., & Lonka, K. (2021). Motivating online learning: The challenges of COVID-19 and beyond. *The Asia-Pacific Education Researcher*, 30(3), 187–190. https://doi.org/10.1007/s40299-021-00566-w

Chung, J., & McKenzie, S. (2020). Is it time to create a hierarchy of online student needs? In S. McKenzie, F. Garivaldis, & K. R. Dyer (Eds.), *Tertiary online teaching and learning: Total perspectives and resources for digital education* (pp. 207–215). Springer Singapore.

Clayton, T. (2023). 15 education software examples 2023. *Rigorous Themes*. https://rigorousthemes.com/blog/educational-software-examples/

Cloonan, M., & Hulstedt, L. (2012). *Taking notes: Mapping and teaching popular music in higher education*. Higher Education Academy. https://www.advance-he.ac.uk/knowledge-hub/taking-notes-mapping-and-teaching-popular-music-higher-education

Coneyworth, L. J., Jessop, R., Maden., P., & White, G. (2019). The overlooked cohort? – Improving the taught postgraduate student experience in Higher Education. *Innovations in Education and Teaching International*, 57(3), 262–273. https://doi.org/10.1080/14703297.2019.1617184

Cope, B., & Kalantzis, M. (2017). *E-learning ecologies: Principles for new learning and assessment*. Routledge.

Corbett, F., & Spinello, E. (2020). Connectivism and leadership: Harnessing a learning theory for the digital age to redefine leadership in the twenty-first century. *Heliyon*, 6(1).

Costa, M. L., Van Rensburg, L., & Rushton, N. (2007). Does teaching style matter? A randomised trial of group discussion versus lectures in orthopaedic undergraduate teaching. *Medical Education*, 41(2), 214–217. https://doi.org/10.1111/j.1365-2929.2006.02677.x

Costley, C., & Fulton, J. (2019). *Methodologies for practice research: Approaches for professional doctorates*. Sage.

Cowan, J. (2010). Developing the ability for making evaluative judgements. *Teaching in Higher Education*, 15(3), 323–334. https://doi.org/10.1080/13562510903560036

Cowan, M. (2023). Flexible assessment: Some benefits and costs for students and instructors. *Assessment and Evaluation in Higher Education*, 1–11. http://dx.doi.org/10.33422/ejte.v3i4.545

Cruwys, T., Greenaway, K. H., & Haslam, S. A. (2015). The stress of passing through an educational bottleneck: A longitudinal study of psychology honours students. *Australian Psychologist*, 50(5), 372–381. https://doi.org/10.1111/ap.12115

Cummins, S., Beresford, A. R., & Rice, A. (2016). Investigating engagement with in-video quiz questions in a programming course. *IEEE Transactions on Learning Technologies*, 9(1). https://doi.org/10.1109/TLT.2015.2444374

Curwood, J. S. (2012). Cultural shifts, multimodal representations, and assessment practices: A case study. *E-Learning and Digital Media*, 9(2), 232–244. https://doi.org/10.2304/elea.2012.9.2.232

Custers, E. J. (2010). Long-term retention of basic science knowledge: A review study. *Advances in Health Sciences Education*, 15(1), 109–128. https://doi.org/10.1007/s10459-008-9101-y

Dao, X. Q., Le, N. B., & Nguyen, T. M. T. (2021, March). Ai-powered moocs: Video lecture generation. In *Proceedings of the 2021 3rd international conference on image, video and signal processing* (pp. 95–102). https://doi.org/10.1145/3459212.3459227

Davies, R. S., Dean, D. L., & Ball, N. (2013). Flipping the classroom and instructional technology integration in a college-level information systems spreadsheet course. *Educational Technology Research and Development*, 61, 563–580. https://doi.org/10.1007/s11423-013-9305-6

Dawson, P., Carless, D., & Pui Wah Lee, P. (2021). Authentic feedback: Supporting learners to engage in disciplinary feedback practices, *Assessment & Evaluation in Higher Education*, 46(2), 286–296. https://doi.org/10.1080/02602938.2020.1769022

Dawson, P., Henderson, M., Mahoney, P., Phillips, M., Ryan, T., Boud, D., & Molloy, E. (2019). What makes for effective feedback: Staff and student perspectives. *Assessment & Evaluation in Higher Education*, 44(1), 25–36. https://doi.org/10.1080/02602938.2018.1467877

Deci, Edward, L., & Ryan, R. M. (1985). *Intrinsic motivation and self-determination in human behavior*. Springer US. https://doi.org/10.1007/978-1-4899-2271-7

Department for Education (DfE). (2011). *Teachers' standards in England, September 2011*. https://dera.ioe.ac.uk/id/eprint/13187/

Department for Education (DfE). (2021). *Teachers' standards in England, September 2021*. https://www.gov.uk/government/publications/teachers-standards

Dodd, R. H., Dadaczynski, K., Okan, O., McCaffery, K. J., & Pickles, K. (2021). Psychological wellbeing and academic experience of university students in Australia during COVID-19. *International Journal of Environmental Research and Public Health*, 18(3). https://doi.org/10.3390/ijerph18030866

Dogan, M. E., Dogan, T. G., & Bozkurt, A. (2023). The use of artificial intelligence (AI) in online learning and distance education processes: A systematic review of empirical studies. *Applied Sciences*, 13(5), 3056. https://doi.org/10.3390/app13053056

Dong, H., Lio, J., Sherer, R., & Jiang, I. (2021). Some learning theories for medical educators. *Medical Science Educator*, 31, 1157–1172. https://doi.org/10.1007/s40670-021-01270-6

Donnon, T., Al Ansari, A., Al Alawi, S., & Violato, C. (2014). The reliability, validity, and feasibility of multisource feedback physician assessment: A systematic review. *Academic Medicine: Journal of the Association of American Medical Colleges*, 89(3), 511–516. https://doi.org/10.1097/ACM.0000000000000147

Dron, J. (2023). *How education works: Teaching, technology, and technique*. Athabasca University Press.

Du, X., Dai, M., Tang, H., Hung, J. L., Li, H., & Zheng, J. (2023). A multimodal analysis of college students' collaborative problem solving in virtual experimentation activities: A perspective of cognitive load. *Journal of Computing in Higher Education*, 35(2), 272–295. https://doi.org/10.1007/s12528-022-09311-8

Eager, B., & Brunton, R. (2023). Prompting higher education towards AI-augmented teaching and learning practice. *Journal of University Teaching and Learning Practice*, 20(5). https://doi.org/10.53761/1.20.5.02

Eldredge, L. K. B., Markham, C. M., Ruiter, R. A., Kok, G., & Parcel, G. S. (2016). *Planning health promotion programs: An intervention mapping approach*. John Wiley & Sons.

Elkington, S. (2019). Assessment: Understanding the basics. In S. Marshall (Ed.), *A handbook for teaching and learning in higher education* (pp. 72–80). Routledge.

Elkington, S. (2021). Scaling up flexible assessment. In P. Baughan (Ed.) *Assessment and feedback in a post-pandemic era: A time for learning and inclusion* (pp. 31–41). Advance HE Pedagogic Innovation Series.

Elkington, S., & Chesterton, P. (2023). The (dis)continuities of digital transformation in flexible assessment practice: Educator perspectives on what matters most. *Studies in Technology Enhanced Learning*, 3(2). https://doi.org/10.21428/8c225f6e.ef49a881

Elkington, S., & Chesterton, P. (2024). Innovation or inhibition? Factors affecting students' experiences of flexible assessment arrangements – A multidisciplinary perspective. *Student Engagement in Higher Education Journal*, 5(3), 103–125. https://sehej.raise-network.com/raise/article/view/1237

Enders, N., Gaschler, R., & Kubik, V. (2021). Online quizzes with closed questions in formal assessment: How elaborate feedback can promote learning. *Psychology Learning & Teaching*, 20(1), 91–106. https://doi.org/10.1177/1475725720971205

Eraut, M. (2006). Feedback. *Learning in Health and Social Care*, 5, 111–118. https://doi.org/10.1111/j.1473-6861.2006.00129.x

Esterhazy, R., & Damşa, C. (2017). Unpacking the feedback process: An analysis of undergraduate students' interactional meaning-making of feedback comments. *Studies in Higher Education*, 44(2), 260–274. https://doi.org/10.1080/03075079.2017.1359249

Falloon, G. (2009). Using avatars and virtual environments in learning: What do they have to offer? *British Journal of Educational Technology*, 41(1), 108–122. https://doi.org/10.1111/j.1467-8535.2009.00991.x

Farmus, L., Cribbie, R. A., & Rotondi, M. A. (2020). The flipped classroom in introductory statistics: Early evidence from a systematic review and meta-analysis. *Journal of Statistics Education*, 28(3), 316–325. https://doi.org/10.1080/10691898.2020.1834475

Fatima, S. S., Amin, B., & Yusuf, M. Z. (2023). Pecha Kucha in medical education: Promoting self-directed learning. *Medical Education*, 57(5), 468–469. https://doi.org/10.1111/medu.15059

Fatima, S. S., Idrees, R., Jabeen, K., Sabzwari, S., & Khan, S. (2021). Online assessment in undergraduate medical education: Challenges and solutions from a LMIC university. *Pakistan Journal of Medical Science*, 37(4), 945–951. https://doi.org/10.12669/pjms.37.4.3948

Favero, T. G., & Hendricks, N. (2016). Student exam analysis (debriefing) promotes positive changes in exam preparation and learning. *Advances in Physiology Education*, 40(3), 323–328.

Fawns, T. (2019). Postdigital education in design and practice. *Postdigital Science and Education*, 1(1), 132–145. https://doi.org/10.1007/s42438-018-0021-8

Fawns, T. (2022). An entangled pedagogy: Looking beyond the pedagogy – technology dichotomy. *Postdigital Science Education*, 4, 711–728. https://doi.org/10.1007/s42438-022-00302-7

Fawns, T., Aitken, G., Jones, D., & Gravett, K. (2022). Beyond technology in online postgraduate education. *Postdigital Science Education*, 4, 557–572. https://doi.org/10.1007/s42438-021-00277-x

Felten, P., & Lambert, L. M. (2020). *Relationship-rich education – how human connections drive success in college*. John Hopkins University Press.

Ferguson, P. (2011). Student perceptions of quality feedback in teacher education. *Assessment & Evaluation in Higher Education*, 36, 51–62. https://doi.org/10.1080/02602930903197883

Festinger, L. (1962). Cognitive dissonance. *Scientific American*, 207(4), 93–106.

Fischer, J., Bearman, M., Boud, D., & Tai, J. (2024). How does assessment drive learning? A focus on students' development of evaluative judgement. *Assessment & Evaluation in Higher Education*, 49(2), 233–245. https://doi.org/10.1080/02602938.2023.2206986

Fisher, K. (2003). Demystifying critical reflection: Defining criteria for assessment. *Higher Education Research & Development*, 22(3), 313–325. https://doi.org/10.1080/0729436032000145167

Fleet, P. (2017). 'I've heard there was a secret chord': Do we need to teach music notation in UK Popular Music Studies? In G. Smith, Z. Moir, M. Brennan, S. Rambarran, & P. Kirkma (Eds.), *The Routledge research companion to popular music education* (pp. 166–176). Routledge.

Fung, D. (2016). *A connected curriculum for higher education*. UCL Press.

Gebre, E. (2013). Students' engagement in technology rich classrooms and its relationship to professors' conceptions of effective teaching. *British Journal of Educational Technology*, 45(1), 83–1. https://doi.org/10.1111/bjet.12001

GeneralMedical Council (GMC). (2018). *Outcomes for graduates*. www.gmc-uk.org/-/media/documents/outcomes-for-graduates-2020_pdf-84622587.pdf

Gerring, J. (2006). *Case study research: Principles and practices*. Cambridge University Press.

Gibbs, G. (1988). *Learning by doing: A guide to teaching and learning methods*. Further Education Unit. Oxford Polytechnic.

Gibbs, G. (2006). Why assessment is changing. In C. Bryan & K. Clegg (Eds.), *Innovative assessment in higher education* (pp. 31–42). Routledge.

Gibson, R. M., & Morison, G. (2021). Improving student engagement and active learning with embedded automated self-assessment quizzes: Case study in computer system architecture design. In *Lecture notes in networks and systems 2021 computing conference*, London, United Kingdom.

Gikandi, J. W., & Morrow, D. (2016). Designing and implementing peer formative feedback within online learning environments. *Technology, Pedagogy and Education*, 25(2), 153–170. https://doi.org/10.1080/1475939X.2015.1058853

Gikandi, J. W., Morrow, D., & Davis, N. E. (2011). Online formative assessment in higher education: A review of the literature. *Computers & education*, 57(4), 2333–2351. https://doi.org/10.1016/j.compedu.2011.06.004

Gilster, P. (1997). *Digital literacy*. Wiley Computer Pub.

Gipps, C. (2002). Sociocultural perspectives on assessment. In G. Wells & G. Claxton (Eds.), *Learning for life in the 21st century: Sociocultural perspectives on the future of education* (pp. 73–83). Blackwell Publishing.

Goncharova, M. S., & Gorbunova, I. B. (2020). Mobile technologies in the process of teaching music theory. *Propósitos y Representaciones*, 8(SPE3), e705. https://doi.org/10.20511/pyr2020.v8nSPE3.705.

Goodyear, P. (2020). Design and co-configuration for hybrid learning: Theorising the practices of learning space design. *British Journal of Educational Technology*, 51(4), 1045–1060. https://doi.org/10.1111/bjet.12925

Goodyear, P., & Carvalho, L. (2014). Framing the analysis of learning network architectures. In L. Carvalho & P. Goodyear (Eds.), *The architecture of productive learning networks* (pp. 48–70). Routledge.

Goodyear, P., Carvalho, L., Hodgson, V., & de Laat, M. (2017). Conclusion – place-based spaces for networked learning: Emerging themes and issues. In L. Carvalho, P. Goodyear, & M. de Laat (Eds.), *Place-based spaces for networked learning* (pp. 242–260). Routledge.

Goodyear, P., Ellis, R. A., Marmot, A. (2018). Learning spaces research: Framing actionable knowledge. In R. Ellis, & P. Goodyear (Eds.), *Spaces of teaching and learning. understanding teaching-learning practice* (pp. 1–11). Springer, Singapore. https://doi.org/10.1007/978-981-10-7155-3_12

Gooneratne, S., & Russell, P. (2021). An investigation into the use of the Microsoft Office 365 toolkit to manage group projects in undergraduate chemical engineering. In *ChemEngDayUK: Making knowledge work* (April, 2021).

Gordon, N. A. (2010). Enabling personalised learning through formative and summative assessment. In J. O'Donoghue (Ed.), *Technology-supported environments for personalized learning: Methods and case studies* (pp. 268–284). IGI Global.

Gordon, N. A. (2014). *Flexible pedagogies: Technology-enhanced learning*. The Higher Education Academy, pp. 1–24. www.advance-he.ac.uk/knowledge-hub/flexible-pedagogies-technology-enhanced-learning

Gordon, N. A. (2015). Sustainable development as a framework for ethics and skills in higher education computing courses. In W. L. Filho, L. Brandli, O. Kuzetsova, & A. M. F. do Paco (Eds.), *Integrative approaches to sustainable development at university level: Making the links* (pp. 345–357). Springer.

Gordon, N. A. (2016). *Issues in retention and attainment in computer science*. Higher Education Academy. www.advance-he.ac.uk/knowledge-hub/issues-retention-and-attainment-computer-science

Gordon, N. A., Brayshaw, M., & Grey, S. (2013). Maximising gain for minimal pain: Utilising natural game mechanics. *Innovation in Teaching and Learning in Information and Computer Sciences*, 12(1), 27–38. https://doi.org/10.11120/ital.2013.00004

Gourlay, L. (2021). There is no "virtual learning": The materiality of digital education. *Journal of New Approaches in Educational Research*, 10(1), 57–66. https://doi.org/10.7821/NAER.2021.1.649

Gourlay, L., & Oliver, M. (2018). *Student engagement in the digital university: Sociomaterial assemblages*. Routledge.

Gravett, K., Kinchin, I. M., Winstone, N. E., Balloo, K., Heron, M., Hosein, A., & Medland, E. (2020). The development of academics' feedback literacy: Experiences of learning from critical feedback via scholarly peer review. *Assessment & Evaluation in Higher Education*, 45(5), 651–665. https://doi.org/10.1080/02602938.2019.1686749

Gravett, K., Taylor, C. A., & Fairchild, N. (2021). Pedagogies of mattering: Re-conceptualising relational pedagogies in higher education. *Teaching in Higher Education*, 29(2), 388–403. https://doi.org/10.1080/13562517.2021.1989580

Gressick, J., & Langston, J. B. (2017). The guided classroom: Using gamification to engage and motivate undergraduates. *Journal of the Scholarship of Teaching and Learning*, 17(3), 109–123. https://doi.org/10.14434/v17i3.22119

Hafner, C. A., & Ho, W. Y. J. (2020). Assessing digital multimodal composing in second language writing: Towards a process-based model. *Journal of Second Language Writing*, 47, 100710. https://doi.org/10.1016/j.jslw.2020.100710

Hager, P. (2006). Nature and development of generic attributes. In P. Hager & S. Holland (Eds.), *Graduate attributes, learning and employability* (pp. 17–47). Springer Netherlands.

Haines, C. (2004). *Assessing students' written work: Marking essays and reports*. Routledge. https://doi.org/10.4324/9780203465110

Hanauer, D. I., & Dolan, E. L. (2013). The project ownership survey: Measuring differences in scientific inquiry experiences. *CBE—Life Sciences Education*, 13(1), 149–158. https://www.lifescied.org/doi/epdf/10.1187/cbe.13-06-0123

Haneda, M., & Wells, G. (2000). Writing in knowledge-building communities. *Research in the Teaching of English*, 34, 430–457.

Handley, K., & Williams, L. (2011). From copying to learning: Using exemplars to engage students with assessment criteria and feedback. *Assessment & Evaluation in Higher Education*, 36(1), 95–108. https://doi.org/10.1080/02602930903201669

Hanesworth, P., Bracken, S., & Elkington, S. (2019). A typology for a social justice approach to assessment: Learning from universal design and culturally sustaining pedagogy. *Teaching in Higher Education*, 24(1), 98–114. https://doi.org/10.1080/13562517.2018.1465405

Haniya, S., & Roberts-Lieb, S. (2017). Differentiated learning: Diversity dimensions of e-learning. In B. Cope & M. Kalantzis (Eds.), *E-Learning ecologies: Principles for new learning and assessment* (pp. 183–206). Routledge.

Harvey, A., Andrewartha, L., Edwards, D., Clarke, J., & Reyes, K. (2017). Student equity and employability in higher education. In *Report for the Australian Government Department of Education and Training*. Centre for Higher Education Equity and Diversity Research, La Trobe University.

Henderson, M., Phillips, M., Ryan, T., Boud, D., Dawson, P., Molloy, E., & Mahoney, P. (2019a). Conditions that enable effective feedback. *Higher Education Research & Development*, 38(7), 1401–1416. https://doi.org/10.1080/07294360.2019.1657807

Henderson, M., Ryan, T., Boud, D., Dawson, P., Phillips, M., Molloy, E., & Mahoney, P. (2019b). The usefulness of feedback. *Active Learning in Higher Education*. https://doi.org/10.1177/1469787419872393

Henderson, M., Selwyn, N., & Aston, R. (2017). What works and why? Student perceptions of 'useful' digital technology in university teaching and learning. *Studies in Higher Education*, 42(8), 1567–1579. https://doi.org/10.1080/03075079.2015.1007946

Henning, J. E. (2008). *The art of discussion-based teaching: Opening up conversation in the classroom*. Routledge.

Herrington, A., & Herrington, J. (2006). *Authentic learning environments in higher education*. Information Science Pub.

HESA. (2023). *Where do HE students study?* Retrieved October 27, 2023, from www.hesa.ac.uk/data-and-analysis/students/where-study

Hinchliffe, T. (2020). The hidden curriculum of higher education: An introduction. In T. Hinchliffe (Ed.), *The Hidden Curriculum of Higher Education* (pp. 2–4). York Advance HE.

Hodgson, D. M., Goldingay, S., Boddy, J., Nipperess, S., & Watts, L. (2021). Problematising artificial intelligence in social work education: Challenges, issues and possibilities. *British Journal of Social Work*, 52(4), 1878–1895. https://doi.org/10.1093/bjsw/bcab168

Hogan, J., & Millard, L. (2022). *Personalised approaches to resilience and community (PARC) – Building academic and social success*: Abertay Discovery Tool. 1. www.enhancementthemes.ac.uk/resilient-learning-communities/flexible-and-accessible-learning/parc#

Hon, A. (2022). *You've been played: How corporations, governments and schools use games to control us all*. Swift Press.

Howell, A. J., & Demuynck, K. M. (2023). Psychological flexibility and the eudaimonic activity model: Testing associations among psychological flexibility, need satisfaction, and subjective well-being. *Journal of Contextual Behavioural Science, 27*, 65–71. https://doi.org/10.1016/j.jcbs.2022.12.002

Hughes, C., & Tight, M. (2021). *Learning gain in higher education* (vol. 14), International Perspectives on Higher Education Research. Emerald Publishing Limited.

Huntley, E., Johnson, L., & Napier, S. (2023). Reflective practice: The core of professional and personal learning. In A. Borrie, C. Chandler, A. Hooton, A. Miles, & P. Watson (Eds.), *The applied sport and exercise practitioner* (pp. 110–121). Routledge.

Hyppönen, L., Hirsto, L., & Sointu, E. (2019). Perspectives on university students' self-regulated learning, task-avoidance, time management and achievement in a flipped classroom context. *International Journal of Learning, Teaching and Educational Research, 18*(13), 87–106. https://doi.org/10.26803/ijlter.18.13.5

Ibrahim, A. K., Kelly, S. J., Adams, C. E., & Glazebrook, C. (2013). A systematic review of studies of depression prevalence in university students. *Journal of Psychiatric Research, 47*(3), 391–400. https://doi.org/10.1016/j.jpsychires.2012.11.015

Ifenthaler, D., & Yau, J. Y. K. (2020). Utilising learning analytics to support study success in higher education: A systematic review. *Educational Technology Research and Development, 68*, 1961–1990. https://doi.org/10.1007/s11423-020-09788-z

Institute for Apprenticeships. (2022). *Academic professional apprenticeship standard.* www.institute-forapprenticeships.org/apprenticeship-standards/academic-professional-v1-0

Irons, A. (2008). *Enhancing learning through formative assessment and feedback.* Routledge.

Irons, A., & Elkington, S. (2021). *Enhancing learning through formative assessment and feedback.* Routledge.

IT Pro. (2022). *Computer science is now the UK's fastest growing degree subject.* Retrieved June 29, 2023, from www.itpro.com/business-strategy/careers-training/368855/computer-science-is-now-the-fastest-growing-degree

Jackson, D., Dean, B. A., & Eady, M. (2023). Equity and inclusion in work-integrated learning: Participation and outcomes for diverse student groups. *Educational Review.* https://doi.org/10.1080/00131911.2023.2182764

Jackson, D., & Trede, F. (2020). The role of reflection after placement experiences to develop self-authorship among higher education students. In S. Billett, J. Orrell, D. Jackson, & F. Valencia-Forrester (Eds.), *Enriching higher education students' learning through post-work placement interventions* (pp. 189–208). Springer. https://doi.org/10.1007/978-3-030-48062-2_11

Jacobson, N. S., & Truax, P. (1991). Clinical significance: A statistical approach to defining meaningful change in psychotherapy research. *Journal of Consulting and Clinical Psychology, 59*, 12–19.

Jandrić, P. (2020). Postdigital research in the time of Covid-19. *Postdigital Science and Education, 2*, 233–238. https://doi.org/10.1007/s42438-020-00113-8

Jandrić, P., & Hayes, S. (2020). Postdigital we-learn. *Studies in Philosophy and Education, 39*(3), 285–297. https://doi.org/10.1007/s11217-020-09711-2

Jandrić, P., Knox, J., Besley, T., Ryberg, T., Suoranta, J., & Hayes, S. (2018). Postdigital science and education. *Educational Philosophy and Theory, 50*(10), 893–899. https://doi.org/10.1080/00131857.2018.1454000

Jaramillo, J. A. (1996). Vygotsky's sociocultural theory and contributions to the development of constructivist curricula. *Education, 3*(13), 117: 133. Gale Academic OneFile. Retrieved August 19, 2024, from link.gale.com/apps/doc/A18960235/AONE?u=anon~5f021275&sid=googleScholar&xid=14cd42c4

Jarrad, T., Dry, M., Semmler, C., Turnbull, D., & Chur-Hansen, A. (2019). The psychological distress and physical health of Australian psychology honours students. *Australian Psychologist, 54*(4), 302–310. https://doi.org/10.1111/ap.12384

Jensen, J. L., Holt, E. A., Sowards, J. B., Ogden, T. H., & West, R. E. (2018). Investigating strategies for pre-class content learning in a flipped classroom. *Journal of Science Education and Technology, 27*, 523–535. https://doi.org/10.1007/s10956-018-9740-6

Jessop, T., El Hakim, Y., & Gibbs, G. (2014). The whole is greater than the sum of its parts: A large-scale student o students' learning in response to different programme assessment patterns. *Assessment and Evaluation in Higher Education*, 39(1), 73–88. https://doi.org/10.1080/02602938.2013.792108

JISC. (2014). *Developing digital literacies*. www.jisc.ac.uk/guides/developing-digital-literacies

JISC. (2021). *Assessment rebooted: From 2020's quick fixes to future transformation*. Assessment Rebooted | Jisc. Retrieved February 25, 2024.

Johnson, G. (2015). On-campus and fully-online university students: Comparing demographics, digital technology use and learning characteristics. *Journal of University Teaching and Learning Practice*, 12, 45–58. https://doi.org/10.53761/1.12.1.4

Jones, E. P., Wahlquist, A. E., Hortman, M., & Wisniewski, C. S. (2021). Motivating students to engage in preparation for flipped classrooms by using embedded quizzes in pre-class Videos. *Innovations in Pharmacy*, 12(1).https://doi.org/10.24926%2Fiip.v12i1.3353

Jong, B., & Tan, K. H. (2021). Using Padlet as a technological tool for assessment of students' writing skills in online classroom settings. *International Journal of Education and Practice*, 9(2), 411–423. https://eric.ed.gov/?id=EJ1295506

Jönsson, A., & Panadero, E. (2017). The use and design of rubrics to support assessment for learning. In D. Carless, S. M. Birdges, C. Ka Yuk Chan, & R. Glofcheski (Eds.), *Scaling up assessment for learning in higher education* (pp. 99–111). Springer.

Jopp, R., & Cohen, J. (2022). Choose your own assessment – assessment choice for students in online higher education. *Teaching in Higher Education*, 27(6), 738–755. https://doi.org/10.53761/1.20.7.11

Jorre De St Jorre, T., Boud, D., & Johnson, E. D. (2021). Assessment for distinctiveness: Recognising diversity of accomplishments. *Studies in Higher Education*, 46(7), 1371–1382. https://doi.org/10.1080/03075079.2019.1689385

Kandlbinder, P. (2014). Constructive alignment in university teaching. *HERDSA News*, 36(3), 5–6.

Kaya-Capocci, S., O'Leary, M., & Costello, E. (2022). Towards a framework to support the implementation of digital formative assessment in higher education. *Education Sciences*, 12(11), 823–835. www.mdpi.com/2227-7102/12/11/823#

Kemmis, S. (2006). Participatory action research and the public sphere. *Educational Action Research*, 14(4), 459–476. https://doi.org/10.1080/09650790600975593

Kemmis, S. (2021). A practice theory perspective on learning: Beyond a 'standard' view. *Studies in Continuing Education*, 43(3), 280–295. https://doi.org/10.1080/0158037X.2021.1920384

Kemp, A., Randon McDougal, E., & Syrdal, H. (2019). The matchmaking activity: An experiential learning exercise on influencer marketing for the digital marketing classroom. *Journal of Marketing Education*, 41(2), 141–153.

King, H. (2016). Learning spaces and collaborative work: Barriers or supports? *Higher Education Research and Development*, 35(1), 158–171. https://doi.org/10.1080/07294360.2015.1131251

Kinsella, G. K., Mahon, C., & Lillis, S. (2017). Using pre-lecture activities to enhance learner engagement in a large group setting. *Active Learning in Higher Education*, 18(3), 231–242. https://doi.org/10.1177/1469787417715205

Kirschner, P. A., & De Bruyckere, P. (2017). The myths of the digital native and the multitasker. *Teaching and Teacher Education*, 67, 135–142.

Klein, E. J., & Riordan, M. (2011). Wearing the "student hat": Experiential professional development in expeditionary learning schools. *Journal of Experiential Education*, 34(1), 35–54. https://doi.org/10.1177/105382591103400104

Klute, M., Apthorp, H., Harlacher, J., & Reale, M. (2017). *Formative assessment and elementary school student academic achievement: A review of the evidence (REL 2017-259)*. U.S. Department of Education, Institute of Education Sciences, National Center for Education Evaluation and Regional Assistance, Regional Educational Laboratory Central. Retrieved from http://ies.ed.gov/ncee/edlabs

Knauf, H. (2016). Reading, listening and feeling: Audio feedback as a component of an inclusive learning culture at universities. *Assessment & Evaluation in Higher Education*, 41(3), 442–449. https://doi.org/10.1080/02602938.2015.1021664

Knight, P. T., & Yorke, M. (2003). *Assessment, learning and employability*. McGraw-Hill Education.

Knox, J. (2019). What does the 'postdigital' mean for education? Three critical perspectives on the digital, with implications for educational research and practice. *Postdigital Science and Education*, 1(2), 357–370. https://doi.org/10.1007/s42438-019-00045-y

Koehler, M. J., Mishra, P., & Cain, W. (2013). What is technological pedagogical content knowledge (TPACK)? *The Journal of Education*, 193(3), 13–19.

Kolb, D. A. (1984). *Experiential learning: Experience as the source of learning and development*. Prentice-Hall.

Kolb, D. A. (2014). *Experiential learning: Experience as the source of learning and development*. FT press.

Kolb, D. A., & Kolb, D. (2017). Experiential learning & teaching in higher education (ELTHE). *A Journal for Engaged Educators*, 1(1), 7–44.

Konopasek, L., Norcini, J., & Krupat, E. (2016). Focusing on the formative: Building an assessment system aimed at student growth and development. *Academic Medicine*, 91(11), 1492–1497. https://doi.org/10.1097/ACM.0000000000001171

Kopp, R., Dhondt, S., Hirsch-Kreinsen, H., Kohlgrüber, M., & Preenen, P. (2019). Sociotechnical perspectives on digitalisation and industry 4.0. *International Journal of Technology Transfer and Commercialisation*, 16(3), 290–309. https://doi.org/10.1504/IJTTC.2019.099896

Krathwohl, D. R. (2002). A revision of bloom's taxonomy: An overview. *Theory into Practice*, 41(4), 212–218.

Kruiper, S. M. A., Leenknecht, M. J. M., & Slof, B. (2022). Using scaffolding strategies to improve formative assessment practice in higher education. *Assessment & Evaluation in Higher Education*, 47(3), 458–476. https://doi.org/10.1080/02602938.2021.1927981

Lai, C. L., & Hwang, G. J. (2016). A self-regulated flipped classroom approach to improving students' learning performance in a mathematics course. *Computers & Education*, 100, 126–140. https://doi.org/10.1016/j.compedu.2016.05.006

Lam, R. (2023). E-portfolios: What we know, what we don't, and what we need to know. *RELC Journal*, 54(1), 208–215. https://doi.org/10.1177/0033688220974102

Lamb, J., Carvalho, L., Gallagher, M., & Knox, J. (2022). The postdigital learning spaces of higher education. *Postdigital Science Education*, 4, 1–12. https://doi.org/10.1007/s42438-021-00279-9

Lameras, P., & Arnab, S. (2021). Power to the teachers: An exploratory review on artificial intelligence in education. *Information*, 13(1), 14. https://doi.org/10.3390/info13010014

Lancaster, T. (2020). Academic discipline integration by contract cheating services and essay mills. *Journal of Academic Ethics*, 18, 115–127. https://doi.org/10.1007/s10805-019-09357-x

Lave, J., & Wenger, E. (1991). *Situated learning: Legitimate peripheral participation*. Cambridge University Press.

Lea, S. J., Stephenson, D., & Troy, J. (2003). Higher education students' attitudes to student-centred learning: Beyond "educational bulimia"? *Studies in Higher Education*, 28(3), 321–334. https://doi.org/10.1080/03075070309293

Lee, P. (2023). Interview with Peter Lee. Hosted by *Zoom*, edited by author. Online: Private Channel.

Leenknecht, M., Wijnia, L., Köhlen, M., Fryer, L., Rikers, R., & Loyens, S. (2021). Formative assessment as practice: The role of students' motivation. *Assessment & Evaluation in Higher Education*, 46(2), 236–255. https://doi.org/10.1080/02602938.2020.1765228

Leganger-Krogstad, H. (2014). From dialogue to trialogue: A sociocultural learning perspective on classroom interaction. *Journal for the Study of Religion*, 27, 104–128.

Leong, K., Sung, A., Au, D., & Blanchard, C. (2021). A review of the trend of microlearning. *Journal of Work-Applied Management*, 13(1), 88–102.

Lim, F. V., & Tan-Chia, L. (2023). *Designing learning for multimodal literacy: Teaching viewing and representing*. Routledge.

Lim, L. A., Dawson, S., Gašević, D., Joksimović, S., Fudge, A., Pardo, A., & Gentili, S. (2020). Students' sense-making of personalised feedback based on learning analytics. *Australasian Journal of Educational Technology*, 36(6), 15–33.

Liu, Y., & Zhang, H. (2022). Exploring the influencing factors and validity of formative assessment in online learning. *Journal of Education and e-Learning Research*, 9(4), 278–287.

Lizzio, A. (2006). *Designing an orientation and transition strategy for commencing students: Applying the five senses model.* https://nanopdf.com/download/designing-an-orientation-and-transition-strategy-for_pdf

Lizzio, A., & Wilson, K. (2008). Feedback on assessment: Students' perceptions of quality and effectiveness. *Assessment & Evaluation in Higher Education, 33*(3): 263-75. https://doi.org/10.1080/02602930701292548

Lockee, B. B. (2021). Online education in the post-COVID era. *Nature Electronics, 4,* 5-6. https://doi.org/10.1038/s41928-020-00534-0

Lockyer, J., & Sargeant, J. (2022). Multisource feedback: An overview of its use and application as a formative assessment. *Canadian Medical Education Journal, 13*(4), 30-35. https://doi.org/10.36834/cmej.73775

Lucas, C., Gibson, A., & Shum, S. B. (2019). Pharmacy students' utilization of an online tool for immediate formative feedback on reflective writing tasks. *American Journal of Pharmaceutical Education, 83*(6).

Lynam, A., & Moira Cachia, S. (2018). Students' perceptions of the role of assessments at higher education. *Assessment & Evaluation in Higher Education, 43*(2), 223-234. https://doi.org/10.1080/02602938.2017.1329928

Macfarlane, B. (2015). Student performativity in higher education: Converting learning as a private space into a public performance. *Higher Education Research and Development, 34*(2), 338-350. https://doi.org/10.1080/07294360.2014.956697

Malecka, B., & Boud, D. (2021). Fostering student motivation and engagement with feedback through ipsative processes. *Teaching in Higher Education,* 1-16. https://doi.org/10.1080/13562517.2021.1928061

Malecka, M., Boud, D., & Carless, D. (2020). Eliciting, processing and enacting feedback: Mechanisms for embedding student feedback literacy within the curriculum. *Teaching in Higher Education.* https://doi.org/10.1080/13562517.2020.1754784

Mansi, G. (2021). Bridging the gap between markers' tacit knowledge and students' assessment literacy. *Compass: Journal of Learning and Teaching, 14*(2), 1-8. https://doi.org/10.21100/compass.v14i2.1224

Margaryan, A., Littlejohn, A., & Vojt, G. (2011). Are digital natives a myth or reality? University students' use of digital technologies. *Computers & Education, 56*(2), 429-440. https://doi.org/10.1016/j.compedu.2010.09.004

Marginson, S., & Dang, T. K. A. (2017). Vygotsky's sociocultural theory in the context of globalization. *Asia Pacific Journal of Education, 37,* 116-129. https://doi.org/10.1080/02188791.2016.1216827

Markauskaite, L., Carvalho, L., & Fawns, T. (2023). The role of teachers in a sustainable university: From digital competencies to postdigital capabilities. *Education Technology Research Development, 71,* 181-198. https://doi.org/10.1007/s11423-023-10199-z

Martin, D. (2020). Providing students with multimodal feedback experiences. *Journal of Curriculum, Teaching, Learning and Leadership in Education, 5*(1), 16-27. https://digitalcommons.unomaha.edu/ctlle/vol5/iss1/2

Marvin, M. C. (2020). Microsoft OneNote provides continuity for undergraduate biochemistry lab during a pandemic. *Biochemistry and Molecular Biology Education, 48*(5), 523-525. https://doi.org/10.1002/bmb.21437

Masters, K. (2013). Edgar Dale's pyramid of learning in medical education: A literature review. *Medical Teacher, 35*(11), 1584-1593. https://doi.org/10.3109/0142159X.2013.800636

Mauri, T., Clarà, M., Colomina, R., & Onrubia, J. (2016). Educational assistance to improve reflective practice among student teachers. *Electronic Journal of Research in Educational Psychology, 14*(2), 287-309.

McAlpine, H., Hicks, B. J., Huet, G., & Culley, S. J. (2006). An investigation into the use and content of the engineer's logbook. *Design Studies, 27*(4), 481-504. https://doi.org/10.1016/j.destud.2005.12.001

McCallum, S., & Milner, M. M. (2021). The effectiveness of formative assessment: Student views and staff reflections. *Assessment & Evaluation in Higher Education, 46*(1), 1-16. https://doi.org/10.1080/02602938.2020.1754761

McLaughlin, T., & Yan, Z. (2017). Diverse delivery methods and strong psychological benefits: A review of online formative assessment. *Journal of Computer Assisted Learning, 33*(6), 562–574. https://doi.org/10.1111/jcal.12200

McNally, B., Chipperfield, J., Dorsett, P., Del Fabbro, L., Frommolt, V., Goetz, S., Lewohl, J., Molineux, M., Pearson, A., Reddan, G., Roiko, A., & Rung, A. (2017). Flipped classroom experiences: Student preferences and flip strategy in a higher education context. *Higher Education, 73*, 281–298. https://doi.org/10.1007/s10734-016-0014-z

Medway, D., Roper, S., & Gillooly, L. (2018). Contract cheating in UK higher education: A covert investigation of essay mills. *British Educational Research Journal, 44*(3), 393–418. https://doi.org/10.1002/berj.3335

Mercer, N., & Howe, C. (2012). Explaining the dialogic processes of teaching and learning: The value and potential of sociocultural theory. *Learning, Culture, and Social Interaction, 1*(1), 12–21. https://doi.org/10.1016/j.lcsi.2012.03.001

Meyer, J. H. F., & Land, R. (2003). Threshold concepts and troublesome knowledge: Linkages to thinking and practice within the disciplines. *ETL Project*. Occasional Report 4, May 2003. www.etl.tla.ed.ac.uk/docs/ETLreport4.pdf

Meyers, C., & Jones, T. B. (1993). *Promoting active learning: Strategies for the college classroom*. Jossey-Bass Inc.

Middleton, A. (2019). *Reimagining spaces for learning in higher education*. Bloomsbury.

Millard, L., Blackwell-Young, J., & Hogan, J. (2023). Designing personalized student development through microcredentials: An institutional approach. In D. Willison & E. Henderson (Eds.), *Perspectives on enhancing student transition into higher education and beyond*. (pp. 122–142). IGI Global. https://doi.org/10.4018/978-1-6684-8198-1.ch006

Mishra, P., & Koehler, M. J. (2006). Technological pedagogical content knowledge: A framework for teacher knowledge. *Teachers College Record, 108*, 1017–1054. https://doi.org/10.1111/j.1467-9620.2006.00684.x

Molloy, E. K., & Boud, D. (2014). Feedback models for learning, teaching and performance. In J. M. Spector, M. D. Merrill, J. Elen, & M. J. Bishop (Eds.), *Handbook of research on educational communications and technology* (pp. 413–424). Springer.

Molloy, E. K., Boud, D., & Henderson, M. (2020). Developing a learning-centred framework for feedback literacy. *Assessment & Evaluation in Higher Education, 45*(4), 527–540. https://doi.org/10.1080/02602938.2019.1667955

Morris, C., Milton, E., & Goldstone, R. (2019). Case study: Suggesting choice: Inclusive assessment processes. *Higher Education Pedagogies, 4*(1), 435–447. https://doi.org/10.1080/23752696.2019.1669479

Morris, R., Perry, T., & Wardle, L. (2021). Formative assessment and feedback for learning in higher education: A systematic review. *Review of Education, 9*(3), 3292. https://doi.org/10.1002/rev3.3292

Morris, T. H. (2020). Experiential learning – a systematic review and revision of Kolb's model. *Interactive Learning Environments, 28*(8), 1064–1077. https://doi.org/10.1080/10494820.2019.1570279

Moss, C. M., & Brookhart, S. M. (2019). *Advancing formative assessment in every classroom: A guide for instructional leaders*. ASCD.

Mullane, J. (2013). Three stars and a wish. *Primary Teacher Update, 27*, 34–35. https://doi.org/10.12968/prtu.2013.1.27.34

Nadeem, N. H., & Al Falig, H. A. (2020). Kahoot! quizzes: A formative assessment tool to promote students' self-regulated learning skills. *Journal of Applied Linguistics and Language Research, 7*(4), 1–20.

Narciss, S. (2013). Designing and evaluating tutoring feedback strategies for digital learning environments on the basis of the interactive tutoring feedback model. *Digital Education Review, 23*, 7–26.

Nash, R. A., & Winstone, N. E. (2017). Responsibility-sharing in the giving and receiving of assessment feedback. *Frontiers in Psychology, 8*, 1518–1519. https://doi.org/10.3389/fpsyg.2017.01519

Nelson, M. M., & Schunn, C. D. (2009). The nature of feedback: How different types of peer feedback affect writing performance. *Instructional Science*, *37*(4), 375–401. https://doi.org/10.1007/s11251-008-9053-x

Nerantzi, C. (2020). The use of peer instruction and flipped learning to support flexible blended learning during and after the COVID-19, Pandemic. *International Journal of Management and Applied Research*, *7*(2), 184–195. www.ceeol.com/search/article-detail?id=883236

Newfield, D. (2014). Transformation, transduction and the transmodal moment. In C. Jewitt (Ed.), *The Routledge handbook of multimodal analysis* (pp. 100–113). Routledge.

Nicol, D., & Macfarlane-Dick, D. (2006). Formative assessment and self-regulated learning: A model and seven principles of good feedback practice. *Studies in Higher Education*, *2*, 199–218. https://doi.org/10.1080/03075070600572090

Nieminen, J. H. (2022). Unveiling ableism and disablism in assessment: A critical analysis of disabled students' experiences of assessment and assessment accommodations. *Higher Education*, *85*(3), 613–636. https://doi.org/10.1007/s10734-022-00857-1

Nieminen, J. H. (2024). Assessment for Inclusion: Rethinking inclusive assessment in higher education. *Teaching in Higher Education*, *29*(4), 841–859. https://doi.org/10.1080/13562517.2021.2021395

Norcini, J. J., & McKinley, D. W. (2007). Assessment methods in medical education. *Teaching and Teacher Education*, *23*(3), 239–50. https://doi.org/10.1016/j.tate.2006.12.021

Norris, J. (2015). Their own voices: Empowering students with choice in writing tasks. *Voices from the Middle*, *23*(2), 43–48. https://publicationsncte.org/content/journals/10.58680/vm201527617

Notion AI. (2023). What is Notion? Available at: https://www.notion.so/help/guides/what-is-notion

Novak, G. M. (2011). Just-in-time teaching. *New Directions for Teaching and Learning*, *128*, 63–73. https://doi.org/10.1002/tl.469

Oc, Y., & Plangger, K. (2022). GIST do it! How motivational mechanisms help wearable users develop healthy habits. *Computers in Human Behaviour*, *128*, 107089. https://doi.org/10.1016/j.chb.2021.107089

O'Donnell, M. (2020). Assessment as and of digital practice: Building productive digital literacies. In M. Bearman, P. Dawson, R. Ajjawi, J. Tai, & D. Boud (Eds.), *Re-imagining university assessment in a digital world* (Vol. 7, pp. 111–125). Springer International Publishing. https://doi.org/10.1007/978-3-030-41956-1_9

O'Flaherty, F., & Phillips, C. (2015). The use of flipped classrooms in higher education: A scoping review. *The Internet and Higher Education*, *25*, 85–95. https://doi.org/10.1016/j.iheduc.2015.02.002

Okoli, J., Arroteia, N., & Barish, O. (2019). Piloting a portfolio of experiential learning activities for international business students. *Journal of Teaching in International Business*, *30*(3), 219–245. https://doi.org/10.1080/08975930.2019.1698393

Oldfield, A., Broadfoot, P., Sutherland, R., & Timmis, S. (2012). *Assessment in a digital age: A research review*. www.bristol.ac.uk/media-library/sites/education/documents/researchreview.pdf

O'Neill, G. (2022). Student choice of assessment methods. Assessment for inclusion in higher education: Promoting equity. In R. Ajjawi, J. Tai, D. Boud, & T. J. de St Jorre (Eds.), *Assessment for inclusion in higher education: Promoting equity and social justice in assessment* (pp. 199–210). Routledge.

O'Neill, G., & Padden, L. (2021). Diversifying assessment methods: Barriers, benefits, and enablers. *Innovations in Education and Teaching International*, *59*(4), 398–409. https://doi.org/10.1080/14703297.2021.1880462

Orsmond, P., Merry, S., & Reiling, K. (2005). Biology students' utilization of tutors' formative feedback: A qualitative interview study. *Assessment & Evaluation in Higher Education*, *30*(4), 369–386. https://doi.org/10.1080/02602930500099177

Panadero, E., & Jonsson, A. (2013). The use of scoring rubrics for formative assessment purposes revisited: A review. *Educational Research Review*, *9*, 129–144. https://doi.org/10.1016/j.edurev.2013.01.002

Panadero, E., Jonsson, A., Pinedo, L., & Fernández-Castilla, B. (2023). Effects of rubrics on academic performance, self-regulated learning, and self-efficacy: A meta-analytic review. *Educational Psychology Review*, 35(4), 113. https://doi.org/10.1007/s10648-023-09823-4

Panopto. (2023). www.panopto.com/

Parker, M. E., & Parkinson, D. (2022). Embedding authentic feedback literacy in design students: A new model for peer assessment. In D. Lockton, S. Lenzi, P. Hekkert, A. Oak, J. Sádaba, & P. Lloyd (Eds.), *Proceedings of DRS. DRS biennial conference series* (pp. 1–15). Bilbao, 25 June–3 July, Bilbao, Spain.

Payne, A. (2023). Beyond telling: A clarion call for technology-mediated feedback conversations in higher education. In V. Rossi (Ed.), *Inclusive learning design in higher education: A practical guide to creating equitable learning experiences* (pp. 274–277). Routledge.

Pebble Learning. (2023). www.pebblepad.co.uk/

Pilkington, R. (2018). Investigating the use of 'professional dialogues' when assessing academic practice: Revealing learning, managing process, and enabling judgements. *International Journal for Academic Development*, 24, 1–14. https://doi.org/10.1080/1360144X.2018.1512496

Pitt, E., Bearman, M., & Esterhazy, R. (2019). The conundrum of low achievement and feedback for learning. *Assessment & Evaluation in Higher Education*, 45(2), 239–250. https://doi.org/10.1080/02602938.2019.1630363

Pitt, E., & Norton, L. (2017). 'Now that's the feedback I want!' Students' reactions to feedback on graded work and what they do with it. *Assessment & Evaluation in Higher Education*, 42(4), 499–516. https://doi.org/10.1080/02602938.2016.1142500

Pitt, E., & Winstone, N. (2020). Towards technology enhanced dialogic feedback. In M. Bearman, P. Dawson, R. Ajjawi, J. Tai, & D. Boud (Eds.), *Re-imagining university assessment in a digital world* (pp. 79–94). Springer.

Pitt, E., & Winstone, N. (2023). Enabling and valuing feedback literacies. *Assessment & Evaluation in Higher Education*, 48(2), 149–157. https://doi.org/10.1080/02602938.2022.2107168

Postman, N. (1992). *Technopoly: The surrender of culture to technology*. Vintage Books.

Prashanti, E., & Ramnarayan, K. (2019). Ten maxims of formative assessment. *Advances in Physiology Education*, 43, 99–102. https://doi.org/10.1152/advan.00173.2018

Price, M., Rust, C., O'Donovan, B., & Handley, K., & Bryant, R. (2012). *Assessment literacy: The foundation for improving student learning*. Oxford Centre for Staff and Learning Development, Oxford Brookes University.

Prince, M. (2004). Does active learning work? A review of the research. *Journal of Engineering Education*, 93(3), 223–231. https://doi.org/10.1002/j.2168-9830.2004.tb00809.x

Pryor, P., & Crossouard, B. (2008). A socio-cultural theorisation of formative assessment, *Oxford Review of Education*, 34(1), 1–20. https://doi.org/10.1080/03054980701476386

QAA. (2014). *UK quality code for higher education part A: Setting and maintaining academic standards*. Gloucester: QAA. https://www.qaa.ac.uk/docs/qaa/quality-code/qualifications-frameworks.pdf

QAA. (2016). *Glossary*. www.qaa.ac.uk/docs/qaas/about-us/qaa-glossary.pdf?sfvrsn=a94bfc81_4

QAA. (2019). *Subject benchmark statement: Music*. edited by QAA Membership. Gloucester: QAA. https://www.qaa.ac.uk/docs/qaa/subject-benchmark-statements/subject-benchmark-statement-music.pdf?sfvrsn=61e2cb81_4

QAA. (2022a). *Characteristics statement: Micro-credentials*. The Quality Assurance Agency for Higher Education. www.qaa.ac.uk/the-quality-code/characteristics-statements/micro-credentials

QAA. (2022b). Subject Benchmark Statement Computing. The Quality Assurance Agency. Available at: https://www.qaa.ac.uk/docs/qaa/sbs/sbs-computing-22.pdf?sfvrsn=ebb3dc81_2

QAA. (2023). *Resilient learning communities*. www.enhancementthemes.ac.uk/resilient-learning-communities

QAA/AdvanceHE. (2021). *Education for sustainable development guidance*. QAA/AdvanceHE Education for Sustainable Development Advisory Group. www.advance-he.ac.uk/knowledge-hub/education-sustainable-development-guidance

Quirke, P., Kreeft Peyton, J., Burton, J., Reichmann, C., & Trites, L. (2021). *Developing teachers as leaders*. Brill | Sense. https://doi.org/10.1163/9789004449169.

Ragupathi, K., & Lee, A. (2020). Beyond fairness and consistency in grading: The role of rubrics in higher education. In S. Sanger & N. W. Gleason (Eds.), *Diversity and inclusion in global higher education. Lessons from across Asia* (pp. 73–96). Palgrave-Macmillan.

Ramlal, A., & Augustin, D. S. (2020). Engaging students in reflective writing: An action research project. *Educational Action Research, 28*(3), 518–533.

Rapanta, C. Botturi, L., Goodyear, P., Guàrdia, L., & Koole, M. (2021). Balancing technology, pedagogy and the new normal: Post-pandemic challenges for higher education. *Postdigital Science and Education, 3*(3), 715–742. https://doi.org/10.1007/s42438-021-00249-1

Rashid, Y., Rashid, A., Warraich, M. A., Sabir, S. S., & Waseem, A. (2019). Case study method: A step-by-step guide for business researchers. *International Journal of Qualitative Methods, 18*. https://doi.org/10.1177/1609406919862424

Reddy, Y. M., & Andrade, H. (2009). A review of rubric use in higher education. *Assessment & Evaluation in Higher Education, 35*(4), 435–448. https://doi.org/10.1080/02602930902862859

Reiss, M., Abrahams, I., & Sharpe R. (2012). *Improving the assessment of practical work in school science*. Gatsby Charitable Foundation.

Rogers, M. R. (2004). *Teaching approaches in music theory: An overview of pedagogical philosophies*. Southern Illinois University Press.

Ross, J. (2023). *Digital futures for learning: Speculative methods and pedagogies*. Routledge.

Ross, J., Curwood, J. S., & Bell, A. (2020). A multimodal assessment framework for higher education. *E-Learning and Digital Media, 17*(4), 290–306. https://doi.org/10.1177/2042753020927201

Rossatto, C. A., & Dickerson, M. E. R. S. G. (2019). Reinventing critical digital literacy to empower student-teachers in cross-cultural, web-based learning environments. In J. Keengwe & K. Kungu (Eds.), *Handbook of research on cross-cultural online learning in higher education* (pp. 138–58). IGI Global.

Rowe, A. D., & Zegwaard, K. E. (2017). Developing graduate employability skills and attributes: Curriculum enhancement through work-integrated learning. *Asia-Pacific Journal of Cooperative Education, 18*(2), 87–99. https://hdl.handle.net/10289/11267

Ryan, R. M., & Deci, E. L. (2017). *Self-determination theory: Basic psychological needs in motivation, development, and wellness*. Guilford Publish.

Sadler, R. (2010). Beyond feedback: Developing student capability in complex appraisal. *Assessment & Evaluation in Higher Education, 35*(5), 535–550. https://doi.org/10.1080/02602930903541015

Sadler, D. R. (2013). Opening up feedback: Teaching learners to see. In S. Merry, M. Price, D. Carless, & M. Taras (Eds.), *Reconceptualising feedback in higher education* (pp. 54–63). Routledge.

Saichaie, K. (2020). Blended, flipped, and hybrid learning: Definitions, developments, and directions. *New Directions for Teaching and Learning, 2020*(164), 95–104. https://doi.org/10.1002/tl.20428

Sambell, K. (2010). Enquiry-based learning and formative assessment environments: Student perspectives. *Practitioner Research in Higher Education, 4*(1), 52–61. https://ojs.cumbria.ac.uk/index.php/prhe/article/view/34

Sambell, K., Brown, S., & Race, P. (2019). Assessment to support student learning: Eight challenges for 21st century practice. *All Ireland Journal of Higher Education, 11*(2).

Sambell, K., McDowell, L., & Montgomery, C. (2013). *Assessment for learning in higher education*. Routledge.

Saputra, D. B., Arianto, M. A., & Saputra, E. (2023). "Will they listen to me?" Investigating the utilization of audio feedback in higher education. *Studies in English Language and Education, 10*(2), 741–755. https://jurnal.usk.ac.id/SiELE/article/view/28173

Schuwirth, L. W., & Van der Vleuten, C. P. (2011). Programmatic assessment: From assessment of learning to assessment for learning. *Medical Teacher, 33*, 478–485. https://doi.org/10.3109/0142159X.2011.565828

Selwyn, N. (2016). *Is technology good for education?* John Wiley & Sons.

Selwyn, N. (2023). There is a danger we get too robotic: An investigation of institutional data logics within secondary schools. *Educational Review, 75*(3), 377–393. https://doi.org/10.1080/00131911.2021.1931039

Shea, P., & Bidjerano, T. (2009). Community of inquiry as a theoretical framework to foster "epistemic engagement" and "cognitive presence" in online education. *Computers and Education*, *52*(3), 543–553. https://doi.org/10.1016/j.compedu.2008.10.007

Shelby, S. J., & Fralish, Z. D. (2021). Using Edpuzzle to improve student experience and performance in the biochemistry laboratory. *Biochemistry and Molecular Biology Education*, *49*(4), 529–534. https://doi.org/10.1002/bmb.21494

Shulman, L. (2005). Signature pedagogies in the professions. *Daedalus*, *134*(3), 52–59. https://www.jstor.org/stable/20027998

Shute, V. J. (2008). Focus on formative feedback. *Review of Educational Research*, *78*(1), 153–189. https://doi.org/10.3102/0034654307313795

Sinclair, C., & Hayes, S. (2019). Between the post and the com-post: Examining the postdigital 'work' of a prefix. *Postdigital Science and Education*, *1*(1), 119–131. https://doi.org/10.1007/s42438-018-0017-4

Smith, A., & Kennett, K. (2017). Multimodal meaning: Discursive dimensions of e-learning. In In B. Cope & M. Kalantis (Eds.), *E-Learning ecologies: Principles for new learning and assessment* (pp. 88–117). Routledge.

Smith, A., McCarthy, S., & Magnifico, A. (2017). Recursive feedback: Evaluative dimensions of e-learning. In B. Cope & M. Kalantis (Eds.), *e-Learning ecologies: Principles for new learning and assessment* (pp. 118–142). Routledge.

Smith, C. D., Worsfold, K., Davies, L., Fisher, R., & McPhail, R. (2013). Assessment literacy and student learning: The case for explicitly developing students 'assessment literacy'. *Assessment & Evaluation in Higher Education*, *38*(1), 44–60. https://doi.org/10.1080/02602938.2011.598636

Sokhanvar, Z., Salehi, K., & Sokhanvar, F. (2021). Advantages of authentic assessment for improving the learning experience and employability skills of higher education students: A systematic literature review. *Studies in Educational Evaluation*, *70*, Article 101030. https://doi.org/10.1016/j.stueduc.2021.101030

Sotiriadou, P., Logan, D., Daly, A., & Guest, R. (2020). The role of authentic assessment to preserve academic integrity and promote skill development and employability. *Studies in Higher Education*, *45*(11), 2132–2148. https://doi.org/10.1080/03075079.2019.1582015

Stallman, H. M. (2010). Psychological distress in university students: A comparison with general population data. *Australian Psychologist*, *45*(4), 249–257. https://doi.org/10.1080/00050067.2010.482109

Stanja, J., Gritz, W., Krugel, J., Hoppe, A., & Dannemann, S. (2023). Formative assessment strategies for students' conceptions – The potential of learning analytics. *British Journal of Educational Technology*, *54*(1), 58–75. https://doi.org/10.1111/bjet.13288

Star, M., & Collette, L. (2010). GPS: Shaping student success one conversation at a time. *Educause Quarterly*, *33*(4). Retrieved August 12, 2024, from www.learntechlib.org/p/109170/

Steen-Utheim, A., & Hopfenbeck, T. N. (2019). To do or not to do with feedback. A study of undergraduate students' engagement and use of feedback within a portfolio assessment design. *Assessment & Evaluation in Higher Education*, *44*(1), 80–96. https://doi.org/10.1080/02602938.2018.1476669

Stommel, J. (2020). An introduction to critical digital pedagogy. In *Policy Insights: The Digitalization of Education*. Network for International Policies and Cooperation in Education and Training (NORRAG) in Collaboration with the United Nations Special Rapporteur on the Right to Education.https://resources.norrag.org/resource/view/719/416?ref=jessestommel.com#accept-cookies

Stuart, G. (2023). ggstuart/classroom-analytics: v0.0.1 (v0.0.1). *Zenodo*. https://doi.org/10.5281/zenodo.7920431

Sweller, J. (1994). Cognitive load theory, learning difficulty, and instructional design. *Learning and Instruction*, *4*(4), 295–312. https://doi.org/10.1016/0959-4752(94)90003-5

Swiecki, Z., Khosravi, H., Chen, G., Martinez-Maldonado, R., Lodge, J. M., Milligan, S., & Gašević, D. (2022). Assessment in the age of artificial intelligence. *Computers and Education: Artificial Intelligence*, *3*, 100075. https://doi.org/10.1016/j.caeai.2022.100075

REFERENCES

Tai, J., Ajjawi, R., Bearman, M., Boud, D., Dawson, P., & Jorre de St Jorre, T. (2023). Assessment for inclusion: Rethinking contemporary strategies in assessment design. *Higher Education Research & Development, 42*(2), 483–497. https://doi.org/10.1080/07294360.2022.2057451

Tai, J., Ajjawi, R., Boud, D., Dawson, P., & Panadero, E. (2018). Developing evaluative judgement: Enabling students to make decisions about the quality of work. *Higher Education, 76*(3), 467–481. https://doi.org/10.1007/s10734-017-0220-3

Tamim, R. M., Bernard, R. M., Borokhovski, E., Abrami, P. C., & Schmid, R. F. (2011). What forty years of research says about the impact of technology on learning: A second-order meta-analysis and validation study. *Review of Educational Research, 81*(1), 4–28. https://doi.org/10.3102/0034654310393361

Tan, J. S. H., & Chen, W. (2022). Peer feedback to support collaborative knowledge improvement: What kind of feedback feed-forward? *Computers & Education, 187*(104467). https://doi.org/10.1016/j.compedu.2022.104467

Tapingkae, P., Panjaburee, P., Hwang, G. J., & Srisawasdi, N. (2020). Effects of a formative assessment-based contextual gaming approach on students' digital citizenship behaviours, learning motivations, and perceptions. *Computers & Education, 159*(103998). https://doi.org/10.1016/j.compedu.2020.103998

Teesside University. (n.d.). *LTE online: Future facing learning [online]*. Retrieved June 15, 2023, from https://blogs.tees.ac.uk/lteonline/future-facing-learning/

Telio, S., Ajjawi, R., & Regehr, G. (2015). The "educational alliance" as a framework for reconceptualizing feedback in medical education. *Academic Medicine, 90*(5), 609–614. https://doi.org/10.1097/ACM.0000000000000560

Thai, N. T. T., De Wever, B., & Valcke, M. (2017). The impact of a flipped classroom design on learning performance in higher education: Looking for the best "blend" of lectures and guiding questions with feedback. *Computers & Education, 107*, 113–126. https://doi.org/10.1016/j.compedu.2017.01.003

Thibodeaux, T., Harapnuik, D., & Cummings, C. (2019). Student perceptions of the influence of choice, ownership, and voice in learning and the learning environment. *International Journal of Teaching and Learning in Higher Education, 31*(1), 50–62. https://eric.ed.gov/?id=EJ1206966

Thomas, L. (2012). Building student engagement and belonging in higher education at a time of change. *Paul Hamlyn Foundation, 100*(1–99), 1–102. https://s3.eu-west-2.amazonaws.com/assets.creode.advancehe-document-manager/documents/hea/private/what_works_final_report_1568036657.pdf

Thompson, M., Pawson, C., & Evans, B. (2021). Navigating entry into higher education: The transition to independent learning and living. *Journal of Further and Higher Education 45*(10), 1398–1410. https://doi.org/10.1080/0309877X.2021.1933400

Tierney, R., & Simon, M. (2004). What's still wrong with rubrics: Focusing on the consistency of performance criteria across scale levels. *Practical Assessment, Research, and Evaluation, 9*. https://doi.org/10.7275/jtvt-wg68

Timmis, S., Broadfoot, P., Sutherland, R., & Oldfield, A. (2016). Rethinking assessment in a digital age: Opportunities, challenges, and risks. *British Educational Research Journal, 42*(3), 454–476. https://doi.org/10.1002/berj.3215

Torrance, H. (2012). Formative assessment at the crossroads: Conformative, deformative and transformative assessment. *Oxford Review of Education, 38*(3), 323342. https://doi.org/10.1080/03054985.2012.689693

Treleaven, L., & Voola, R. (2008). Integrating the development of graduate attributes through constructive alignment. *Journal of Marketing Education, 30*(2), 160–73. https://doi.org/10.1177/0273475308319352

Tsai, Y. S., Rates, D., Moreno-Marcos, P. M., Muñoz-Merino, P. J., Jivet, I., Scheffel, M., Drachsler, H., Kloos, C. D., & Gašević, D. (2020). Learning analytics in European higher education – Trends and barriers. *Computers & Education, 155*, 103933. https://doi.org/10.1016/j.compedu.2020.103933

Tusa, N., Sointu, E., Kastarinen, H., Valtonen, T., Kaasinen, A., Hirsto, L., Saarelainen, M., Mäkitalo, K., & Mäntyselkä, P. (2018). Medical certificate education: Controlled study between lectures and flipped classroom. *BMC Medical Education, 18*, 1–6. https://doi.org/10.1186/s12909-018-1351-7

UK Foundation Programme Assessments. (2023). *Team assessment of behaviour*. https://foundationprogramme.nhs.uk/curriculum/assessments

UNESCO. (2017). *Education for sustainable development goals: Learning objectives*. UNESCO, Paris.

UNESCO. (2021). Recovering lost learning: What can be done quickly and at scale. *UNESCO COVID-19 Education Response: Education Sector 7*. UNESCO, Paris.

University of Aberdeen's Strategic Plan 2040. www.abdn.ac.uk/2040/

Van Wyk, J., & Haffejee, F. (2017). Benefits of group learning as a collaborative strategy in a diverse higher education context. *International Journal of Educational Sciences*, 18(1–3), 158–163. http://dx.doi.org/10.1080/09751122.2017.1305745

Varga-Atkins, T. (2024). *Multimodal Learning: A practitioner guide*. Advance HE.

Vasilienė-Vasiliauskienė, V., Butvilienė, J., & Butvilas, T. (2016). Project-based learning: The complexity and challenges in higher education institutions. *Computer Modelling & New Technologies*, 20(2), 7–10. www.cmnt.lv/upload-files/ns_66art01_Butvilas.pdf

Vaughan, R. (2015). UK among world's worst for 'teaching to the test', research finds. *TES*, 18th December. https://www.tes.com/magazine/archive/uk-among-worlds-worst-teaching-test-research-finds

Wainwright, E., Chappell, A., & McHugh, E. (2020). Widening participation and a student "success" assemblage: The materialities and mobilities of university. *Population Space and Place*, 26(3). https://doi.org/10.1002/psp.2291

Wanner, T., Palmer, E., & Palmer, D. (2024). Flexible assessment and student empowerment: Advantages and disadvantages – research from an Australian university. *Teaching in Higher Education*, 29(2), 349–365. https://doi.org/10.1080/13562517.2021.1989578

Watling, C. J., & Ginsburg, S. (2019). Assessment, feedback and the alchemy of learning. *Medical Education*, 53(1), 76–85. https://asmepublications.onlinelibrary.wiley.com/doi/pdf/10.1111/medu.13645

Watson, P., Borrie, A., Chandler, C., Hooton, A., & Miles, A. (2023). Professional practice in sport and exercise. In A. Borrie, C. Chandler, A. Hooton, A. Miles, & P. Watson (Eds.), *The applied sport and exercise practitioner* (pp. 1–4). Routledge.

Wegerif, R. (2011). Towards a dialogic theory of how children learn to think. *Thinking Skills and Creativity*, 6(3), 179–190. https://doi.org/10.1016/j.tsc.2011.08.002

Welch, D., Mandich, G., & Keller, M. (2020). Futures in practice: Regimes of engagement and teleoaffectivity. *Cultural Sociology*, 14(4), 438–457. https://doi.org/10.1177/1749975520943167

Wenger, E. (1998). *Communities of practice: Learning, meaning, and identity*. Cambridge University Press.

Weurlander, M., Söderberg, M., Scheja, M., Hult, H., & Wernerson, A. (2012). Exploring formative assessment as a tool for learning: Students' experiences of different methods of formative assessment. *Assessment & Evaluation in Higher Education*, 37(6), 747–760. https://doi.org/10.1080/02602938.2011.572153

Whitehouse, A., Hassell, A., Bullock, A., Wood, L., & Wall, D. (2007). 360-degree assessment (multisource feedback) of UK trainee doctors: Field testing of team assessment of behaviours (TAB). *Medical Teacher*, 29(2–3), 171–176. https://doi.org/10.1080/01421590701302951

Whitfield, R., & Hartley, P. (2019). Assessment strategy: Enhancement of student learning through a programme focus. In A. Diver (Ed.), *Employability via higher education: Sustainability as scholarship* (pp. 237–253). Springer.

Wiliam, D. (2011). What is assessment for learning? *Studies in Educational Evaluation*, 37(1), 3–14. https://doi.org/10.1016/j.stueduc.2011.03.001

Wilkie, B., & Liefeith, A. (2022). Student experiences of live synchronised video feedback in formative assessment. *Teaching in Higher Education*, 27(3), 403–416. https://doi.org/10.1080/13562517.2020.1725879

Willcoxson, L., Wynder, M., & Laing, G. K. (2010). A whole-of-program approach to the development of generic and professional skills in a university accounting program. *Accounting Education*, 19, 65–91.

Winstone, N. E. (2019). Facilitating students' use of feedback: Capturing and tracking impact using digital tools. In M. Henderson, R. Ajjawi, D. Boud, & E. Molloy (Eds.), *The impact of feedback in higher education* (pp. 225–242). Springer.

Winstone, N. E., & Boud, D. (2022). The need to disentangle assessment and feedback in higher education. *Studies in Higher Education*, 47(3), 656–667. https://doi.org/10.1080/03075079.2020.1779687

Winstone, N. E., & Carless, D. (2019). *Designing effective feedback processes in higher education: A learning-focused approach*. Routledge.

Winstone, N. E., & Carless, D. (2021). Who is feedback for? The influence of accountability and quality assurance agendas on the enactment of feedback processes. *Assessment in Education: Principles, Policy & Practice*, 28(3), 261–278. https://doi.org/10.1080/0969594X.2021.1926221

Winstone, N. E., Nash, R. A., Parker, M., & Rowntree, J. (2017a). Supporting learners' agentic engagement with feedback: A systematic review and a taxonomy of recipience processes. *Educational Psychologist*, 52(1), 17–37.

Winstone, N. E., Nash, R. A., Rowntree, J., & Parker, M. (2017b). 'It'd be useful, but I wouldn't use it': Barriers to university students' feedback seeking and recipience. *Studies in Higher Education*, 42(11), 2026–2041. https://doi.org/10.1080/03075079.2015.1130032

Winter, R. (2003). Contextualising the patchwork text: Addressing problems of coursework assessment in HE. *Innovations in Education and Teaching International*, 40(2), 112–122. https://doi.org/10.1080/1470329031000088978

Woitt, S., Weidlich, J., Jivet, I., Göksün, D. O., Drachsler, H., & Kalz, M. (2023). Students' feedback literacy in higher education: An initial scale validation study. *Teaching in Higher Education*. https://doi.org/10.1080/13562517.2023.2263838

Wong, B. T., & Chiu, Y. (2021). *The ideal student: Deconstructing expectations in higher education*. Open University Press.

Wong, B. T., & Li, K. C. (2020). A review of learning analytics intervention in higher education (2011–2018). *Journal of Computers in Education*, 7, 7–28. https://doi.org/10.1007/s40692-019-00143-7

Wood, J. (2021). A dialogic technology-mediated model of feedback uptake and literacy. *Assessment and Evaluation in Higher Education*, 46(8), 1173–1190. https://doi.org/10.1080/02602938.2020.1852174

Wood, J. (2022). Making peer feedback work: The contribution of technology-mediated dialogic peer feedback to feedback uptake and literacy. *Assessment & Evaluation in Higher Education*, 47(3), 327–346. https://doi.org/10.1080/02602938.2021.1914544

Wood, J. (2023). Enabling feedback seeking, agency and uptake through dialogic screencast feedback. *Assessment & Evaluation in Higher Education*, 48(4), 464–484.

Woodfield, R. (2014). *Undergraduate retention and attainment across the disciplines*. Higher Education Academy.

Wright, G. B. (2011). Student-centred learning in higher education. *International Journal of Teaching and Learning in Higher Education*, 23.

Wyosocki, R., Udelson, J., Ray, C. E., Newman, J. S. B., Matravers, L. S., Kumari, A., Gordon, L. M. P., Scott, K. L., Day, M., Baumann, M., Alvarez, S. P., & DeVoss, D. N. (2019). On multimodality: A manifesto. In S. Khadka & J. C. Lee (Eds.), *Bridging the multimodal gap* (pp. 17–29). Utah State University Press. https://doi.org/10.7330/9781607327974.c001

Yan, Z., & Boud, D. (2022). Conceptualising assessment-as learning. In Z. Yan & L. Yang (Eds.), *Assessment as learning: Maximising opportunities for student learning and achievement* (pp. 7–21). Routledge.

Yancey, K. B. (Ed.). (2019). *E-portfolio as curriculum: Models and practices for developing students' e-portfolio literacy*. Stylus Publishing.

Yeoman, P., & Wilson, S. (2019). Designing for situated learning: Understanding the relations between material properties, designed form and emergent learning activity. *British Journal of Educational Technology*, 50(5), 2090–2108. https://doi.org/10.1111/bjet.12856

Yeung, K., & O'Malley, P. J. (2014). Making "the flip" work: Barriers to and implementation strategies for introducing flipped teaching methods into traditional higher education courses. *New Directions in Institutional Research*, 10, 59–63. https://doi.org/10.11120/ndir.2014.00024

Zeichner, K. M., & Liston, D. P. (1996). *Reflective teaching: An introduction*. Lawrence Erlbaum Associates.

Zheng, L., Zhong, L., & Niu, J. (2022). Effects of personalised feedback approach on knowledge building, emotions, co-regulated behavioural patterns and cognitive load in online collaborative learning. *Assessment & Evaluation in Higher Education*, 47(1), 109–125. https://doi.org/10.1080/02602938.2021.1883549

Ziegenfuss, D. H., & Furse, C. M. (2021). Flipping the feedback: Formative assessment in a flipped freshman circuits class. *Practical Assessment, Research, and Evaluation*, 26(8). https://doi.org/10.7275/007t-dj06

Zimmerman, B. J. (2000). Attaining self-regulation: A social cognitive perspective. In M. Boekaerts, P. R. Pintrich, & M. Zeidner (Eds.), *Handbook of self-regulation* (pp. 13–39). Academic Press.

Index

Note: Page numbers in *italics* indicate figures, and page numbers in **bold** indicate tables in the text.

ABE101 Being Successful at Abertay 196–198; microcredential options *197*
ABE107 Planning Your Future Career 201
Abertay Discovery Tool 196, 197, 199, 201; aim of 200; sections of 198–199
Abertay University 196
ABE108 Your Student Life 197
Academic Professional Apprenticeship/ Postgraduate Certificate in Learning and Teaching in higher education (APA/PGCLTHE) course 203–205; assessment strategy 206, **206**; challenges 210; formative feedback media 207; student engagement with formative feedback 207, **208**; student outcomes 209, **209**
Academic Professional Apprenticeship (APA) standard 203, 206, 207, 209
academic safety net, for inducted undergraduate medical students 127–134
Acosta, D. 155
action-oriented approach 60
active blended learning (ABL) frameworks 187, 188, 193
active learning technique 100, 159, 160, 187
adaptive learning management systems 225
affective challenge 93
Ajjawi, R. 27

application programming interface (API) 181
artificial intelligence (AI) text-to-video technology 120–126
'assessment and feedback learning' 45
assessment-as-learning 11, 79
assessment-centred learning environments 180
assessment feedback 9, 19, 218; rubrics helping students understand 81
assessment-for-learning 9, 11, 18, 23, 129; literature 20; opportunities 24, 28, 212, 215, 217, 219, 221–223; practice 21
assessment literacy 9, 20, 79
assessment-of-learning 10
assessments: critical commentary 63–64; embedding assessment flexibilities 15–18; essay plan 64; for, as, and of learning for sustainable development 60, *61*; library retrieval 63; participatory multimodal 23–27; perceptions of 73–75; in post-digital environments 4–5, 15; reframing for international trainee teachers 69–76; standardisation and moderation of 74; structure of 62; *see also* formative assessment
asynchronous formative feedback: on assessment preparation 167; on project activity 167–168

audio-visual formative feedback 23, 26
Auralia 31
authentic assessments 78, 193
authentic feedback 220
authentic feedback literacies 91–98; framework for *94*
autonomy 52; and intrinsic motivation 57–58

Bath programmes 188, 193
Bearman, M. 27
bi-directional feedback mechanism 160
biological sciences, practical skills in 149–157, *152*, *153*
Black, P. 60
block-based approach 175
blogs 64
Bloomsbury Learning Environment (BLE) 62
Bloom's taxonomy 159, 161
Boud, D. 9, 25, 45, 79, 86, 92, 93, 115, 116
Brookhart, S. M. 120
Buber, M. 72
Burton's Reflective Writing Typology 36, **37**, 38, 41

CA *see* constructive alignment (CA)
Canvas Speedgrader 78
Carless, D. 9, 10, 45, 92, 93, 115, 116
Carvalho, L. 13, 216
Cavalcanti, A. P. 112
Centre for Development, Environment and Policy (CeDEP) 59; change in practice 60; context and needs of students 60–61; promote change towards sustainability and climate action 61–62
CGP *see* computer games programming (CGP)
ChatGPT 27, 123
Climate Change and Development 62
cloud-based computing platforms 181
cognitive challenge 93
cognitive learning theory approach 129
collaborative smart editing tools 22
common-sense approach 211
competence 52
computational thinking 176–177
computer games programming (CGP) 179, 180; authentic facilitation method for 184; cloud-based computing platforms 181
computer science (CS) education: enhancing learning and employability skills in 186–194; first-year professional skills and development 175–176; growth in computing 173; mathematics and computational thinking 176–177; scaling up and automating formative assessment in 172–178
constructive alignment (CA) 44, 190, *191*
Contemporary and Critical Perspectives in Education module 77
contemporary assessment and feedback research 20
Content Knowledge (CK) 30
continuing professional development (CPD)-style activities 177
contract plagiarism 77, 78
Cope, B. 17
course-wide approach 187
Coventry University (CU) 100
COVID-19 pandemic: data-driven approach 180; Foundation module 128, 133; ipsative feedback process 89; students transitions and success through personalised guidance 195–196; use of Microsoft Forms 104–105
CS education *see* computer science (CS) education

data-driven approach, to student support 179–185
Davies, R. S. 160
Dawson, P. 93, 220
De Bruyckere, P. 169
decision-making, staged development of expertise in 20
De Montfort University (DMU) 179
'designed' formative assessment processes 17
developmental feedback 19
dialogic assessment 73, 75
differentiated learning 221–223
digital assessment methods 139–141
digital-human divide 125–126
digital learning environments 11, 17, 109
digital learning tools and technologies: advancement of 1–2, 4–5, 12, 15, 211; advantage of affordances 213; contribution to formative assessment and feedback practices 212; during face-to-face sessions 21; practical illustration of 212; proliferation of 2–3, 223
digital literacy 16
'digital native' fallacy 169–170
direct assessment 149–157
direct-entry program (DEP) 84–90
discussion-based teaching (DBT) 138–140
distance learning, practicalities of 71
distributed formative process 22
distributed learning 223

DREAM Educational Management and Leadership approach 35, 39; ten principles of 35–36
DREAM Management course 39
dual-level evaluation process 117

early career academics: development of 203; formative feedback approach to support 202–210
educational environments 1–2
educational technology, change and innovation in 15
educator-AI-student paradigm 122
educators 13, 15, 16, 18, 22; challenge for 215, 222; communicative relationships and actions of 212; developing students' numeracy skills 106; interactions between students and 122; ipsative feedback practice 90; learner-focused designs 217; role in scaffolding and designing assessment 19–20; shared responsibility between students and 86; students and 213; written feedback 26
educator-student-software trialogue 32, 34
effective formative assessment 13, 20
effective technology-enabled assessment 15
EL *see* experiential learning (EL)
Elai 123
e-learning theory 29–34
Elkington, S. 9, 11, 60, 120
'embarrassment-free' formative feedback 170
employability-related skills 187
Employer-Led Interdisciplinary Project 42, 44, **46**, 47
enactment of feedback 93
end-of-course assessment 128
End Point Assessment (EPA) 204–207, 209
English higher education (HE) environment, fee structure in 173
EPA *see* End Point Assessment (EPA)
epistemic artefacts/knowledge representations 219
e-portfolios 25, 26, 86–89, 143, 144, 148; learning 139–140; ownership and confidence 140; postgraduate students' development 135–141
ESD principles 60; learning objectives for 60
e-tivities 62; forms and functions of 62–64
evaluative judgement 93
Evans, C. 151
evidence-based course-wide formative assessment 188
evidence-based educational approach 193

experiential formative assessment activity, GIST framework 107–113
experiential knowledge 71, 72, 75
experiential learning (EL) 118; learning cycle approach for 118, *119*
experimental systems project (ESP) 189–191, *191*

Falloon, G. 121
Favero, T. G. 167
Fawns, T. 12, 61, 222
feedback information 10, 21, 22, 25; sources of 19; use of 23
feedback intervention theory (FIT) 116
feedback literacy 19, 91–98, 115, 116, 193, 210; appreciating feedback 95–96; features of *92*; making judgements 96; managing effect 97; realism 97; taking action 97
feedback process 5–7, 21–22; AI-generated videos 124; computer science education 186–194; as connected and coherent process 10; defined as 9; effectiveness of 211; in ESP 190; flexible instructional design 215–216; generative constraints 214; human interaction within 147; ipsative feedback process, direct-entry program 84–90; performance 22–23; preparatory 20–21; process 21–22; reconceptualising 213–225; reflexive praxis 214–215; regularity of 40–41; scope and purposes of 212; shared practice of 214; student learning development and improvement of instruction 217–218; sustainability of 215; tutor-led discussion and 21; *see also* formative feedback
feedback-rich environments 19
feedforward 138
flexed rubric 80
flexible assessments 226; designs 218, 220
'flexible learning environments' 3
flipped classroom approach 158–163; expected learning 160–161; objectives of 158; positive and negative aspects of 159; technology in delivery of 160
flipped-classroom lectures 190–191; case study and group discussion on *191*
formative assessment 5–8, 49; AI-generated teaching assistant for enhancing 120–126; for CeDEP's transformation 60; competency, practical skills in biological sciences 149–157, *152*, *153*; computer science education 186–194; in computer science, scaling up and automating

172–178; defined as 9; development of rubrics 79–80; effectiveness of 211; e-portfolios 135–141; flexible instructional design 215–216; in flipped statistics classroom 158–163; generative constraints 214; primary goal of 101; reconceptualising 213–225; reflexive praxis 214–215; scope and purposes of 212; shared practice of 214; student employability through 42–49; students transitions and success, personalised guidance 195–201; sustainability of 215; through post-digital lens 12–15; for UK postgraduate education studies module 77–83
formative assessment tool, in teacher leadership development 35–41
formative e-assessments 112
formative exercises 13, 21
formative feedback 10, 159; data-driven approach 179–185; for international supply chain post-graduate students 114–119, *119*; near-real-time impact of 116; student engagement with 165; students wellbeing, scaffold and manage 50–58; to support early career academics 202–210; through differentiated instruction using Microsoft OneNote 164–171
formative-feedback trialogue 29–34
formative reflective writing assignments 35–41
'forward moving' formative assessment design 120
Foundation module 128, 131; COVID-19 pandemic 128, 133; student evaluation of formative assessments and feedback in 131, **132**
future facing learning (FFL) initiative 165

gamification 109, 110, 111
GDPA programs 51; student wellbeing in 51
General Medical Council (GMC) 142, 143
generative artificial intelligence (GenAI) 2, 27, 224
generative constraints 17
Gibson, R. M. 161
GIST framework, experiential formative assessment activity 107–113
GitHub 181–182
Git repository 182
Goodyear, P. 13, 216
GoogleDocs 87, 88
Gordon, N. A. 177
group-based assignment 14

Haines, C. 205
Handley, K. 165
Henderson, M. 86
Hendricks, N. 167
Hon, A. 34
HTML5 (H5P) 130
Hull University 77
hybridisation, of higher education 3

iGeneration 33
in-class activities 138; synchronous formative feedback on 166–167
informal peer support groups 210
information and communication technology (ICT) 160
'in-process' assessment information 217
integrated assessment designs: activating learning processes through 18–23; performance feedback 22–23; preparatory feedback 20–21; process feedback 21–22
integrated formative assessment feedback practices 20
Intended Learning Outcomes 150
international English language competency tests 85
International English Language Testing System (IELTS) 85
International Initial Teacher Training (IITT) programmes 70
international postgraduate taught (PGT) student 114
international supply chain post-graduate students, formative feedback for 114–119, *119*
international trainee teachers, reframing assessment for 69–76
intrinsic motivation 52, 53, 55–58
ipsative feedback process, direct-entry program 84–90
Irons, A. 9, 11, 60, 120
iterative formative feedback 115

Jandrić, P. 3
Jill Watson, AI chatbot 121
Journal Article Reporting Standards (JARS) 53
just-in-time teaching process 63

Kahoot 129, 130
Kalantzis, M. 17
Kemmis, S. 12
Kennett, K. 17
Khan Academy 121
Kirschner, P. A. 169

knowledge production 23–24
Knox, J. 222
Koehler, M. J. 30
Kolb, D. A.: experiential learning theory 112

Land, R. 204
learner-centred approaches 84
learner-centred feedback paradigm 19
learning: activities and outcomes 64, *65*; digital assessment methods 139–140; experiential 109, 111, 118, *119*; flexibility in 224; game-based 111; personalised learning experiences 125; resources, activities, and assessments 64, *65*; structure of 62
learning analytics (LA) approaches 180, 183
Learning and Teaching Strategy 150
learning community, social norms of 26
learning-focused assessment strategies 16
learning outcomes 10, 16, 19–21, 30, 32
Learning Skills 32–34
learntime 13, 216
lecture-centric teaching method 108
Lee, P. 31
life science degree, structure of 150–151

Macfarlane-Dick, D. 165
Marketing Communication 107–108
marketing simulation game 107–113; development and implementation of 111–112; on-campus classes 110–111; QR code to access *110*, *113*
mathematics 176–177
Mcalpine, H. 167
Mclaughlin, T. 159
Mentimeter 129, 130
Meyer, J. H. F. 204
Microsoft Forms 100–104, 106; integrating open-ended questions in *103*; integrating research-based questions in *104*; during pandemic 104–105; practical application of *102*
Microsoft OneNote 115–117, 119, 164–171; cloud-based operation 168; use of 168
mid-module written formative examination 129, 130
module attainment data 183
module intended learning outcomes 44
Molloy, E. 86
Moodle platform 85, 87, 151, *152*, 154, 156; learning management system 62
Morison, G. 161
motivation 161; intrinsic 52, 53, 55–58
motivational interviewing (MI) 139
multi-modal assessment-for-learning approach 129

multimodal assessment literacy 24
multimodal assessments 23–27
multimodal formative feedback 27
multisource feedback, medical students 142–148
music theory courses 29, 31
Musition 31–33

narrative feedback 133
Nash, R. A. 86
National Student Survey 91
near-real-time feedback 116
Nelson, M. M. 154
Newfield, D. 24
Nicol, D. 165
non-pitched instrumentalist 32, 33
Notion platform 35; benefits of 41; impact of dialogic journals 38; use as platform for formative reflective assignments 36

Objective Structured Clinical Examinations (OSCEs) 150
O'Malley, P. J. 159
OneDrive 181
OneNote Class Notebooks (ONCNs) 166, **166**, 167; 'embarrassment-free' formative feedback 170; manage logbooks for PG students 168; use for formative feedback 169; video guides 169–170
one-size-fits-all curriculum 18
online distance learning (ODL) programmes 59–68; CeDEP 59; demand for 60; formative assessment and feedback on 67; transformation process 64
online learning 51, 71, 72, 123; for CeDEP students 59; competitive environment 110; formative assessment and self-regulated learning in 126
online peer assessment and feedback exercises 91–98
online research course 50–58
online survey tool 80–81
OpenLearning platform 85
Open Science Framework (OSF) 56
oral formative feedback, biological sciences 149–157, *152*, *153*
Orsmond, P. 170
OSCEs *see* Objective Structured Clinical Examinations (OSCEs)
other-directed formative feedback 53; scaffolded summative assessments 54, *55*; weekly group/individual tutorials 53
Our Education Faculty Dialogue Journals Café 37

Padlet exercise 22, 43, 129–130
PARC *see* Personalised Approaches to Resilience and Community (PARC)
patchwork assessment 205
Pearson Test of English (PTE) 85
PebblePad 136–138, 140
PechaKucha approach 129–131
Pedagogical Knowledge (PK) 30
peer-feedback exercise 97
peer instruction 21
peer-to-peer feedback 64
peer-to-peer group pedagogy 115
performance feedback 22–23
personal and professional development (PPD) 142, 143
Personalised Approaches to Resilience and Community (PARC) 197, 201
PGCE Early Years Teaching (EYT) distance learning programme 69, 70, 74, 75
PGCE iQTS team 69, 75
plagiarism 77, 78
post-digital education 2–4
post-digital era, benefit of 174
post-digital learning environments 27, 89; assessment in 4–5
post-digital reality for 85, 125–126
Postgraduate Certificate in Education (PGCE) distance education programmes 69
postgraduate teaching assistants (GTAs) 152, 153
Postman, N. 71
practical skills tracking *153*, 154, 155
practitioners, in higher education 173
"pre-lecture preparation kit" 160
preparatory feedback 20–21
pre-recorded lecture videos 159–161
problem-based-learning 127
process-focused learning 140–141
'process view' feedback framework 206
productive diversity 221–223
professional degrees 150
Professional Standards Framework 203
programme portfolio approach 187
project-based learning 44, 48
psychology, graduate diploma of 50–51
psychology honours 51

Quality Assurance Agency: Scotland collaborative group 201; Scotland Enhancement Themes 197; synoptic assessment 204–205
Quizizz 161

Rapanta, C. 34
realism 93, 97

real-time formative feedback strategy 117, 118
real-time monitoring, of student progress 180, 184
reflective learning process: depth of reflection 41; ground reflection in practice 40; learner's role in 38; volume of reflection 40–41
reflective practice (RP) 137, 139
reflective writing 36, 37
relatedness 52
relationships: building of 71–73; connotations of 72; student-mentor 147
Reliable Change Index (RCI) 56, *56*
responsive assessment designs 218
responsiveness 215–216
RESTful interface 181, 182
Ross, J. 24
Royal Society of Biology (RSB) 150, 151
rubrics, for UK postgraduate education: assessment feedback helping students understand 81; formative assessment, development of 79–80; summative assessment, development of 80

scaffolding 187, 214; for internalisation 189–191, *191*
scaffolding instructional strategy 99–106
School of Oriental and African Studies (SOAS) 59; Learning and Teaching Enhancement team 64
Schunn, C. D. 154
Self-Assessment Quizzes (SAQs) framework 161
self-determination theory (SDT) 51–52
self-regulated learning: AI-generated teaching assistant for enhancing 120–126; positive impact on 126
self-regulation skills 159
shared feedback literacy 215
Smith, A. 17
Smith, C. D. 79
social distancing 169
social science curriculum, virtual project learning in 42–49
Software Process and Modelling (SPAM) unit 189
Soler, R. 25
sport and exercise science (SES) 135, 140
strengths, weaknesses, opportunities, and threats (SWOT) analysis 199
student assessment activity 13, 14
student-centred learning 15, 69, 180

student-directed formative feedback 52–53; conference-style feedback on oral presentation 54–55; modularised course content 53, *54*
student learning development 10, 11
student-mentor relationship 147
student reflection, support for 139
student-situated learning practices 61
students wellbeing: in accelerated online research course 50–58; in GDPA 51; link between need satisfaction and 53
Subject Benchmark Statement 30
subjectivity 92
summative assessments 45; in biological sciences 149–157; development of rubrics 80; e-portfolios 136, 137; essay plan 64; for UK postgraduate education studies module 77–83
summative feedback 53, 55
synchronous formative feedback: on in-class activity 166–167; on project activity 167–168
Synthesia 123
systems-based modules 128

TCK *see* Technology Content Knowledge (TCK)
teacher leadership development, formative assessment tool in 35–41
Teachers' Standards 69, 70, 72, 75
Team Assessment of Behaviour (TAB) 143, 144; annual programme-wide assessment 144; aspect of 144; challenges 148; complexity of 144–145; digital planning and support 146–147; evolution of process 148; importance of human interaction within feedback process 147; requirements *145*; student evaluation responses 146; student's professional behaviour 145–146; training 147
team-based formative assessments 49
technological pedagogical content knowledge (TPACK) framework 30, 31, 34
Technological Pedagogical Knowledge (TPK) 31
Technology Content Knowledge (TCK) 31
technology-enhanced flipped classroom 160
Technology Knowledge (TK) 30–31
Teesside University (TU) 164; future facing learning initiative 165

Test of English as a Foreign Language (TOEFL) 85
Thibodeaux, T. 141
Timmis, S. 139
TK *see* Technology Knowledge (TK)
TPK *see* Technological Pedagogical Knowledge (TPK)
traditional assessment 72
'transmodal moments' 24
tutor feedback 22, 39, 63, 167, 170, 220
tutor-student interactions 165

UK postgraduate education studies module 77–83
undergraduate finance students, scaffolding instructional strategy 99–106
undergraduate medical education (UGME) program 127–134
Understanding Sustainable Development 62
university learning management systems 219
University of Glasgow 150; life science degree, structure of 150–151
user-generated content, idea of 174

values-driven approach 60
video presentations 49
video reflections, students' personal and professional development 135–141
virtual learning environment (VLE) 19, 30–31, 69, 78, 79, 176, 190
virtual learning platforms 19, 22
virtual project learning: across Scotland 43, **43**; formative assessment and feedback practice in 45, **46**; in social science curriculum 42–49

Wiliam, D. 60
Williams, L. 165
Winstone, N. E. 86, 170
Winter, R. 71, 205
work-integrated learning 42–43
work-related stress 51
World Economic Forum 60

Yan, Z. 79, 159
Yeung, K. 159

Zara 120–126

9781032418940